THE POLITICAL ECONOMY OF TOLERABLE SURVIVAL

The Political Economy of Tolerable Survival

Edited by
MAXWELL GASKIN

CROOM HELM LONDON

Croom Helm Ltd, 2–10 St John's Road, London SW11

British Library Cataloguing in Publication Data

Gaskin, Maxwell
The political economy of tolerable survival.
1. Great Britain – Social conditions – 1945–
– Congresses
I. Title
309.1'41'0857 HN385.5

ISBN 0-7099-0266-2

Papers presented to Section F (Economics) of the 1979 Annual Meeting of the British Association for the Advancement of Science.

Typeset in Great Britain by
Pat Murphy Composition, Highcliffe-on-sea, Dorset
Printed and bound in Great Britain by
Biddles Ltd, Guildford, Surrey

CONTENTS

INTRODUCTION

The title of this book is that of the Presidential Address to Section F of the British Association at its 1979 Meeting in Edinburgh. But the title of that address was itself chosen as providing a theme for the whole programme of the Section, and the papers presented at the meeting and now collected in this volume address themselves to conditions and developments in the present which have important bearing on the economic and social predicaments in which we find ourselves and which will shape the future that lies ahead. It will hardly need saying that the theme of 'tolerable survival' was suggested by the contemporary mood of perplexed pessimism and apprehension about the course of events in Britain, and for that matter in Western society as a whole. There is much genuine perplexity, among economists no less than others, about the causes and cures of dominating economic problems: inflation and unemployment are compelling ones, but they are two among many. And this state of mind is overcast by forebodings about the outcome of present trends.

However, whilst prompted by this mood the theme did not produce a series of messages of woe. With whatever misgivings individual contributors might regard particular attitudes or policies, all clearly accept the opening statement of the first chapter that we do not in Britain face 'imminent social or economic catastrophe'. 'Survival' is not in question: the issue for all is that of securing tolerable outcomes from our difficulties by open-minded analysis of problems and a search for practical policies.

Although a majority of the papers in this volume are by economists, we have been fortunate in the contributions from fellow social scientists, and the collection as a whole will, I hope, strike the reader as markedly interdisciplinary. This was certainly the intention, reflecting a personal conviction that our present problems are susceptible neither to analysis nor remedies that are exclusively derived from economics. But also, like my predecessor when the British Association last met in Scotland – Professor Sir Kenneth Alexander – it seemed to me entirely appropriate that on Scottish soil Section F's programme should reflect that broad view of the social economy which the Scottish pioneers of political economy placed before their contemporaries.

The chapters are arranged in two sections. The first and shorter of these contains three papers which set out general perspectives, economic, political and social, on the theme of the book. The first chapter presents a view of the dimensions of two dominating problems facing society, inflation and unemployment, and of the directions in which solutions must be sought. David Marquand follows this with an analysis of our problems as viewed by a political scientist with a considerable practical experience of economic affairs. In the third chapter, David Reisman, himself an economist, presents an account and critique of the essentially sociological and moral standpoints taken by the late Fred Hirsch in his *Social Limits to Growth*, a book which has had a considerable impact well beyond the confines of economics.

The second and longer section consists of a series of chapters directed to specific issues in present economic and social life. The issues, all major ones, fall into two broad groups. One group arises from conditions affecting the economy at its most general levels. Thus, Colin Crouch, a sociologist with a clear appreciation of present economic debate, gives a sociologists's view of modern inflation, a position from which he inevitably criticises some prominent economic approaches and notably that of the monetarists. But the monetarist view is represented in lively fashion by Patrick Minford in a chapter which focuses on the processes of international monetary adjustment. In an intervening chapter, Colin Robinson considers one of the few apparent springs of aid and comfort in our present troubles, North Sea oil, and takes a critical look at some suggestions for using its monetary benefits to reverse the adverse trends in the British economy.

The other group of papers in this second section is concerned with aspects of economic and social change. Tom Stonier is among those who foresee imminent technological changes of large dimensions, and his chapter is addressed to the implications of this and the steps necessary to meet it. Then in the two following chapters Edward Cunningham and Duncan Maclennan look at complementary aspects of regional problems: Cunningham dissects regional development policy and explores the directions it should take, whilst Maclennan takes a wide-ranging, critical look at the position of the city, and the policies which have created or attempted to grapple with its problems. Both these papers reflect the authors' close experience of the Scottish scene, and this applies also to the final two chapters in which aspects of change and development in Scottish society are examined. But, like the Cunningham and Maclennan papers, Ian Carter's case study of community development in the Scottish Highlands and Geoff Payne's and his colleague's presentation of some results of the Aberdeen study of social and occupational mobility in Scotland convey messages of quite general significance. Indeed, some of the conclusions of Payne, Ford and Ulas about the relation between social mobility and structural change in the economy suggest questions about their bearing on the social conflict thesis discussed in some of the earlier, more general chapters.

In this book there are no unanimously supported answers to the questions suggested by the title. Differences of diagnosis and prescription are clearly evident, and in any case some major problems are scarcely touched on. What is hoped is that it contributes to that wide approach to our problems which is clearly required if Britain is to remain a tolerable as well as a tolerant society.

M. Gaskin

PART ONE

THE DIMENSIONS OF TOLERABLE SURVIVAL

1 THE POLITICAL ECONOMY OF TOLERABLE SURVIVAL

Maxwell Gaskin

When I chose this theme in early 1979 I intended the key word of the title to be 'tolerable', not 'survival'; and whilst on a wider, non-insular view the events of 1979 itself, especially those in the world energy economy, might suggest doubts about that emphasis, in early 1980 it remains my position: that is, I do not subscribe to any thesis of imminent social or economic catastrophe in Britain. In view of this it may legitimately be asked if simply to use the term 'tolerable survival' is not to overdramatise the situation facing us, since it does by implication lend support to the mood of pessimism and apprehension, as it was certainly suggested by it. We do well, therefore, to ask at the outset if in thinking these thoughts we are not allowing ourselves to be deceived by the eternal myopia of the present. For example, the historically-minded critic might argue that every age finds the going difficult and is prone to apocalyptic fears, and he might well proceed to show – as periodically someone does – that despite the worrying trends in the present-day economy, it is not difficult to draw favourable comparisons between the present and some past period.

A comparison ready to hand is with the inter-war years. So far as we have faith in statistical comparisons over a period of half a century, the level of income per head in the United Kingdom today is possibly two and a half times what it was in 1930; and even if our faith is weak, it is undeniable that in the mass the British are better housed, better clothed and fed, and enjoy greater economic security than their counterparts of the 1930s. And whilst it is true that unemployment is high, and only just below its post-war peak, up to early 1980 it had not reached one-third of its 1932 rate.

But, of course, comparisons of this kind do not remove the doubts, particularly in Britain where we contemplate a long phase of absolute political decline and a much longer period of relative economic decline. The last thirty years have seen our economy grow at faster rates than at any time in our history, but for many this is outweighed by the fact that we have fallen behind most of our fellow members of the Western economy in some major economic quantities. This pessimism is reinforced by doubts about future growth rates, although these are not confined to Britain, and by our apparent inability to produce the flexibility and dynamic response that a highly competitive and rapidly changing world demands. Added to all this, we are in the midst of an inflationary episode which whilst also not confined to Britain, is for us historically unique in its intensity and duration, and which some believe to be linked with fundamental social and political changes.

In fact, to the criticism that we may be taking a blinkered and present-centred view of our predicament one compelling answer actually flows from an alternative historical stance. Dr John Goldthorpe, having given a sociologist's view of the roots of modern inflation, at a recent conference, was reportedly provoked by critical economists into remarking: 'It's a historical situation, not an intellectual problem, that we are confronting here' (1978, p. 216). Taken in context, the remark was not an attack on the intellectual approach as such, but on one species of it – that of the analytically-minded economist. As I read him, here and in his preceding paper, Goldthorpe was asserting the necessity of viewing modern inflation in its socio-historical dimension, not simply as an economic puzzle. But the point can be turned against the more simplistic forms of historically-based criticism of modern pessimism: applied to the example taken here, the inference is that despite the statistically-measurable advances of the last half century, the attitudes and responses of people today are different from those of their counterparts of the 1930s. Higher incomes and more social welfare are not irrelevant to a prognosis of our present state, but they can be detached neither from the economic trends that have produced them, nor from the changed social and political environment in which they are enjoyed. As Heilbronner reminds us, 'each generation takes for granted the standard of living it inherits and feels no debt of gratitude to the past' (1976, p. 45). And whether or not we agree, what does emerge here is that there is more than one historical perspective on our present problems, and some of the alternatives are not calculated either to dispel unease, or to support a dismissive attitude to the issues raised in our title.

The 'Tolerability' of the Future

This returns me to my theme, and to the need to say what I mean by the 'tolerability' of whatever future lies ahead. Clearly, with such a subjective word, one cannot proceed by definition, and the most serviceable approach is to indicate those conditions of social existence which, at this point in time and with my values and preconceptions, I regard as marking the bounds of a tolerable future – or, from another point of view, as setting limits within which solutions must be sought. Because any such selection is so subjectively determined, it is best to keep these conditions few in number and fundamental in character. They should also be relevant to the problem to be considered for which reason I will at this point say briefly what these are to be. With so many candidates for examination, and given the necessity to restrict the number discussed, it was clear that two, inflation and unemployment, were so dominant in their effects on events and apprehensions as to pre-empt the discussion, and this can be further justified in that, as conditions of economic and social existence, their *bearing* on the tolerability of the future would command a wide assent.

One condition that I postulate as an essential part of a tolerable future is that we should as a society continue to enjoy a liberal political order, that is, one in which the degree of personal liberty is not less than is now enjoyed in the societies of Western Europe and North America, and which – having regard to the need to maintain its own stability and liberal nature – allows the maximum amount of freedom to individuals and groups to pursue their legitimate objectives. This is a criterion of so fundamental a nature that some might be disposed to think it should be taken as read, but this I would dispute because, without prejudging whether or not or how far the liberal order is actually endangered, by no means everyone is convinced that present circumstances allow it to be taken for granted. In some countries, including Britain, the intensity of recent inflation has been accompanied by a manifest increase in social stress, a fact which is one origin of the apprehensions referred to earlier. Some of the present tensions in our society are clearly the product of inflation as various groups feel themselves made relatively or absolutely worse off by the inflationary process; and such reactions are bound to be sharper the higher the rate of inflation, since high inflation rates increase the penalties of being a loser in the process. Again, in recent years inflation has coincided with a disposition on the part of some groups to challenge the authority of established institutions like Parliament and even the Law. And whilst some of the fears aroused by these actions may proceed from misapprehensions about the nature and locus of authority in a liberal society – as political scientists tell us – the fears are nevertheless there, and the actions themselves are both causes and effects of social tension.

But there is another reason for not taking the political order for granted. There is an important school of thought, represented in all the social sciences, which sees modern inflation as itself the product of conflict – a conflict produced either within the competitive market system itself, or by a discordance between that system and the liberal political order. On this view, inflation is now endemic in our society, with the implications that a cure is only conceivable through changes either in the political or the economic order.[1] This view will be considered at greater length later. Here it may simply be remarked that the emphasis on social stress and the growing preoccupation with the conflictual elements in inflation raise one further possibility, remote though it may appear in the British context. It could be envisaged that in some situations arising out of an economic condition like inflation, a government might feel compelled to act in a way that would curtail political liberties. Probably few would regard the actions proposed by the present government to reverse recent legislation favouring the trades unions – the 'roll back' policy – as falling into this class. Nevertheless the test of the effect on the political order is a relevant one to apply to any such measure, since the preservation of that order implies certain limits which policy in a would-be liberal regime should respect.

Inflation is not the only economic condition that gives rise to social tensions which could conceivably be politically disruptive. Unemployment, the other major question to be considered here, might also be cast in this role. An estimation of unemployment as a political threat is however more difficult because the evidence is slight and prognosis proceeds on even more uncertain ground than in the case of inflation. But more to the point, I think that here another criterion of tolerability supervenes: the condition of what is morally tolerable. Given the undesirable human and social effects of unemployment, it is not difficult to argue that a tolerable future should preclude unemployment of certain kinds. Having defined those kinds, and broadly all are types of involuntary unemployment, and having accepted that we may not practically be able to eliminate all such unemployment, the argument then turns on tolerable levels of unemployment and involves our ability or otherwise to affect those levels. But this is for later discussion: having, as promised, confined myself to few, in fact two, very fundamental conditions of tolerability, I turn now to the problems themselves.

The Inflation Prospect

Among the present problems of the British economy, inflation is the one which most arouses apprehensions about the future. These apprehensions are not always clearly focused, but one can detect in them fears for the integrity of our social and political institutions as inflation rates have accelerated, and as industrial conflict and other socially-divisive accompaniments of inflation have intensified.

The present inflation is the latest phase in one of the most sustained inflationary processes in modern British history. Money incomes and prices have been rising continuously, if at varying rates, since the economic revival of the early 1930s. However, the duration of this process is less significant than its divisibility into fairly distinct sub-periods. The differences in character and causation between the price movements of the 1930s and those of the 1940s, and between those of the 15 years before 1966 and the dozen or so years since, are more significant than the similarities. Even the post-1966 period may be subdivided into at least two distinct phases, and we may indeed now be entering a third. However, whilst it is important to note the distinctions between these phases one must also consider the possibility, very relevant to the present theme, that each of these sub-periods has bequeathed a legacy of experience and expectations which has affected the shape of those that follow. In my view, such inter-period effects were not particularly significant before the post-1966 period. There is no generally agreed explanation of why inflation began to accelerate in the late 1960s, but there is little evidence to suggest that it was materially affected by price expectations generated in the preceding period of creeping inflation. This is not to say that there were no such transmitted effects, between these phases: the accustoming of the working population to regular upward income adjustments could be singled out as a significant legacy of the 1940s and 50s to the post-1966 years.

In contrast, since the late 1960s there is evidence of a more significant spillover of effects from one period to the next. It is admittedly impressionistic evidence, but the impressions are strongly derived from observed events and attitudes. It suggests that the ground of experience that we occupied in 1979 is very different from that on which we stood in 1969. In 1969, when inflation had only recently begun to accelerate from the low and variable rates of the 1950s and early 1960s, it was still possible to believe that inflation in most Western countries, Britain included, had not produced any changes in social and economic attitudes that would be particularly resistant to a reverse movement. Indeed, looking back, it is arguable that as late as 1971, had world events turned out differently, we might well have returned to the modest inflation rates of the 1950s. But even then some changes had occurred: income settlements, modest by later standards but high in comparison with previous figures, had been won by some groups; and this caused a shift in attitudes to pay claims as well as resentments over disturbed comparabilities. These changes undoubtedly prepared the way for the succeeding episode, in 1974–5, of what were for Britain unprecedented rates of wage and price inflation – an episode the proximate causes of which must be largely sought in the world boom in commodity prices, capped by the massive rise in oil prices in 1973–4, with monetary expansion greasing the skids (to use Professor Arthur Brown's words – 1979, p. 6).

Three years of remarkably successful controls over money incomes and prices, from 1975–8, brought inflation down dramatically, but since then the climate of pay claims and pronouncements strongly suggests that the earlier episode is far from forgotten and that the rates of income and price inflation experienced then have moved society over a significant threshold of experience. In that period it was demonstrated that various groups in society could demand and get pay rises of very high orders, up to 30 per cent, and that whatever the remoter effects might be, the economy would not immediately collapse about their ears. And that lesson appears to have impressed itself more firmly on the mind of the average wage- or salary-earner than the well-denounced futility of pursuing 'confetti money'.

The 'Threshold' Hypothesis

In a recent critique of the concept of a natural rate of unemployment – that rate of unemployment which in monetarist doctrine will tend to obtain in equilibrium (and monetarily undisturbed) conditions, and which will be determined by frictions and other imperfections in the labour market (see Friedman, 1968, p. 8) – Professor Tom Wilson has questioned the monetarist view that the unanticipated price increases, which it is argued will result from any attempt to reduce unemployment below the 'natural rate', will inevitably lead to *accelerating* wage and price rises. In making the point, he remarked: 'Presumably there is some kind of threshold before that danger becomes really serious' (Wilson, 1976, p. 103), the implication being that it is only beyond a certain point that perception of price rises causes income earners to raise the supply price of their labour and so precipitate the accelerating effect. The more moderate monetarists would possibly accept this modification, though in the light of price history it might be seen as greatly foreshortening the period to which monetarist emphasis on price expectations as an influence on labour market behaviour has much relevance. However the nature and implications of a threshold effect, for which I think there is strong evidence in the 1970s, strike me as having a much wider significance than as a modification of the price expectational element in monetarist doctrine.

First, however, let it be said that no one would argue that the noticeable rise in inflation rates in many countries after 1966 and more especially after 1971 marked a divide between an era when price expectations were entirely absent and one when they came sharply into play. Whilst there was no apparent tendency for inflation to accelerate before 1966, some econometric work has turned up evidence of an influence of prices on wage changes in the 1950s and 60s, and for that matter in the inter-war period (Lipsey, 1960, pp. 24–30).

But if there was some kind of threshold effect, such as Tom Wilson suggests, in the late 1960s or early 1970s – and the pattern of preceding and succeeding events seems to me to support this – did it do any more than heighten people's perception of price changes so that they began to take much more account of them in their expectations about the future, and in the contracts into which they were prepared to enter? In the language of the debate over the nature of the Phillips curve, was the effect simply to increase the size of the price expectations coefficient, with a consequent steepening of the curve, possibly to the extreme situation where, except in a shrinking short-run, that curve becomes a vertical line offering no trade-off between inflation and unemployment as some of its earlier exponents had claimed?[2]

Clearly, that is a possible effect of a movement over a significant threshold of price increases; certainly, I would not argue against the proposition that sharp movements of prices over a detectable range alert people to the distinction between real income and money income. But to regard this as the sole or even the principal effect of the 1970s experience may be to take too narrow a view, and I would argue that that experience has probably produced qualitative effects describable in simpler, less sophisticated terms than those of the theorists of expectations, namely that it has removed inhibitions that had previously restrained collective economic behaviour. And one example of such an inhibition is the assumption which Sir Henry Phelps Brown tells us was widely accepted from 1920 onwards, that 'wages would be adjusted from time to time, by small margins downwards and by larger but still modest amounts upwards' (1975, p. 15). In short, the unions and other groups of the workforce are now much less inhibited in the pursuit of all the objectives that they attempt to achieve through pay claims – including, for example, distributional objectives. This does not mean that there is necessarily less rationality in collective behaviour, but it does imply that some accounts of 'rationality' may overestimate its firmness as a basis for predictability.

One question suggested by this interpretation of the threshold effect is whether it might not in the end be self-reversing: could accelerating inflation eventually produce a social trauma that would radically alter the conditions in which, for example, control might operate? Here the evidence, necessarily drawn from other countries, is mixed. Hyper-inflations of the kind experienced by Germany in the 1920s seem capable of producing very durable anti-inflationary attitudes; and the drastic monetary reforms which some countries were able to apply in the aftermath of World War II convey a similar message. On the other hand, the experience of Latin America suggests that some societies at least can live with rates of inflation very much higher than we have so far seen, though few of these have done so under what we would regard as tolerable political orders.

The threshold hypothesis thus presents a possible and persuasive account of the way in which the present British inflation has developed, one that cannot be ignored in surveying the outcomes we may have to face and which we would wish to avoid.[3] It suggests more than one possible profile of future inflation, including the disturbing one of a progression of discontinuous leaps as successive layers of inhibitions in money income demands are shed. In itself it says nothing about the ultimate causes of inflation, or about the mode of monetary management necessary to sustain it. The monetary conditions of inflation, regarded simply as permissive conditions, are well understood, though there is an area of questions only now being opened up about the political motivations that allow them to exist (see e.g. Gordon, 1975; also David Marquand and Colin Crouch in this volume). In the account of the causes of inflation to which I now turn, the monetary factor is explained in terms of an unwillingness of government to go beyond certain limits in opposing the forces which are the ultimate engines of inflation. This account belongs to the group of explanations which finds these causes in social or institutional forces: specifically, it is the one that connects inflation with a social conflict over income distribution.

Inflation, Distribution and Conflict

The suggestion that modern inflation may arise from conflicting claims on the national cake, and may indeed be the best available means of accommodating them, was made at least as long ago as 1966, by Professor Reddaway,[4] and has since been stated by other economists. More recently a sociological account of the sources of inflation, emphasising the role of social conflict in various forms, has been widely elaborated by thinkers in almost all the social sciences. John Goldthorpe has found the roots of such conflict in the decay of status groups and the spreading realisation of the egalitarian implications of citizenship (1978). Political economists like the late Fred Hirsch (1977, especially Ch. 12) and Robert Heilbronner (1976) have pointed to the competitive ethos and other aspects of the market system itself as a source of tensions in liberal societies. Even an economist of such monetarist hue as Samuel Brittan has explored the inflationary tendencies in the democratic process itself (1975) – though such an exercise is of course by no means inconsistent with monetarist views.

Almost all these approaches, whether from economists or sociologists, see a distributional conflict as a major cause of modern inflation. One writer goes so far as to represent the creeping inflation of the 1950s and 1960s as a unique period when Western society was able to avoid 'a harsh distributional conflict between classes' by means of economic growth, and indeed refers to the idea of growth as 'a surrogate for redistribution', as the 'great conservative idea of the last generation' (Maier, 1978). In the light of the British record of two to three per cent real growth *per annum*, as well as recollections of the period itself, I find this particular gloss implausible.[5] But this does not detract from the distributional conflict thesis *per se*.

Indeed, if one weighs the evidence for the conflict diagnosis in the present circumstances of this country, it does appear depressingly heavy. At the present time, having passed through a succession of incomes policies, from guidelines, through mandatory limits and negotiated limits, and back to no limits, we are witnessing a widespread and barely contained action by many groups to achieve large pay increases. Since all movements in pay inevitably decide income distributions, one could view present pressures as supporting the social conflict theory. Of course, the motives actuating the claimants clearly vary. Some of the traditionally better-paid workers, wearing both white and blue collars, are reacting against a perceived erosion of conventional relativities and differentials, caused partly by the form of recent incomes policies, partly by the effects of inflation itself working on a progressive tax structure. They are ostensibly, and in many cases actually, motivated by a desire to 'catch up'.

Some groups however are exhibiting a simple determination to use a strong bargaining position to push themselves up the relative income ladder. This is also evident among a sector of the workforce which in the past has not been regarded, by others or themselves, as having a strong bargaining position: the lower-paid workers. The more militant determination of many low-paid groups to improve their economic position through higher incomes from work – particularly groups in the public sector where some have proved to have more muscle than they had realised – is an important development of this decade. Furthermore, it is a clear cause of conflict in that it meets, head on, the equally strong determination of other groups, at all levels in society, to maintain established relativities. If the income objectives of the low-paid related to absolute income levels, an eventual resolution of this conflict through economic growth might be envisaged, if not optimistically anticipated in the British case. But despite the expression of these aims as specific levels or figures, there is no question of there being any illusions about absolute levels, and in the end such aspirations must return to relative incomes, so that a resolution of the contest through growth is unattainable – at any rate at any levels of growth we could reasonably count on in the UK.

It is a notable feature of the present pay situation, as of all similar phases, that most groups whether of the lower paid or the higher paid see their respective positions in terms of 'fairness', that is social justice, or in the closely related terms of 'deserts'. This lends colour to the pessimistic view of Samuel Brittan (1975) that in the face of the destructive contradictions within liberal democracy it is fruitless to seek criteria of distributive justice, or alternatively for acceptance of income differences at the practical level. Brittan presents a very formidable case, and I am not disposed to dispute his analysis. But as he presents himself in that paper, I part company with him, as I do with the implied conclusions of the conflictual diagnosis of modern inflation, on the question of practical action.

There are no certain, indeed no apparent solutions to the dilemmas of our present inflation. The fundamental choice offered us is between a paralysing pessimism and taking action which is bound to be based on a mixture of faith and of arguments that can be as easily refuted as supported. Particular action may not be a sufficient, or at any rate the *right*, condition of tolerable survival; but some action is surely necessary. We have to act in the belief that we can contain the conflicts, which may be causes and are certainly effects of inflation, within limits that will prevent social or economic breakdown. At the practical level everything points to the need to seek a moderation of conflict in the area of relativities and differentials. One necessary condition of this is that the trade union movement should more openly recognise the contradictions within its own ranks on this question. But candour and insight are not solely for the unions: all income earners, however organised or represented, must be brought to a recognition that pay claims concern the sharing out of income, and that apart from insignificant numbers and comparatively trivial sums, it is the sharing of income between the various sections of the employed population that is at issue, not that between employees and employers.

In effect what this argues is that to find a viable way forward we have to create an awareness and appreciation of the distributive issues involved in pay negotiations – issues which are very imperfectly perceived at present. Two recent developments increase the urgency of this exercise. One is the increasing unpredictability of world economic events, especially events like the imposition of large price changes by OPEC or similar cartels which may arise, which can perceptibly affect the amount of income to be shared out. The second is the point on the bidding scale at which competing income claims are now made: having crossed a significant threshold in the early 1970s, the contest has moved on to an altogether more dangerous plane with much severer penalties for the losers than in earlier periods. As Charles Maier puts it: 'Beyond a certain rate . . . inflation . . . aggravates the very distributional conflicts it helped assuage' (1978).

Along with increasing an awareness of the issues, it is vital to seek as wide an area of agreement on relativities as possible. This implies an incomes policy of some sort, and despite the difficulties and failures of past policies, I think it would be folly to abandon the search for an improved system for regulating changes in money incomes. Given the comparative crudity of our attempts so far there is much room for improvement, and the principal improvement to seek is a system which is sensitive to the relativities problem with the associated problem of entry into the policy. One of the most interesting suggestions for an institutionalised approach to an incomes policy is Sir Henry Phelps Brown's proposal for a Central Consortium incorporating all the major pay negotiating bodies – about 300 of them, including all individual firms with 5,000 or more employees – which would administer a controlled but flexible system of comprehensive collective bargaining

(1972).[6] A difficult prescription, you may say, and the problems are certainly daunting. Indeed Samuel Brittan could claim that he has already destroyed it; to which the only reply must be that his 1975 paper effectively destroys all prescriptions, including the one of which he is such a noted proponent, monetarism. For it is clear that the market mechanism to which monetarists pin their faith, and which unquestionably at its functioning best disposes of many of the problems for which incomes policies have yet to produce even imperfect solutions, is a subtle and difficult instrument for men and women to comprehend. As other contributors to this volume point out, there are no grounds for assuming that in modern conditions society will assent to its outcomes more readily than to those of any other piece of social mechanism. What it comes down to is that in terms of common understanding the great divide in economic thought is marked by Adam Smith. Most men are pre-Smithian in their conception of how the economic system works, and to put it at its lowest – and the case can actually be put at a much higher level[7] – the essentially mercantilist solution of an incomes policy is required in a world where mercantilist assumptions are the norm, and where 'le Smithianisme' can no longer be imposed by a wise élite on a deferential populace.

Unemployment and a Tolerable Future

I turn now to my other major problem for tolerable survival, unemployment. At the present time high unemployment is, of course, connected in various ways with high rates of inflation, and the moderation of inflation is unquestionably a necessary – though not so clearly a sufficient – condition of its reduction. But this is not the angle from which I approach unemployment here.

Unemployment is neither apparently nor, I think, actually a cause of social stress and conflict in the way that inflation is. Probably most people assume that somewhere on the scale of possible rates of unemployment there is a level that could threaten political order, but there is no evidence of where at the present time that point lies. Even in the 1930s, a very different world from today, but one with fiercely high unemployment rates, social disorder on account of unemployment was remarkably absent. There is of course ample evidence that unemployment at what are now regarded as high rates, or in any case at rising rates, *has* a political effect in putting the party in power electorally at risk. But though this is practically important, and frequently what people have in mind when they invoke the spectre of a 'politically intolerable' level of unemployment, it is not relevant to the present theme of tolerable survival, which is concerned with more fundamental conditions of society. As I stated at the outset I think that here we have to fall back on the hazier and subjective – though not, for that, inferior – criterion of what is morally tolerable.

Though present unemployment rates are low by some past standards, few would deny that unemployment is a serious problem. Many – Professor Stonier, a contributor to this volume, among them – see a prospect of increasingly intractable types of structural unemployment, extending well beyond the short-term. In some aspects, unemployment presents a more difficult problem than inflation: it is affected by a wider range of factors, including inflation itself, and it is a surprisingly ill-understood phenomenon. Even the figures by which we measure and interpret it are not always what they seem. The proportion of the population of working age who join the workforce can and does vary, and can thereby affect measured unemployment either by displacing an existing worker or by raising the number of those registering themselves as unemployed. Another factor which has recently come under theoretical and empirical scrutiny is the effect on measured unemployment of changes in the cost of being unemployed. With more generous unemployment benefits and redundancy payments these costs have declined, in Britain as in other countries. This is not to invoke the 'scrounger' thesis, but simply to note that, on *a priori* grounds, it would be entirely normal and legitimate for respectable working people to be more choosey, and therefore take more time, in seeking a new job when they become unemployed; and the effect of this would be to increase the quantity of unemployment at any given time. Most observers feel that this has had some effect on the British figures since the late 1960s, although quantifying it is very difficult. However, the evidence suggests that it is not a major element in the present unemployment.

But besides the statistical puzzles, unemployment poses conceptual difficulties, ostensibly of classification but more fundamentally of causation. The old – admittedly over-simplified – categories with which we worked during the Keynesian ascendancy – frictional unemployment, structural unemployment and cyclical or demand-deficient unemployment – are presumably unacceptable to the monetarist school. They would not quarrel with 'frictional' and 'structural' unemployment, as subsumed in their 'natural rate of unemployment', though they do not say very much about the place of structural unemployment within the natural rate, and it may not fit in as comfortably as might appear. What monetarists do reject is the Keynesian category of involuntary unemployment resulting from a general deficiency of demand. It would take more space than remains to me to review this controversy so I will simply state that I do believe in the possibility and indeed the present reality of demand-deficient unemployment. However I would certainly accept that the old tripartite classification is inadequate and incomplete, partly for reasons which monetarists would probably accept.

For example, some part of current unemployment is undoubtedly due to a relative price effect, with the price of labour being too high in relation to the market value of its output, *at the margin.* Geoffrey Maynard (1978) has recently argued that such an effect has been produced by the relative rise in the price of raw material inputs in production, and especially energy, *without* a compensating fall in the prices of other inputs, notably labour. Finding a cause of unemployment in a relative price effect of this kind is by no means inconsistent with a Keynesian stance, and given its classical flavour it would presumably be acceptable to monetarists. A relative price effect of a different kind has been suggested by Professor Arthur Brown (1979). In Brown's analysis a combination of cost-push inflation and an ingrained, if diminishing, habit of firms of basing prices on historic costs squeezes profits; this, he suggests, is a major cause of the generally low profitability of British industry. Professor Brown is not directly concerned to explain unemployment but his relative price effect, if intensified by accelerating inflation, would be similar in outcome to Maynard's, and would indeed reinforce it. It would not commend itself to monetarists since it is founded on a cost-push view of modern inflation. In neither case however is the resulting unemployment of a kind that might be called 'demand-deficient' in the traditional Keynesian sense.[8]

To turn now from conceptual questions to the facts of the present and prospective unemployment problem in this country, these have been brought together most usefully in a recent publication by the Cranfield School of Management (Fishwick, 1979). One contributor to this notes how the widespread pessimism about unemployment is based on the outlook both for the supply and demand sides of the market (Dean, 1979). The demand side of the equation is not difficult to appreciate in the light of uncertainties overhanging world economic growth, the apparent speeding up of technical and other changes affecting many industries and the specific problems of British industry.

The outlook on the supply side gets less prominence, at least in popular discussion.

The developments here can be illustrated by a brief analysis of present unemployment. We are in a recession from which, for the last 18 months, there has been some recovery which is itself now in jeopardy from recent world events. But take the situation in 1979 with unemployment averaging 1.3 million, and compare that with the average position in 1971. On that comparison unemployment was up by about 500,000: but it is noteworthy that the number employed was up by 350,000, whilst the total population at work (employed plus self-employed) had increased by over 670,000. The explanation of this conjuncture is that since 1971 the labour force has grown, by rather more than one million. The interpretation of these figures is complicated by the fact that the greater part of the increase has been in part-time women workers. But even allowing for this (and the part-time figures affect unemployment as well as employment) it does appear that during the 1970s the economy has not failed to *maintain* employment, and it has in fact probably increased it in terms of full-time equivalent workers; but it has not done so fast enough to compensate for the continuing loss of jobs and to absorb the increased labour force. (Also, it must be conceded that the concentration of employment growth in the service sector is not a reassuring development.)

For the future the important point is that this growth trend in labour supply will continue. The Department of Employment in its latest forecasts (DoE *Gazette*, April 1978 and June 1979) projects a growth of 2.25 million between 1976 and 1991; a rough adjustment of this period to a 1979 start modifies the figure to 1.75 million. Rather more of this growth will come in the next five years than in the following seven, whilst – and this is most important – unlike much of the growth in the 1970s it will contain a sizeable male contingent.

On past comparisons this forecast growth is by no means immense, but in the context in which it will occur it could add seriously to our problems. One estimate of the extra net annual investment needed to 'equip' this increased labour force, puts it at £2 billion (at 1976 prices), an increase of well over 20 per cent on the 1976 level of net investment (Ermisch, 1979). The actual total would depend very much on the activities into which the new labour might be absorbed, but in any case whilst the amount is not negligible, at under two per cent of present GDP neither is it unthinkable. What is in doubt is the existence of the necessary incentives to the private sector to undertake its share.

To Keynesians of whatever vintage this situation illustrates the thesis of market failure. Increased human resources will become available, resources whose employment could generate at least some of the demand on which that employment would depend; but this demand is in the future and the future cannot transmit the appropriate signals to the present. Of course where so many factors adverse to investment are present one hardly needs to seek others. Furthermore, too much stress on demand as the source of the incentive to invest can obscure the relationship between investment, growth and market development which is a much more organic and integral one than phrases like 'investment-led' or 'export-led' growth suggest. Indeed the chief criticism of post-war Keynesian demand-management policy is not that it produced modern inflation, which it did not, but that for too long it deflected attention from the roots of Britain's economic problems in the supply side of the market, and at the micro-economic level.

Be that as it may, the immediate and even the medium-term future in unemployment looks bleak, and whilst it is no part of my present purpose to discuss current policy at any length, one cannot avoid noting that the policy stance now adopted can only worsen it in the short-term. The policy may or may not succeed in its aim of mitigating our difficulties by improving the business environment. But regardless of that, and despite my earlier critical comments on demand-orientated policies, to regard demand-management as having *no* further part to play in mitigating unemployment and from time to time providing a more favourable outlook for business activity and investment, is no less doctrinaire and simplistic than some of the earlier expressions of the demand management philosophy itself. On general policies to meet a possible long-term unemployment problem, I have no difficulty in rejecting the facile solution of work-sharing as almost certain to produce harmful and irreversible effects on efficiency and thus eventually to make the problem worse (see Dean, 1979). Whilst willing to suspend judgement on some aspects of current policy, and even to wish them well, I think that the recent history of this country offers no ground for optimism about the ability of the free market economy, unaided, to reverse present trends. Hence, without being blind to the imperfections and difficulties of state-inspired action, I consider that interventionism as manifested in such bodies as the NEDC, and the EDCs and Sector Working Parties that function under its aegis, in the Scottish and Welsh Development Agencies operating in their regions, and in positive Government assistance and stimulus to the modernisation and redirection of industry, is a vital ingredient of a policy to contain any long-term tendency to increasing unemployment.[9]

Conclusions

In this chapter I have concentrated on two problems only of the British economy, treating even these very selectively. But they are the problems which seem most to threaten the tolerability of our future, in the one case by producing or intensifying stresses which could eventually weaken the liberal order, in the other by producing a waste of human resources that could exceed what is morally and socially tolerable. On inflation, which is unquestionably the key problem, the solution of which would facilitate much else, I have opted for more openness in confronting the issues of distribution involved pursued through newly-devised arrangements within which a wider consensus can be aimed at. This conclusion is advanced in full awareness of the scepticism to which any proposal for a new agency or body is exposed, and with an equal conviction that there are no ready panaceas to the problems of our social economy.

The consortium proposal of Sir Henry Phelps Brown, which I see as a promising suggestion on these lines, is symptomatic of a wider trend of thought which calls for a closing remark. There is a growing recognition of the vulnerability and indeed inadequacy of our present political organs, and especially Parliament, in the face of the organisations and pressure groups which contend with one another and make life uncomfortable and threatening for the ordinary citizen. The late John Mackintosh, in a penetrating analysis of the political dimensions of our predicament, proposed a reconstitution of the Upper Chamber so that these modern equivalents of the feudal barons might be brought within a reformed institutional framework which would 'encourage co-operation and help confer legitimacy on what is decided' (1974, p. 98). Professor Ralf Dahrendorf, arguing along parallel lines, has said: 'We have to organise organisations and give people control at the same time if we want to be governable' (1975, p. 96). But Dahrendorf has pointed to another important condition of improving our prospects of survival, the 'creation of a new political public'. I would gloss that prescription by making 'political' embrace 'economic', but also by drawing attention to the responsibilities of the public towards the bodies which represent their organised interests. It is little use organising the organisations if the barons who head them have little influence over their tenantry. This shifts the problem to a deeper level and underlines the crucial role of education. Without a public that has more understanding of the underlying economic and political realities of modern society than people presently possess, institutional changes will achieve nothing. If the people are to remain the masters of government, as in a liberal order they should, society needs more than ever to educate its masters.

Notes

1. It is only fair to say that in the exchange referred to, Goldthorpe's economist critics were challenging him to admit that this was the practical upshot of his diagnosis (Hirsch and Goldthorpe, 1978, p. 216).

2. The 'Phillips curve' derives from the empirical study of wage rate changes and unemployment by A. W. Phillips, reported in his classic paper, 'The Relationship between Unemployment and the Rate of Money Wages in the United Kingdom, 1861–1957', *Economica* (November 1958).

3. Compare Colin Crouch's thesis of increased 'labour mobilisation', arising from full employment and stronger trade union organisation, as a factor in recent inflation. This is clearly a separate argument from the threshold hypothesis advanced here, but it could be taken as complementing it.

4. Colin Crouch notes a reference to this interpretation by Aujac in 1950: see his chapter in this volume.

5. I should make it clear that like David Marquand I attach great importance to a resumption of growth in the British economy, and to the pursuit of policies designed to increase its rate. But I must admit to scepticism about the contribution that resumed growth could make, even on an optimistic forecast of its possible trend, to the present and foreseeable inflationary problem of the British economy.

6. Compare David Marquand's comments on the Phelps Brown proposals, and also on those of John Mackintosh which I refer to later.

7. In a recent letter to *The Times* (4 March 1980) Sir Henry Phelps Brown has pointed to the constructive and educative role of an incomes policy. In contrast to the avowedly 'low level', mercantilist argument suggested in the text, this is the positive and high level case for an incomes policy and, particularly in the light of the closing remarks of this chapter, one which I fully support.

8. On the other hand, such unemployment should not be described as 'voluntary'. In fact, the terms 'voluntary' and 'involuntary' strike me as so loaded with meanings relating to individual behaviour as to be highly misleading as classifications of unemployment in the essentially *social* situations depicted by Maynard and Brown.

9. As has been pointed out by Mr Geoffrey Chandler, Director-General of NEDO, in a recent address to the Aberdeen Chamber of Commerce (January 1980), our international competitors have not been content to rely on policies restricted to improving the general business environment. See also Hugh Stephenson's telling criticism of some recent remarks by Milton Friedman on Japanese economic development, in *The Times*, 26 February 1980.

References

Brittan, S. (1975), 'The Economic Contradictions of Democracy' in Alexander, K. J. W. (ed.), *The Political Economy of Change* (Oxford: Blackwell)

Brown, A. J. (1979), 'Inflation and the British Sickness', *Economic Journal* (March)

Dahrendorf, R. (1975), *The New Liberty: Survival and Justice in a Changing World* (London: Routledge & Kegan Paul)

Dean, A. (1979), 'A Survey of the Current Employment Situation' in Fishwick

Ermisch, J. (1979), 'Trends in Labour Supply and their Implications' in Fishwick

Fishwick, F. (1979), *Labour Economics* (Cranfield Research Papers in Managerial Economics, Cranfield Institute Press)

Friedman, M. (1968), 'The Role of Monetary Policy', *The American Economic Review* (March)

Goldthorpe, J. H. (1978), 'The Current Inflation: Towards a Sociological Account' in Hirsch and Goldthorpe

Gordon, R. J. (1975), 'The Supply and Demand for Inflation', *Journal of Law and Economics* (October)

Heilbronner, R. L. (1976), *Business Civilisation in Decline* (London: Marion Boyars; New York: W. W. Norton)

Hirsch, F. (1977), *The Social Limits to Growth* (London: Routledge & Kegan Paul; Cambridge, Mass.: Harvard University Press)

Hirsch, F. and Goldthorpe, J. H. (eds.) (1978), *The Political Economy of Inflation* (London: Martin Robertson)

Lipsey, R. (1960), 'The Relation between Unemployment and the Rate of Change of Money Wage Rates in the United Kingdom, 1862–1957 – A Further Analysis', *Economica* (February)

Mackintosh, J. (1974), 'Political Institutions', Chapter 5 in *Reshaping Britain: A Programme of Economic and Social Reform* (PEP Broadsheet no. 548, December)

Maier, C. S. (1978), 'The Politics of Inflation in the Twentieth Century' in Hirsch and Goldthorpe

Maynard, G. W. (1978), 'Keynes and Unemployment Today', *The Three Banks Review* (December)

Phelps Brown, E. H. (1972), 'A Workable Incomes Policy for Britain' in Blackaby, F. (ed), *An Incomes Policy for Britain* (London: Heinemann, for NIESR and SSRC)

——— (1975), 'A Non-monetarist View of the Pay Explosion', *The Three Banks Review* (March)

Reddaway, W. B. (1966), 'Rising Prices for Ever?', *Lloyds Bank Review* (July).

Wilson, T. (1976), 'The "Natural" Rate of Unemployment', *Scottish Journal of Political Economy* (February)

2 TOLERABLE SURVIVAL AND POLITICS

David Marquand

For me, as for Maxwell Gaskin in chapter 1, the key word in the title is 'tolerable', not 'survival'. I take it for granted that we shall survive: or, rather, I intend for the purposes of what follows to take it for granted that we shall survive. The questions I shall be trying to answer are whether we can survive in a tolerable fashion, and, if so, what policies are needed to ensure that we do. Clearly, the concept of tolerability is a fuzzy one. If we were talking about bare, physical survival, we could agree fairly easily on what we meant, even if we disagreed about the means necessary to achieve it. It is obviously more difficult to agree on what we mean by 'tolerable' survival: one man's 'toleration' may be another's 'endurance' and a third's 'acquiescence'. In this country today, most – though not all – of us would probably agree that a form of survival which entailed sacrificing free elections, freedom of speech and freedom of association would not be tolerable. But suppose we were offered survival at the cost of five million unemployed. Would that be tolerable or not? Or suppose that we could survive *either* with full employment *or* with free elections, freedom of speech and freedom of association but not with both. Which could seem more tolerable – or, at any rate, less intolerable?

That second question is particularly pertinent, since, in practice different aspects of tolerability almost certainly have to be traded off against each other. Most of us would probably agree that, for the foreseeable future, we shall have to go on trading desired levels of employment off against desired levels of inflation. Many of us believe that we shall also have to go on trading desired amounts of freedom in collective bargaining off against desired levels of wage settlements. We may also have to make other, less familiar, trade-offs as well – for example, between an incoming government's freedom to pursue its ideological predelictions and the level of industrial investment, or between the United Kingdom's willingness to transfer sovereignty to the European Community and its capacity to safeguard the interests of its citizens in trade negotiations. On none of these matters is there anything approaching a national consensus: most of them are, and will remain, fiercely controversial.

Any definition of tolerability, in short, is bound to be arbitrary. My own is fairly close to – though not quite identical with – Professor Gaskin's (chapter 1). The word 'tolerable', it seems to me, carries at least some moral overtones. It is not a synonym for the word 'endurable'. A prisoner at Auschwitz would probably have had to endure torture. It would not follow that he had tolerated it. Survival at the cost of the moral and political values which I believe to be right might be the only kind of survival open to me, but I would not be obliged, or perhaps even entitled, to consider it 'tolerable'. Three practical conclusions seem to me to follow. 'Tolerable' survival implies for me the survival of a stable world order and the survival of pluralist democracy, at any rate in the countries where it already exists. It also implies that the present recession must somehow be ended and economic growth resumed – if possible, at a rate closer to that of the rest of the industrialised world than in the past. Finally, it implies that inflation must somehow be contained, if possible at a level lower than the present British one.

The first conclusion will probably command general agreement, and I do not think it needs further discussion here. The second is more controversial. Now that no economic growth is actually taking place, the notion that continued growth is positively undesirable is not quite as fashionable as it was a few years ago, when growth seemed to be availabe for the asking. Even so, it survives in some quarters. It seems to me misconceived. I do not believe that it is possible – or, for that matter desirable – to return to the *pattern* of economic growth which we knew in the fifties and sixties. We shall obviously have to be more sparing in our use of energy, and we shall probably face other resource constraints as well. In common with other industrialised countries, we shall have to accept that the newly industrialising countries now have a comparative advantage in the mass production of industrial goods; and we shall have to shift resources out of them and into activities with a higher skill content, in which, if we play our cards well, the comparative advantage would lie with us. All this will test our political and social ingenuity to the utmost. But the fact that the resource-wasting, environment-damaging growth of the fifties and sixties cannot go on does not imply that growth *per se* must come to a stop. Still less, of course, does it imply that it is undesirable. It is, I believe, a prerequisite, certainly of continued world stability and perhaps of the survival of liberal democracy as well. It is also morally desirable on its own account.

As Max Gaskin has pointed out, there is now a great deal of evidence to suggest that distributional conflicts lie at the heart of the inflationary crisis from which this country has been suffering for the last ten years or so. I shall turn later to the dangers which inflation at the present level poses to the survival of pluralist democracy. For the moment, I merely assert that it does pose dangers: and that the longer it lasts, the greater the dangers are likely to be. The point that concerns me now is that distributional conflicts are, almost by definition, harder to resolve in a stagnant economy than in a growing one. Growth provides a margin for manoeuvre. It makes it possible to change relativities without leaving anyone absolutely worse off. If there is no growth, there is no margin; and redistribution becomes a zero-sum game. To say that inflation cannot be brought down to a tolerable level unless growth resumes would be to beg a whole series of questions, on which a non-economist would pronounce at his peril. But few economists would deny that social and institutional pressures are, at any rate, partly to blame for the inflation of the seventies: and it seems to me equally hard to deny that these pressures have been exacerbated by the current stagnation in real incomes.

At a different level, I also believe that growth is a precondition of lower unemployment – not a sufficient condition, perhaps, but certainly a necessary condition. Like Max Gaskin, I doubt if the present level of unemployment poses a direct threat to liberal democracy. The evidence of the inter-war years points, if anything, in the opposite direction. Indeed, the most sophisticated social historian of the period argues, I think convincingly, that so far from producing political instability or demands for change, the main effect of the Depression was to make working-class people less unwilling to accept their lot (Runciman, 1966). But although high levels of unemployment are almost certainly compatible with social and political stability, they are, I believe, incompatible with the moral values on which the liberal democratic system is ultimately based. Though we may one day live in a society from which the last vestiges of the Protestant work ethic have disappeared, and in which idleness is thought to be no less meritorious than labour, we do not live in such a society yet. In our society, most people are esteemed – by themselves as well as by others – in accordance with the work they do. It follows that if unemployment remains for long at its present level, a large number of people will have been denied an important attribute of full citizenship through no fault of their own. Survival at such a cost, it seems to me, would clearly not be 'tolerable' in the sense in which I am using the term. Last, but by no means least, I also believe that prosperity is better as well as more pleasant than poverty and that it is easier to pursue the fundamental liberal aim of the greatest happiness of the greatest number in a rich society than in a poor one.

The case for growth has to be argued: the case for a lower and more stable rate of inflation is often taken for granted. In fact, it is a more complex case than is sometimes realised, and it deserves more careful discussion than it sometimes receives. It is often said, as though the proposition were self-evident, that liberal democracy cannot survive a high rate of inflation: and the Weimar Republic is often used as an example. In reality, one of the most striking features of the great German hyper-inflation of the early twenties was precisely that it did *not* destroy the Weimar Republic and that the Republican regime proved strong enough to bring inflation to an end, without using authoritarian methods. I do not, of course, suggest that inflation is good for liberal democracy. I do suggest that it is facile, and perhaps even dangerous, to assume that liberal democracy is doomed unless inflation falls below a certain, arbitrarily-chosen, figure.

The truth, it seems to me, is more complicated, and in a way less comforting. Inflation at its present rate is a fairly recent phenomenon. As recently as fifteen years ago, the rate was a whole dimension lower than it is now. This suggests that, if those of us who think that the roots of the current inflationary crisis lie in distributional conflicts are right, the conflicts concerned must have become more acute. If this is so – and there is obviously a good deal of impressionistic evidence to suggest that it is – the central question facing the analyst of inflation is, 'Why?' I have already suggested that part of the explanation probably lies in the failure of real incomes to grow. No doubt, part lies in those deep-seated sociological factors, like the erosion of old status barriers, explored by John Goldthorpe (1978). But I find it hard to believe that these provide the whole explanation. What has to be explained, after all, is not a slow, gradual change, but a sharp and perhaps accelerating one. If real incomes had been rising rapidly for a long period, and had then suddenly ceased to rise, dramatic changes in behaviour might be expected to follow. But in Britain, as we all know, the rise was never rapid. By the same token, I can see how old status barriers, and the inhibitions they imposed, might erode gradually over a period. I cannot see why the pace of the erosion should suddenly speed up, unless other factors are at work as well.

Another explanation, it seems to me, is that group conflicts not only cause inflation, but are in turn caused by it. Inflation, according to the group-conflict theory, can be regarded as a sort of safety valve: leap-frogging wage claims as, so to speak, the moral equivalent of civil war. But of course, inflation, is not only a safety valve. It is also a boiler. It redistributes income in favour of those who get their blow in first, and against those who hold back: in favour of the queue jumper, and against those who are prepared to wait patiently in line. And, because of this, it is apt to turn the queue into a stampede, to set off a Hobbesian war of all against all, or rather of all organised groups against all other organised groups, in which the only way to prevent oneself from being trampled on is to trample on everyone else. The higher the rate of inflation, moreover, the greater are the penalties for being left behind; and the stronger is the incentive, not just to catch up, but to forge ahead. In such a climate, it seems to me, group consciousness and group loyalties are almost bound to become stronger, while consciousness of the interests of the wider society, and perhaps even loyalty to the wider society, are almost bound to fade.

I believe that it is here, rather than in the simple fact of inflation itself, that the real danger to liberal democracy lies. Once again, it is important to avoid over-simplification. Liberal democracy is about group conflicts, or at any rate about the peaceful regulation of group conflicts, and the last thing I want to do is to suggest that group conflicts are, in themselves, fatal to it. But the key word in that sentence is 'peaceful'; and group conflicts can be regulated peacefully only if the protagonists are prepared to accept the regulator's verdict even when it goes against them. This is much more likely to happen if the group conflicts are mild than if they are bitter, and if the groups concerned share strong common loyalties than if the loyalties they have in common are weak. If group conflicts become more bitter and if, at the same time, wider social loyalties are attenuated, the strain on the liberal democratic system must become heavier, and the system's capacity to cope with the strain must become weaker. Stable inflation, it seems to me, need not have these consequences, provided everyone believes that it will remain stable. But accelerating inflation – or, to put it more precisely, inflation which is generally expected to accelerate – is almost bound to have them. And, as we have seen more than once over the last fifteen years, slow inflation has an alarming propensity to turn into fast inflation.

'Tolerable' survival, then, implies the resumption of economic growth and the containment of inflation. But both these objectives have been loudly proclaimed and assiduously pursued by governments of both parties, and neither has been achieved. Indeed, the British record on the two taken together is the worst in the developed world. Unless we are to believe that British governments are uniquely unlucky – and a run of bad luck on that scale would require an explanation of some sort – this suggests that, in this country, the obstacles in the way of achieving them must be particularly formidable. An obvious prerequisite of a policy of tolerable survival, it seems to me, is to identify and understand these obstacles. Since my brief is the politics of tolerable survival rather than the economics, I shall be concerned with the political obstacles rather than with the economic ones. But since the politics and economics overlap, two fairly obvious economic points – one concerning growth and the other inflation – must be made first.

The first is that, although growth is in the general interest, it is not necessarily in everyone's particular interests, at any rate not in the short term. Growth entails change; and change is almost always painful to someone. The history of industrial society is a history of contraction as well as of expansion, of death as well as of birth. Old skills, old habits, old concerns disappear to make way for new ones: and the new ones cannot appear unless the old ones disappear. But those who have learned the old skills, who have become used to the old habits, or who work in the old concerns, are rarely content to see them disappear. Even if they are willing to change their ways – and they are often exceedingly unwilling – the change is almost always costly, in effort and emotion if not in money. Resistance to the changes without which growth is impossible is therefore almost inevitable; and the question that matters is not whether it occurs, but whether the resisters have their way. In a society in which the resisters generally win – and, still more, of course, in a society in which resisters are so likely to win that changes are not attempted in the first place – growth will be slow or non-existent. Growth can be rapid only if society is so organised that the resisters do not win, and if the general interest of the community which stands to gain from change prevails over the particular interests of those who stand to lose. That, of course, is what the market was supposed to do in the *laissez-faire* economies of the nineteenth century, and it is what the state is supposed to do in a command economy. The crucial question, so far as growth is concerned, is not who does it but whether it is done.

The point concerning inflation is more complicated. The causes of inflation are, of course, fiercely disputed: and a non-economist ventures into the disputed territory only with great trepidation. In one important respect, however, it seems to me that the rival explanations have more in common with each other than appears at first sight. As I understand it, there are two main explanations. Keynesians lay the blame for inflation on cost-push pressures in the labour market. Monetarists lay it on excessive growth in the money supply. The distributional-conflict theory of inflation can obviously be assimilated into a Keynesian model very neatly. Inflation, the argument would go, has risen because cost-push pressures have become more intense: cost-push pressures have become more intense because the deeper distributional conflicts which give rise to them have become more acute.

At first sight, it is harder to assimilate the distributional-conflict theory into a monetarist explanation. What, it might be objected, have distributional conflicts to do with the money supply? The answer, it seems to me, is that the monetarist explanation, even if it is valid as far as it goes, obviously does not go far enough. It tells us that inflation occurs when the money supply grows excessively. It does not tell us why governments cause the money supply to grow excessively. Unless the reason is simply that ministers are stupid and cowardly – and even if it is, it is necessary to explain why some ministers in some countries are more stupid and more cowardly than other ministers in other countries – the answer is presumably that there is something about the political process which causes governments to behave in this way. That, of course, is exactly what monetarists interested in political economy in fact say. Governments, they point out, are subject to pressures from the political market-place. Because of the nature of this market-place, because, above all, the individual voter does not have to trade off different wants against each other in the way that the individual consumer in the real market-place has to do, these pressures are almost bound to be inflationary in character (for a good expression of this view see Brittan, 1977). The practical implications of this view, it seems to me, are really very close to those of the Keynesian view. Keynesians say that inflation is caused by pressures on costs, at work in the labour market. Monetarists of this stamp say that it is caused by pressures for a lax monetary policy, at work in the political market. Both agree that inflationary pressures are at work somewhere; and both views are consistent with the theory that these pressures arise ultimately from conflicts over the distribution of resources. If the distributional-conflict theory is right, both therefore point towards the same policy conclusion – that, if inflation is to be contained, the protagonists in these conflicts will have to be prepared to moderate their demands.

A worthwhile policy of tolerable survival must, in other words, have two central aims. In the first place, it must try to ensure that the general interest in economic growth outweighs the particular interests of those who, at any given moment, do not want the changes without which growth cannot happen. Secondly, it must try to ensure that the general interest in price stability outweighs the particular interests of those who, at any given moment, want to start a new round in the distributional battle. The detailed policies needed to stimulate growth may, and often will, differ from the policies needed to contain inflation; not the least of the problems facing contemporary British governments is the genuine technical difficulty of deciding which mix of policies is appropriate at which moment. But measures needed to stimulate growth and measures needed to contain inflation have one crucial characteristic in common. Both depend for their success on the capacity of the general interest to override a series of particular interests.

And that, it seems to me, is where the political problem lies. I do not believe that there is some special British disease which leads us actually to prefer low growth and high inflation to high growth and low inflation. Most of the alleged symptoms of this putative disease – and symptoms vary wildly from diagnostician to diagnostician – are to be found in more successful economies as well. The notion that our troubles stem from too much social and economic equality does not stand up to a comparison with Sweden; the notion that they stem from too little does not stand up to a comparison with France (Brittan, 1978). The notion that our status and value systems are uniquely hostile to entrepreneurial dynamism squares badly with the fact that, in the nineteenth century, they were thought to be uniquely favourable to it. The notion that our economy has grown slowly because, as a nation, we prefer leisure to work – and still more, of course, the complementary notion that we are, in fact, right to sacrifice growth to that preference – square as badly with the fact that working hours are shorter and holidays longer in countries where growth is faster. Even the more plausible notion that our rate of inflation is high because our historical experience has made us more willing to tolerate inflation than, say, the Germans seems to be dubious. It is true that we have never experienced hyper-inflation of the sort that the Germans experienced in the early twenties. But we did experience a fairly long bout of accelerating inflation in 1974–5, and there is not much doubt that the experience was extremely disagreeable. If historical experience were the crucial factor, fresh British memories of what happened five years ago might be expected to have a stronger influence on behaviour than faint German memories of what happened more than fifty years ago. The fact that the British rate of inflation is higher than Germany's requires a more sophisticated explanation.

But although I do not believe that we suffer from some special

British disease, which leads us to spurn growth and tolerate inflation, I do believe that the antibodies which, in more fortunate countries, help to keep growth-inhibiting and inflation-generating diseases at bay are less effective here than elsewhere. The explanation, I believe, is that we find it unusually difficult to ensure that the general interest does override the particular interests that stand in its way. This is partly because the organised groups which articulate and promote such particular interests have more political weight here than elsewhere. It is also because the authorities whose job it is to articulate and promote the general interest find it unusually difficult to do so successfully. There are, I believe, four main reasons for all this, one socio-economic and three political.

In a penetrating analysis of the causes of Britain's low rate of growth, which has influenced my own thinking a great deal, the American economist, Maneur Olson, suggests that one of the main determinants of the rate of growth in any society is the role played by its organised producer groups – what he calls 'common-interest organisations' (1979). Such organisations, Professor Olson argues, need time to establish themselves, since in their early stages they are too weak to give significantly more benefits to their members, who have to bear all the costs of their operations, than to non-members, who do not share in the costs. It follows that they will be stronger in societies which have enjoyed long periods of peace and stability than in societies which have experienced invasion, revolution or totalitarian rule. Strong or weak, however, they exist to pursue the interests of their own members, not to serve the general interest. If they are highly 'encompassing' – if, that is, their members are widely dispersed through society – they are likely to pursue their members' interests in a way that also serves the general interest. If not, they are likely to do so in a way that damages the general interest. In Sweden, the 'common-interest organisations' are both strong and highly 'encompassing'; thus, they do not retard economic growth and may even foster it. In most continental countries, their development has been inhibited by war, totalitarianism and/or foreign occupation; thus they are not strong enough to constitute a serious obstacle to growth. Britain's long history of peace and stability has given such organisations the time they need to establish themselves, but in Britain they are not usually very 'encompassing'; thus, in Britain, they constitute a very formidable obstacle.

Professor Olson's analysis is not wholly convincing, particularly in relation to the crucial concept of 'encompassingness'. If he were right, one would expect Mr Moss Evans – the leader of the most 'encompassing' trade union in this country – to display noticeably more sensitivity to the general interest than any other trade-union leader. It is arguable that some of his predecessors did so, but unfortunately for the theory, they did so most conspicuously when the union was less 'encompassing' than it is now. At a deeper level, Professor Olson does not explain why Britain's 'common-interest' organisations have failed to become as 'encompassing' as the Scandinavian ones. But although there are weaknesses in the theory, the central insight seems to me highly convincing. Other countries have strong producer groups, and yet others have fragmented producer groups. British producer groups exhibit a unique combination of strength and fragmentation; and that combination goes far to explain why it is that, in Britain, the particular so often outweighs the general.

It does not, however, provide a complete explanation; and it seems to me that political factors have to be taken into account as well. The most obvious, though not necessarily the most important, of these political factors is the peculiarly secretive, not to say collusive, character of the relationship between government and the producer groups. Systems of consultation between government and the two sides of industry – what is sometimes called 'tripartism' – have been established in most developed democracies (cf. van Beyne and Ionescu, 1977). Indeed, where the producer groups are strong, government cannot achieve its aims unless it can normally count on their acquiescence even when it does not have their support; in order to do this it has to consult them. The fact that tripartism is practised in this country is therefore neither surprising nor alarming. But there are dangers in tripartism as well as advantages. Almost by definition, really powerful producer groups are in practice conservative. They derive their economic strength, and therefore their political influence, from their weight in the economy as it is; they therefore have a built-in tendency to want the economy to stay as it is. They want prosperity and growth, of course, but in a general, diffuse sort of way. They do not want the particular, detailed disruptions without which growth is impossible. The trade unions call loudly for higher investment, but they fight to maintain the manning levels which make new investment unprofitable. Business leaders proclaim the virtues of free competition, but they scurry to Whitehall for help when competitive pressures threaten them with bankruptcy. In practice, therefore, the producer groups are almost bound to deploy their weight in favour of the *status quo.* Government, as the guardian of the general interest, ought to deploy its weight in favour of change. But almost by definition, government is under strong pressure to reach agreement with the producer groups; all too often, it is apt to sacrifice the general interests to its own interest in a politically popular compromise.

These dangers might be offset in an open form of tripartism, in which the positions of the producer groups were subject to public scrutiny and appraisal and in which the issues discussed between the government and the producer groups were generally known. But, in Britain, the bargaining process is generally shrouded in secrecy – albeit in secrecy punctuated by leaks. No one knows precisely what the producer groups have asked for or what concessions they have been prepared to make; and the issues at stake percolate to the ordinary newspaper reader – or even to the ordinary backbencher – only through heavy, unattributable briefing of the press by those involved in the negotiations. If an agreement is reached at the end of the process, it is presented to Parliament and the public as a *fait accompli*; and all the government's weight and authority are staked on getting it through. If the negotiations break down without an agreement, the air is loud with recrimination as each party in the negotiations does its best to shuffle off the blame on to the others. Since the general public has no way of knowing who is telling the truth, the net result is to discredit all concerned and to corrode public confidence in the system.

This state of affairs seems to me wrong in principle – perhaps even 'intolerable' – since it flouts the fundamental liberal axiom that power should be accountable. Right or wrong, it clearly strengthens the forces of economic inertia and perhaps also the forces of inflation. But it is much easier to diagnose than to put right, for it is bolstered by some of the most powerful elements in our political tradition. There is not much doubt about what is needed. Somehow or other, the producer groups have to be made more aware of, and more sensitive to, the public interest; to put the point another way round, the public interest must somehow or other be given more weight in the bargaining process. This cannot be done, it seems to me, unless the process is opened up: unless we devise a more accountable form of tripartism to replace the present secretive and collusive form. The trouble is that open tripartism necessitates open government; and, as anyone who has followed the recent debate over official secrecy will know, the notion of open government still arouses fierce opposition in some quarters. Though that opposition is sometimes expressed in an irrational way, moreover, it is not irrational in origin. Open government would be in the public interest. It would not necessarily be in the interests of particular ministers at particular moments, or, of course, in the interests of their officials. The point of a more open form of triparitism would not simply be to add to public enlightenment. It would be to create a constraint on the freedom of action of the partners which does not exist at present. The producer groups would be constrained because they would have to defend their positions in public. But government would be constrained as well. Indeed, part of the object of the whole exercise would be to make it more difficult for governments to make deals with the producer groups which run counter to the public good. But governments sometimes want to make deals which run counter to the public good; and they are unlikely to welcome proposals designed to make it harder for them to do so. Their resistance is likely to be fortified by cultural factors as well. The notion that government is a mystery, the 'Queen's business' into which the ordinary public and even ordinary Members of Parliament should not be allowed to pry, still goes deep. It is not observed in practice, of course, as the development of tripartism itself shows. But a secretive, collusive form of tripartism, which allows the government to pretend that it is a free agent even though everyone knows that it is not, is much easier to square with the notion than an open form would be.

All this applies with particular force to the most obvious technique through which our form of tripartism might be opened up. The easiest way in which the public interest could be given more weight in the process and, for that matter, the easiest way in which the public could be made aware of what is being done in its name, is to strengthen the capacity of the House of Commons to scrutinise the working of the executive and to give it a larger role in the crucial, early stages of the legislative process. But would-be parliamentary reformers inside and outside the House of Commons have been asking for this for more than fifteen years; and although the present government recently agreed to implement at least some of the latest set of such demands (see *Select Committee on Procedure*, 1977–8), the reformers' achievements have so far been very limited. The reason, it seems to me, is not just the governments are reactionary and obstructive, nor yet that backbenchers are feeble and pusillanimous. It is that worthwhile measures of parliamentary reform would necessarily make it more difficult for governments to have their way (cf. Walkland, 1978): and that the suggestion that governments ought to find it more difficult to have their way runs counter to a deep-seated British belief in the virtue of 'strong government'. In arguing for open tripartism and open government, I am, in effect, arguing for an open and explicit form of power-sharing. We are used to the notion that power should be limited, but not to the notion that it should be shared.

Yet, by a curious paradox, the second reason why our political arrangements favour the particular against the general and the sectional against the social is that British governments are, in an important sense, too weak. They dispose, of course, of an enormous panoply of formal power: so enormous that the present Lord Chancellor has described the system as one of 'elective dictatorship' (Hailsham, 1978). But it is a dictatorship in which the dictator cannot do what he most wants – or, at any rate, what he most needs – to do. So long as its backbenchers obey the whip, a British government with a majority in the House of Commons behind it can force through whatever legislation it likes, even on matters which in all other democracies would require an amendment to the constitution. Though the courts have become more willing to challenge the executive than they used to be, their ability to resist a determined government is severely limited (Lester, 1977). Yet in their dealings with the producer groups – and above all in their dealings with the unions – government after government has suffered a series of more or less bloody defeats.

Part of this reason, no doubt, is that government was normally condemned to fight on unfavourable terrain. Defence is almost always easier than attack; and government usually had to attack positions which the producer groups were defending. Partly because of this it was inherently more difficult for government to mobilise its forces than it was for the producer groups to mobilise theirs. The producer-group leaders were appealing to their members whose interest in the matter was strong and direct, to fight for their right to go on doing what they had always done. Government's task was much more daunting. It had to appeal to the general public, nearly all the individual members of which had a much weaker and less direct interest in the outcome, to support the proposition that a group of its fellow citizens should no longer be allowed to do what it had done in the past. But it would be dangerous to push this argument too far. Governments were bound to find it difficult to overcome producer-group opposition. To conclude that they were bound to find it impossible is to succumb to a determinism which the facts do not warrant. To succeed, governments would have had to appeal more successfully to rank-and-file producer-group members than they actually did, and/or to win more determined and more consistent support from the general public than they actually won. No recent British government has succeeded in doing this, but it does not follow that no conceivable British government could have done so in the past, or that no conceivable British government could do so in the future. The most obvious reason why British governments have failed to defeat the producer groups when they have come into conflict with them is that they have lacked the necessary moral authority: that the general public and ordinary producer-group members have not had sufficient confidence in government's good faith or competence to give it the kind of backing which it would have had to receive to win. The moral of that is not that we should reconcile ourselves to an endless series of producer-group victories and government defeats. It is that we should alter our political arrangements so as to ensure that future governments have more authority than government has had in the recent past.

That, I take it, is the real – though sometimes only half-acknowledged – purpose of proposals like those put forward by the late John Mackintosh and Sir Henry Phelps Brown to which Max Gaskin has referred in the last chapter. Two tacit assumptions, it seems to me, underlie both sets of proposals. The first is that government alone cannot win enough public support to implement the policies it believes to be necessary in the national interest if the producer groups resist them. The second is that the best way to increase public support for such policies is to remove them from the realm of ordinary party politics by giving them a stamp of approval from respected public figures who are known to stand aloof from the party battle. Under Sir Henry Phelps Brown's proposal the stamp would be given by the Central Consortium of pay-negotiating bodies; under John Mackintosh's by the reconstituted Upper House. These proposals should not be dismissed out of hand. The first of the two assumptions underlying them seems to me unquestionably right. The second might turn out to be right as well. But I do not think that either proposal goes to the heart of the problem. In a liberal democracy, government is the guardian of the public interest; and it cannot share that responsibility with anyone else. Even if government policies originated from Sir Henry Phelps Brown's pay consortium, and were endorsed by John Mackintosh's reconstituted Upper Chamber, they would still be government policies and it would still be up to government to get them through and to defend them before the public. If the elected government is too weak to do this – and that is what these proposals presuppose – it is unlikely that support from unelected bodies, however eminent and authoritative, would make a decisive difference. Indeed, it seems to me more likely that the unelected bodies would be dragged into the realm of party controversy, as in fact happened first to the

National Board for Prices and Incomes and later to the Pay Commission. If government is too weak to discharge its responsibilities properly, government should be strengthened; and that should be done directly as well as – perhaps even rather than – indirectly.

I do not pretend that this would be an easy thing to do. Governments have been losing authority all over the democratic world. Indeed, some political scientists have suggested that a tendency to what they call 'overload' is built into liberal-democratic politics, since governments in a competitive party system are bound to attempt more than they can perform and to raise expectations which they cannot satisfy (King, 1975). If this is true, a decline in government's authority may be built into the system as well. But even if it is true, it is unnecessarily pessimistic to assume that there is nothing we can do to improve this position in this country. Not all modern governments have less authority than their predecessors: government in the Fifth Republic in France clearly has much more moral authority than government had in the Fourth Republic. One obvious reason why British governments lack authority, it seems to me, is that they rarely represent more than a minority of the electorate, yet all too often behave as though they represented a majority – another example of the perverse combination of apparent strength and real weakness which characterises so many aspects of our polity. If the electoral system were changed so as to make the House of Commons more representative of the real preferences of the voters, governments representing only a minority of the total electorate could no longer be formed. The constituent parties of any government with a parliamentary majority would *ipso facto* have had to receive, between them, a majority of the votes cast in the polling booths. I do not share the view that electoral reform is a kind of panacea which will put all our political ills right. But it would mean that a government appealing for public support against producer-group opposition would have been elected by a majority of the public to which it was appealing. This would at least give it a better chance of success.

This brings me to the third – and in my view the most damaging – political component in our economic failure. I said a moment ago that recent British governments have lacked authority because, having been elected by minorities, they have insisted on behaving as though they represented majorities. I attach even more importance to the second part of that proposition than to the first. As the economist, Michael Stewart (1977), has shown in his brilliant study of the development of British economic policy in what he calls 'The Jekyll and Hyde Years' –

the period from 1964 to 1976 – the range of policy options open to British governments is in fact very narrow. All governments, irrespective of party, have been obliged sooner or later to operate a prices and incomes policy of some kind. All governments, irrespective of party, have discovered that no incomes policy, whether statutory or voluntary, can work without trade-union co-operation; and all governments, irrespective of party, have therefore had to tailor their social policies with an eye to trade-union reactions. All governments, irrespective of party, have discovered that in a mixed economy, business confidence is a prerequisite of investment; no government, irrespective of party, has been able to defy the City of London or to ride roughshod over the CBI. Finally, all governments, irrespective of party, have discovered that they need a mix of industrial and regional policies to deal with the supply side of the economy, and that they cannot solve the problems of the supply side by relying on market forces alone. But although all governments have discovered these things, all oppositions have forgotten them – or, at any rate, those of them which do not fit their ideological predelictions. Hence, the 'Jekyll and Hyde' label. In opposition, the restraints of government are thrown off. The sober, consensual, moderately interventionist, confidence-upholding, incomes-policy-pursuing Dr Jekyll is replaced by the roaring ideologist, Mr Hyde. The Conservative Hyde, full of guilt at his Jekyll's flirtations with 'socialism', persuades himself that next time market forces will be given their head. The Labour Hyde, even more full of guilt at *his* Jekyll's flirtations with 'capitalism', resolves that next time the bankers will be defied and a new range of industries nationalised. Each Hyde turns his back on what his Jekyll did in government: each Jekyll has to betray what his Hyde said in opposition.

It seems to me beyond dispute that this pattern is largely responsible for the erosion of governmental authority which I discussed earlier. It means that all governments are attacked for doing what the attackers did when they were in government, and that all oppositions create expectations among their own party supporters which they cannot fulfil. It means that policy lurches from one end of the ideological spectrum to the other, and that institutions are destroyed before they have had time to work. Above all, it means that government has to fight against producer-group opposition with one hand tied behind its back. For each party has to pretend, in its 'Jekyll' phase, that it is still doing what it said it would do in opposition, even though everyone can see that it is not. In 1972 the Heath Government, and in 1975 the second Wilson Government, broke decisively with the policies on which they were elected. But because neither was willing to face a head-on conflict with its party supporters, neither was able to make it clear how total the break was or to explain, clearly and unambiguously, what its new policies meant or what they were designed to do. It was as though the Grand Old Duke of York had insisted that he was still marching up the hill when his men could see perfectly well that they were marching down. This was not a good way to maintain morale or foster understanding among the troops.

It is true, of course, that party politics is a rough game everywhere; and that it is a rough game because democratic self-government is a rough business. But although there are deep party divisions and fierce party battles in other countries, it is hard to think of any other developed democracy where Stewart's 'Jekyll and Hyde' syndrome is as marked as it is here. The reason, I believe, is that, with the possible exception of France – and in France the parties have not alternated in power – it is difficult to think of any other developed democracy where serious contenders for office are so prone to reject the basic assumptions of the mixed economy which they are trying to manage, and to cling to ideologies which have no relevance to the problems which they face in government. Twenty years ago, when Hugh Gaitskell led the Labour Party and Harold Macmillan the Conservative Party it looked as though both big parties were slowly abandoning the ideologies which had inspired them in the past in favour of doctrines more appropriate to the present and future. In this event, the old ideologies seem as firmly entrenched as ever. Since both are ultimately derived from social theories worked out in the early years of the industrial revolution, neither can provide guidance to those called upon to tackle the problems of the last quarter of the twentieth century. The result is that both parties are under constant pressure to focus their attention on dead issues at the expense of living ones. They do not always succumb to the pressure, of course: reality has a habit of breaking through. But it is apt to break through tardily, spasmodically and, all too often, disruptively. If we are to survive tolerably, it seems to me, we shall have to ensure that it does so more easily and more smoothly. A good way to begin would be to acknowledge that Adam Smith and Karl Marx both died a very long time ago.

References

van Beyne, K. and Ionescu, G. (1977), 'The Politics of Employment Policy in Germany and Great Britain', *Government and Opposition* (Spring)

Brittan, S. (1977), *The Economic Consequences of Democracy* (London: Temple Smith)
——— (1978), 'How British is the British Sickness?', *Journal of Law and Economics* (October)
Goldthorpe, J. H. (1978), 'The Current Inflation: Towards a Sociological Account' in Hirsch, F. and Goldthorpe, J. H. (eds.), *The Political Economy of Inflation* (London: Martin Robertson)
Hailsham, Lord (1978), *The Dilemma of Democracy* (London: Collins)
King, A. (1975), 'Overload: Problems of Governing in the 1970s' in Ridley, F. (ed.), *Studies in Politics* (Oxford: Oxford University Press)
Lester, A. (1977), 'Fundamental Rights in the United Kingdom: Law and the British Constitution', *University of Pennsylvania Law Review* (March)
Olson, M. (1979), 'The Political Economy of Comparative Growth Rates' (mimeo)
Runciman, W. G. (1966), *Relative Deprivation and Social Justice* (London: Routledge & Kegan Paul)
Select Committee on Procedure, First Report of, Session 1977–8, vol. 1
Stewart, M. (1977), *The Jekyll and Hyde Years: Politics and Economic Policy Since 1964* (London: Dent)
Walkland, S. (1978), 'The Politics of Parliamentary Reform' in Mackintosh, J. P. (ed.), *People and Parliament* (Farnborough: Saxon House)

3 SOCIAL LIMITS TO TOLERABLE SURVIVAL

David Reisman

The argument in Fred Hirsch's controversial book *Social Limits to Growth* is both a simple and an important one: analogous to the much-discussed physical resources constraint on future growth in the GNP, there exists a parallel social resources constraint on expansion. The latter is more immediate, less 'distant and uncertain' (p. 4), than the former, and has two dimensions: first, the adding-up problem that when it comes to social scarcity there exist a number of goods whose function is 'positional', whose income-elasticity of demand is high but whose price-elasticity of supply is either low or zero; secondly, the ethical problem that a decay in friendliness, generosity and even honesty is likely to occur in a world where economic men see clearly and correctly that a sense of moral obligation bears no significant (or predictable) rate of return.

In this chapter we shall attempt an examination of Fred Hirsch's arguments concerning social limits to growth. In the first section we shall consider the adding-up problem; in the second, the problem of moral decline; in the third some policy inferences; and in the final section some criticisms and extensions of the thesis.

The Adding-up Problem

Economics has traditionally been concerned with that maximisation of collective welfare which results, as if guided by an invisible hand, when each member of society tries rationally but without central co-ordination to maximise his own individual or household welfare. Hirsch maintains, however, that 'the stage may now have been reached where the analytical framework that the economist has come to take for granted . . . has become a hindrance in understanding some key contemporary problems' (p. 2), problems of which the sociologist has for long been aware and which include the following.

First, interdependence of preference-patterns. The satisfaction derived from the consumption of a commodity depends not only on the intrinsic utility yielded by the thing consumed but also on its symbolic function within the consumer's reference-group; for 'a part (but only a part) of satisfaction from positional goods relates to their scarcity as such, implying criteria of status that are inherently comparative' (p. 113). Both Veblen's theory of 'conspicuous consumption' and Duesenberry's 'relative income hypothesis' refer to cases of social scarcity and remind us that economic growth need not imply increased happiness to the extent that relative rather than absolute deprivation is concerned. The concept of interdependence applies not simply to consumer goods, moreover. Top jobs too, for instance, are a scarce social resource, for they serve as desirable means to the socially-valued end of high status: 'Even if you don't like performing as the boss, you may still want to show that you can, that you can have and do what others cannot have and do' (p. 22).

Secondly, interdependence of decisions made. Turning from considerations of social status to those involving purely individual utility, we once again encounter the problem of social scarcity, a dimension of excess demand over supply related not to the production of final utilities but to their absorption:

> The value to me of my education depends not only on how much I have but also on how much the man ahead of me in the job line has. The satisfaction derived from an auto or a country cottage depends on the conditions in which they can be used, which will be strongly influenced by how many other people are using them. (p. 3)

Private consumption has in truth an inevitably social dimension in that the sum of individual decisions made differs substantially from that outcome that might reasonably have been anticipated had we focused exclusively on individual actions in isolation; for 'what each of us can achieve, all cannot' (p. 5).

The implications of the adding-up problem are four in number. First, reduction in amenity-value. Whilst I as an individual might be able to drive my car on a congestion-free highway to my weekend retreat surrounded by unspoiled countryside, I might nonetheless as a social actor be unable to do so where in a growing economy more and more people have cars and crowd the roads in an attempt to reach similar retreats in countryside progressively more overbuilt and aesthetically less pleasing.

Secondly, inflation. Economic growth is accompanied by a rise in the price of positional goods as part of the process of allocating limited supplies in conditions of excess demand. This in turn means a regressive windfall gain to current owners of scarce commodities, who acquired them before rising standards of living and the massification of consumption so dramatically increased their prices relative to the prices of those goods whose supply can be expanded (the price of, say, land suitable for vacation homes near a beauty spot relative to the price of colour televisions, cars or basic foodstuffs). Since all cannot in the positional sector have what some have, economic growth is then accompanied by a distributional struggle and exacerbated social tensions rather than heightened social integration; and consequently accompanied by wage inflation associated with a new beggar-my-neighbour code in the labour market. The increasing power of manual workers and their unions, and the escalated leap-frogging of claims and expectations, is however a threat not simply to the 'harmony and anonymity of the market system' but perhaps to 'its stability and efficiency' (p. 172) as well; for it means that unions increasingly compete with one another for the greatest successes in collective bargaining arenas (since, after all, 'the normal channel of self-improvement for workers in occupations with no career structures is through collective bargaining' (p. 172)) and yet do not see that even a successful if disruptive strike will still lead rather to bitterness than to *embourgeoisement* where such a strike yields the workers money but not the minority goods on which to spend it (since – and here Hirsch is insistent – 'the extension of middle-class objectives has outdistanced middle-class opportunities' (p. 173) in a world of widening reference-groups).

Thirdly, frustration. What some can have, all cannot; and a distributional struggle oriented towards elbowing one's way nearer the front of the queue can never fully choke off total disappointment and false hopes (to say nothing of resentment and anxiety on the part of those already at the head of the queue who come to feel increasingly beleaguered in the face of onslaught after onslaught on relative place) simply because 'the sum of benefits of all the actions taken together is nonetheless zero' (p. 7). Furthermore, the distributional struggle is a struggle for more than money: hence the enormous resistance to the introduction of comprehensive schooling on the part of those parents whose children already attend superior schools, fearful of a reduction in relative social position as well as of an absolute fall in material standards of living.

Fourthly, waste. In a world of scarce positional goods, resources must be wasted on defensive consumption, as in the case of sprawling suburbs (where the desire of more and more people to live in the suburbs leads to reduced access to air and open spaces for the inhabitants of present suburbs, and consequently to an increasing wastage of time and petrol in an attempt to reach a destination ever more distant from the cultural and occupational opportunities of the town centre) and the inflation of paper qualifications (where increased access to formal education has meant increased demand for screening-of-potential rather than primarily training or cultural-humanitarian reasons, educational certification being one of the principal requirements for access to well-paid, satisfying, prestigious but scarce positions of leadership and responsibility). Such cases are cases of waste which mean either more input for the same output (cases where 'the race gets longer for the same prize' (p. 67), since 'if everyone stands on tiptoe, no one sees better' (p. 5)) or even more input for an inferior output (as where a PhD today yields less *entrée* to top jobs than an MSc did yesterday, and is in addition skewed in its social distribution towards wealthy families best able to finance the lengthening obstacle-course of education).

The conclusion then follows: economic liberalism for success presupposes a modest level of absolute income (so that the market mechanism is chiefly allocating material rather than positional goods, and the latter sector remains uncrowded) and a stratified rather than a classless social structure (so that different groups seek different things). In a society where absolute incomes are high and the distribution of relative incomes is somewhat egalitarian, however, social constraints arise and constitute a problem for which decentralised decision-making mechanisms are simply incapable of providing a solution (a problem similar to that which arises in the Keynesian model, where rational pursuit of individual self-interest does not keep the economy at full employment and provides no alternative to explicit state management and co-ordination in the public interest):

> More wealth of the kind attainable by all paradoxically means an increased scramble for the kind of wealth attainable only by some . . . It is now questionable whether the road to the carefree society can run through the market economy, dominated as it is by piecemeal choices exercised by individuals in response to their immediate situation. (p. 26)

The Moral Nexus

Hirsch identifies as a second social limit to growth the decline in friendliness and increase in selfishness which he believes to be associated once again with increasing affluence. Here two social facts are of primary causal significance.

First, the rising marginal cost of time associated with the increasing supply of material goods per hour worked means that 'time becomes scarcer in relation to goods' (p. 73), men are under pressure 'to do more things in – and at – the same time' (p. 73), and time-saving goods and services are developed as a means (a form of defensive consumption) of economising on the scarce resource of time. Since more time is needed for consuming more material goods, and since a further quantity of time is wasted in 'the scramble to acquire larger shares of fixed availabilities' (p. 71), there is a decreased quantity of time available for the time-consuming activities of sociability and friendliness (including the search element of starting contacts which may not 'pay off').

Secondly, a market economy enlists and legitimates individual self-interest and focuses it on monetary exchanges. Commercial advertising, for example, directs its appeal to the consumer's greed rather than to altruistic concern for the welfare of unknown strangers ('Commercial advertising comprises a persistent series of invitations and imperatives to the individual to look after himself and his immediate family; self-interest becomes the social norm, even duty' (p. 82)); and the blandishments of advertisers are reinforced, albeit for different reasons, by the consumerist movement of Ralph Nader and others (where 'the individual is urged to secure maximum value for money for himself or herself. The approach is to the individual as maximising consumer, rather than as cooperating citizen' (p. 82)). Simultaneously, at the same time as material prosperity and consumption increase in importance, so contact, concern and sociability reveal themselves to be inferior goods; for they 'do not, by their nature, have the character of private economic goods: which is to say that the costs and benefits of specific actions do not fall primarily on those undertaking them' (p. 78). In a closely-knit community, bonds are those of reciprocity and mutual aid (as where gift and counter-gift directly imply one another, even if in the long-run rather than the short-run – the case for example, of a lifetime friendship) and/or effects (as where, for emotional reasons, the partner's happiness adds to one's own rather than detracting from it in the way that the exchange model presupposes). In a more loosely-articulated and mobile society, however, the gift is unlikely directly and bilaterally to yield a return-gift to the donor (since one has increasingly to deal with unknown strangers), contacts are in general too casual to generate lasting ties of mutual sympathy and genuine concern, and people find it tempting – and rational – to behave in the manner of free riders with respect to public goods and to seek to take without giving.

The implications of moral decline are again four in number. First, to the extent that altruistic conduct is a necessity rather than a luxury, its decay will bring with it negative externalities in so far as the community is underprovided as a result with free gifts such as blood for transfusion, willingness to help a stranger attacked in the street, or the security of mutual support in a marriage founded on something more durable than calculation of costs and benefits. In area after area of social life, 'the Good Samaritan remedies a market failure' (p. 79); and thus a decline in social involvement resulting from the 'tyranny of small decisions' impoverishes each because it impoverishes all (since that which is a public good to all can easily become a public good to none where people become so money-minded that no citizen is prepared to budget time and effort for the unilateral transfer). Hence we encounter the phenomenon that friendship and sociability, being public goods whose benefits are diffuse rather than specific, tend to be under-supplied relative to demand in rich countries: 'We may want sociability more than ever; yet we cannot, individually and separately, express that want in a way that secures it. This analysis helps explain a frequent casual observation, which otherwise appears economically puzzling: that human contact in advanced economies is increasingly sought but decreasingly attained' (p. 81). Individuals *qua* individuals, in short, may be expected rationally to underproduce the amount of sociability they desire to consume.

Secondly, and turning from quantity to quality of relationships, here again a preoccupation with individual utility has a deleterious effect on the nature of the product. To take one instance, just as sex with a prostitute (bought sex) is inferior to sex based more on congruence of interest than exchange of equivalents, so a highly commercialised form of marriage contract based on rational calculation of costs and benefits is likely similarly to convert friends into merchants (if only because 'the more that is in the contracts, the less can be expected without them' (p. 80); and because in any case 'orgasm as a consumer's right rather rules it out as an ethereal experience' (p. 101). Again, the quality of treatment provided by a doctor in a system of bilateral exchange is likely both to be different from that treatment provided where the *quid pro quo* is not implicit (as where the doctor removes a healthy appendix purely in order to maximise his profits) and to be perceived to be different (witness the rise in malpractice suits in the United States, an indication of diminished trust in doctors on the part of patients). All of this reminds us that the characteristics of a good or service are closely correlated with its mode of provision, and that supplying and demanding are activities substantially dependent on the social environment within which they are situated (so that *what* we have may be no more important than *how* we obtained it).

Thirdly, many choices nowadays presuppose a collective intervention which may not be forthcoming; for the erosion in the moral nexus makes the formulation of effective social policy progressively more difficult. A society with a market bias tends to overproduce goods which can be packaged and sold and to underproduce those which must be consumed in common; but public goods can often be made available in no other way but via public provision, or at the very most via a mode of provision which alters their fundamental character for the worse compared with those features which people would have chosen if given a free choice (consider, for example, a museum charge which removes not only an entrance fee from the pockets of users 'but also the pleasure derived by some visitors from the existence of a part of the cultural heritage as common property available freely to all' (p. 91); or a turnstile restricting access to a pub dartboard to those who have paid a fee, thereby narrowing a game to a small number of effective demanders which up to then had been 'inextricably bound up with open socializing' (p. 90)). The escalating pressures of positional competition (implying as they do both fear of losing one's place relative to others and greater selfishness in consequence) generate resentment on the part of the well-to-do towards subsidising poorer members of the community (e.g. 'formation of new suburbs with homogeneous residents has been a well-documented means for richer residents of big cities to escape from supporting less fortunate citizens' (p. 103)); and greater mobility also induces increased privatisation of facilities on the part of those best situated to pay for them (e.g. 'the substitution of the country club for the village common or city park, or of the effectively private school for the effectively public school' (p. 103)), with a corresponding unwillingness to finance those still dependent on common access, non-exclusive environments and informal exchange. Such privatisation always harms the poor (since they are increasingly asked to pay for what previously was a free good or accept second-rate safety-net provision instead) and is yet another example of the preoccupation with self which characterises the affluent society: 'As general prosperity grows, the difficulty of arranging redistributive transfers through the national or local fiscal system does not diminish. On the contrary, it may even increase' (p. 103). In a world of crowding and commercialisation, in other words, the rate-payers' revolt is fully predictable.

Fourthly, at the very time that new externalities are being generated which can only be dealt with on a collective basis, the very selfishness which gave birth to those externalities is now acknowledged to extend to the political market as well, at least in the Schumpeter-Downs economic approach to politics. According to that approach, the consumer shops for a political leader with desired characteristics (which nowadays, as we have already noted, are increasingly likely to include a preference for the individual and the specific as opposed to the collective and the general) and the producer seeks to match policies supplied to policies demanded purely so as successfully to compete in the market-place for votes (with the result that, precisely because it is in the interests of *each* citizen to do what is not in the interests of *all*, politicians will fear to tackle the adding-up problem lest this harm their personal promotion prospects). More generally, corruption and abuse of power are to be expected from politicians interested exclusively in the maximisation of their own utility; for honesty and a sense of responsibility repose on moral absolutes which both pre-date exchange society and are the precondition for it, but which are increasingly being threatened by the utilitarian perspective and the substitution for morality of rational self-interest. Should judges and politicians truly come to regard themselves as merchants selling their services to the highest bidder, then the 'logical error' (p. 140) in the utilitarian system becomes immediately apparent: in a world where there are no higher values than market-determined costs and benefits, the market system itself becomes unstable – since even private property is not secure from 'the first entrepreneur to be able to raise enough credit to buy the judge' (p. 143).

Early liberalism (the liberalism, for instance, of Adam Smith) 'was predicated on an underlying moral-religious base' (p. 137) which constrained self-interest by ethics as rigidly as others have said it ought to be constrained by laws and the police. Christianity, for example, enjoined altruistic behaviour, and this was a good thing: 'While such cooperation can, in some cases, be replaced by coercive rules, or stimulated through collectively imposed inducements to individuals' private interests, this will rarely be as practicable and efficient as when it is internally motivated' (p. 139). Christianity, moreover, provided external legitimation for absolute values such as devotion to duty, restraint of passion, service to the collectivity, truthfulness and honesty, and these values then became public goods for the whole community – a useful spillover benefit since they are also 'necessary inputs for much of economic output' (p. 141) in a mobile, anonymous, large-scale society where individual behaviour is free of the continuous scrutiny that characterises more traditional communities. Historically speaking, 'the market system was, at bottom, more dependent on religious binding than the feudal system, having abandoned direct social ties maintained by the obligations of custom and status' (p. 143); and yet, ironically perhaps, it is the market system itself which has done most to undermine the unseen source of support that results from the internalisation of social norms over and above that of buying cheap and selling dear.

Early capitalism, in short, was able successfully to rely on the market mechanism precisely because early capitalism was buttressed by social values dating from an earlier stage of social development. Those values are now in decay, and the result is a moral vacuum. Hence the paradox: just at a time when 'the responses of isolated individuals to the situation that faces them have become a less sure guide to promoting the objectives of individuals taken together', yet 'the weakening of traditional social values has made predominantly capitalist economies more difficult to manage, that is, to guide by indirect state intervention' (p. 118). Management is today increasingly necessary; the individualistic ethos makes it increasingly difficult.

Policy Inferences

Hirsch stresses that policy inferences concerning social limits to growth ought to be kept 'guarded and modest' (p. 178), both because there is a restricted amount that we know and because there is a restricted amount that we can do.

At the level of *knowledge*, there is indeterminacy reflecting 'the lack of a precise criterion for economic efficiency through use of collective action' ('We do not have a firm grasp on the full implications of collective action') and also reflecting 'the lack of a quantitative dimension of the critique' ('it has not been found possible to estimate over what proportion of economic activity social limits to growth are in play') (p. 181). This indeterminacy calls in turn for further research into the nature of social limits (and Hirsch emphasises that his book is 'little more than a starting point' (p. vii) with 'no clear-cut implications for immediate policy' (p. 10), especially important since collective intervention imposes costs of its own. In connection with research, moreover, it must be noted with regret that the national accounts as yet provide no statistical measures of positional competition, just as they provide no measure of the 'bads' associated with, say, pollution; and yet, just as 'expenditure on extra laundry services made necessary by a smokier atmosphere' (p. 57) only negates a previous deterioration in individual welfare and merely restores the *status quo ante*, so additional education acquired solely 'so as to safeguard one's access to a particular job at a time that general educational expansion is raising the level of required credentials' (p. 57) ought to be netted out of value added so as to avoid double counting. All human activities do not yield satisfaction to oneself (the case of defensive consumption in the form of, say, extra time wasted in getting to work, the concomitant of the need to dwell in increasingly distant suburbs so as to enjoy constant benefits in terms of amenity); some activities generate dissatisfaction for others (the case of road-congestion); and a reconsideration of the link between statistical value added and psychic pleasure supplied (involving the development of additional social indicators) is urgently needed.

More generally, such knowledge as we have concerning social limits to growth ought to be more widely disseminated, so that members of the public come to appreciate the threat to individual welfare implied by the new adding-up problem and the decay of the moral nexus. One by-product of such awareness is in turn likely to be greater scepticism with respect to salesmanship, and this is a healthy development. After all, 'to the extent that marketing and advertising appeal to individuals to isolate themselves from . . . group or social effects – to get in ahead or to protect their positions – they are socially wasteful. They are then also socially immoral on the mundane level of the morality concerned with social stability and consistency. If all are urged to get ahead, many are likely to have their expectations frustrated' (p. 109).

At the level of *action*, there is a need for explicit central co-ordination of objectives in the field of positional goods, where the discrete, decentralised, piecemeal, marginal adjustments of the market mechanism simply cannot take into account the interactive effects of combined decisions and where each individual in consequence ends up with a social environment significantly different from that which he would have preferred. One course of action which the state can take is land zoning so as to restrict access to the countryside for purposes of constructing new suburbs (and thus to prevent suburban sprawl and protect scenic beauty). Another course of action is social provision of goods and services in areas where all individuals benefit but no single individual can make the relevant rational decisions, as in the case of road-congestion brought about by the absence of a viable alternative mode of transport: 'As public transportation deteriorates, we are given an extra incentive to use our own private mode of transport which in turn results in further deterioration and a worsened position of public vis-à-vis private transportation' (p. 19). Negatively speaking, the public sector must guard itself against escalating claims for public services complementary to positional goods (roads, for example, or education in its screening role), such public services being (and here Hirsch disagrees with Galbraith) not a solution but 'a part of the problem' (p. 106): 'The flaw in the affluent society lies not in the false values of affluence but in its false promise' (p. 110). Within the realm of social scarcity, in summary, individuals come closer to attaining their desired ends the less they seek to attain in isolation their goals:

> In this sense, a shift in the invisible hand from the private into the public or communal sector is needed. Rather than pursuit of self-interest contributing to the social good, pursuit of the social good contributes to the satisfaction of self-interest. The difficulty is that the latter pursuit needs to be deliberately organized under existing standards and instincts of personal behaviour. So the invisible hand is presently unavailable where it is newly needed. (p. 178)

Collective means are now needed in many areas of social life if individual ends are to be attained, but the free market mechanism too has a role to play in solving the problems associated with positional goods. In the labour market, for example, top jobs ('the most important positional sector' (p. 183)) might be allocated by what Hirsch terms a 'Dutch auction' (i.e. an auction which would, in his formulation, reduce Marshall-like, the pay-differentials of those who in compensation have the greatest power, status and job-satisfaction in the community). Although such a method of paring demand (a variable) down to supply (a constant) would be opposed by groups now in power (and their unions), supported by those who favour the career structure, the established pay hierarchy and the traditional differential, it would in truth have a valuable secondary function of reducing social tensions on balance by providing an ethical validation and justification for differences in the capacity to earn and spend. The reduction in differentials could result from the introduction of a totally free market for labour; but, perhaps more realistically, it could also come from discriminatory taxation of highly-paid jobs up to the point where demand equals supply and where those applicants who have not dropped out of the market in disgust are by a process of elimination those who want particular jobs for their intrinsic attractions and not those attractions *plus* the supplementary benefit of superior net renumeration. Reduction in differentials would in turn have beneficial effects for educational institutions, which could then concentrate on educational rather than allocative objectives:

> If education were made a less sure means to acquisition or perpetuation of financial advantages, there would be less reason to restrict competition and diversity within education on distributional grounds. People would then be more likely to choose a particular school or course of education because it fitted their individual needs, rather than as a fast track to high-paying jobs. (p. 187)

And the revised function of educational institutions would then reduce that social waste represented by excessive investment in the acquisition of formal credentials and also have progressive implications for social policy (since the lengthening of time-periods spent in formal education naturally favours the children of past winners in possession of present wealth).

Sharing of advantages is necessary where supply of the scarce utility cannot significantly be expanded; and while the state can do much to equalise access (say, by the provision of free goods such as parks and beaches open to all regardless of income), nonetheless 'it is the haves who expect too much' (p. 188) and who must learn to adapt to the new constraint of positional scarcity. One example of this adaptation is greater power-sharing at work, where (even at the cost of some material inefficiency, and recognising that 'the pains of subordinate status, and the pleasures of superior status, may thereby be reduced a little, with a corresponding diminution in excess demand for superior positions' (p. 42)), leadership roles might be more democratically exercised. A second example is integrated schooling. In a hypothetical society fragmented into an intellectual meritocracy on the one hand and a class of frustrated helots (the 'idiotariat' (p. 126)) on the other, resentments potentially capable of threatening the security of the whole collectivity could be averted should some of the favoured groups agree 'to give up their isolation and perhaps also some of their advantages' (p. 149); and one form that this renunciation could take is the acceptance of the comprehensive school. Parents whose children now attend superior institutions will protest that comprehensivisation will reduce their child's life-chances, and they will be right; for, top jobs being positional goods, it is of value to those having access to superior entry qualifications to protect their interests. Yet what is of advantage to some cannot be of advantage to all; and people must come to accept the need to put social interest (in this case, the reduction of racial and class segregation) above private orientation (in this case, privileged access to a trade). This presupposes state organisation of the process, of course, so as to prevent free riders from abusing their neighbours' generosity ('People may be willing to put social interests first at a modest sacrifice of their individualistic interests, but they cannot act out this preference on their own' (p. 151)), but it also presupposes, most importantly, a willingness to act with an eye to collective obligation and communal needs.

To some extent, this willingness can be justified in terms of rational recognition of interest ('Action that would entail a heavy cost to the individual if undertaken by himself alone could involve imperceptible costs, or even benefits, if similar action were taken by his fellows' (p. 150)), as where citizens all detesting litter all, independently, behave *as if* they care about the damage done by litter to others' contentment and decide rationally not to litter. Yet the internalisation of new moral norms must nonetheless accompany the self-interested altruism of *as if*, precisely because so much of social action takes place in situations where only internal (and not external) restraint is practicable and efficient ('The controllers usually have a large handicap of relevant information. Only *I* can see everywhere I litter' (p. 139)). It is not, of course, entirely clear whence these new moral norms are to spring; but Hirsch suggests they may be associated with a greater belief in the justice of the social system as a whole.

One thing, however, is in Hirsch's view certain: social limits to growth will not be eliminated by the mere process of material growth itself. Expansion may be an alternative to redistribution in the material sector of the economy (where technological progress permits of an increase in supply of goods and services without any deterioration in quality of product). It cannot be an alternative in the positional sector, where one man's gain remains another man's loss and relative as well as absolute values are central to the drama. Hence the dilemma:

> What the wealthy have today can no longer be delivered to the rest of us tomorrow; yet as we individually grow richer, that is what we

> expect. The dynamic interaction between material and positional sectors becomes malign. Instead of alleviating the unmet demands on the economic system, material growth at this point exacerbates them. (p. 67)

Criticisms and Extensions

Hirsch's argument is in three parts concerned, respectively, with the emergence of an adding-up problem, the decay of the moral nexus, and the policy inferences to be drawn from social limits to economic growth. Of these three parts, however, the second would appear central and the first and third essentially derivative from it.

Consider first the adding-up problem. Here the dilemma encountered by the reader is that the beggar-my-neighbour scramble for inclusion appears to extend only to a small percentage of utilities pursued in an affluent society; and that, because most of incremental demand in the foreseeable future is likely to be concentrated in the material rather than the positional sector, it is difficult to believe that today's poor will not be able to have tomorrow many even if not all of the pleasures currently enjoyed by today's rich. It is, in other words, somewhat misleading to argue as if there is an inevitable march in the course of social evolution from the material to the positional; for while some people do, as they become better-off, demand country cottages (which cannot be infinitely replicated), and others demand a Rembrandt original (a case where my gain is truly your loss since the commodity is in totally inelastic supply), still others demand colour televisions, cassette recorders, refrigerators, dishwashers, restaurant meals, dormer windows, electric carving-knives and clothing rather distinctive than durable (commodities which can be mass-produced without encountering social limits) or simply choose to substitute leisure for work by refusing overtime or avoiding promotion in order to have more time to potter in the garden, enjoy a hobby, play with their children or entertain friends. All people, in short, do not want precisely the same things in life even now; and this social pluralism is likely much to be encouraged by greater tolerance of alternative lifestyles and differentiated preference-patterns in an increasingly heterogeneous and complex future.

Even where the demand for positional goods does rise as incomes rise, moreover, it would still be wrong to underestimate the extent to which effective supply can be increased. Technology, for instance, while it admittedly cannot significantly increase the number of holiday-makers on Brighton beach, can nonetheless make available to those holiday-makers at modest cost a wide range of other beaches throughout the world; and while it cannot infinitely augment the number of private cars travelling in to the city-centre at the height of the rush-hour, can provide alternative modes of transport (including devices now in their infancy such as the tele-copier and the video-telephone, which transport not the workers to the work but the work to the workers and thereby allow people – perhaps the parents of small children, perhaps merely lovers of secluded countryside, or perhaps energetic enthusiasts keen to fill the traditional three hours of leisure enjoyed at the place of work by growing vegetables and baking bread – to carry on at home a full business life complete with all necessary office communication, and as a result without ever having to venture forth at all on to congested highways). Social usages clearly have a part to play alongside technological improvements in increasing the effective supply of positional goods, as where flexihours reduce congestion on the roads, flexiweeks raise the weekday productivity of Brighton beach, sharing (which can in practice mean nothing more socialist than renting instead of buying) increases access to the services of otherwise unemployed country cottages, and decentralisation of industry and trade does something to combat the problem of suburban sprawl. The fact that so many concerned citizens, aware of the nuisances associated with (even if not the social limits to) economic growth, have already proposed measures along these lines shows evidence of a healthy recognition of the extent to which men are the masters, not the prisoners, of their social fate.

A distinction must in addition be made between the diminished utility of the few and the augmented utility of the many; for while Jack might feel marginally deprived at having now to share his previously-unspoilt Greek island with other tourists, he nonetheless still obtains much pleasure from it, and so now does Jill. Total happiness is likely to have increased; and while one does sympathise with Jack, it is hard to believe that his deprivation suggests that economic growth *on balance* yields disappointing fruits as more and more people benefit from it. Similarly, while Tom might feel marginally deprived at no longer being able to drive unimpeded by congestion to his office in the City, it is likely that his deprivation is more than offset by the pleasure Dick now obtains from being able to drive home from a party rather than waiting in the rain for a bus, or the satisfaction Harry now experiences of being able to motor with his family in the Highlands of

Scotland. More fundamentally, however, inter-personal and inter-temporal comparisons are fraught with difficulties; for, just as no one can say for certain whether people were happier or less happy before new goods such as the television were invented, so no one can say for certain how happy each or all of the three families today housed in a converted Victorian villa are compared with the single family which lived there a century ago. Things have changed and, as Hirsch would be the first to remind us, static analysis must not be applied to dynamic situations: 'No comparison of welfare can be made where tastes vary' (p. 62). Social progress is slow and gradual, human experience limited and contingent, and it is in practice meaningless to ask the tourist queuing today for an hour to see the Tower of London if he was not in essence happier in 1850: he was not alive in 1850 and, had he been, would have been a different person with different expectations.

In cases where crowding does exist, action does itself in many cases generate the necessary reaction and set into motion, without state intervention, forces tending automatically to correct the abuse. Hirsch himself gives two examples. The first concerns roads where, should access be left unchecked,

> the increased supply then entails a reduction in quality, in the sense that a congested road is of lower quality than a clear one, which is a restraining influence on demand. The classical example of this process in economic literature is the crowding of a new highway that proceeds to the point at which travel along it is no faster than on the old road. (p. 31)

The second concerns top jobs and associated differentials:

> Some responsiveness in relative salary levels to shifts in potential supply and demand undoubtedly exists. The great expansion in supply of college graduates in the United States in the 1950s and 1960s eventually led to a surplus, and between 1969 and 1973 the excess in average mean income of male college graduates over high school graduates was reduced from 50 to 41 per cent. (p. 43)

Our purpose in drawing attention to these two examples is not necessarily to advocate self-regulating allocative mechanisms or the internalisation of information and adjustment costs, only to point out that substitution at the margin evidently extends to positional as well as material sectors and that the existing system does to some extent already provide its own turning-points.

Naturally, it might be objected that the existing system involves waste and frustration, and is for those reasons less acceptable on philosophical grounds than the planned alternative. Yet Hirsch's approach both to waste and to frustration is in truth problematical. Regarding waste, it is important to draw a qualitative distinction between that waste which he associates with the process of competitive educational upgrading and that waste which he identifies as the cost of reaching increasingly distant country cottages (for while both are in his view to be included in the 'deadweight element' (p. 64) in consumption, one would like to think that at least part of the experience of education, even in the eyes of students, is a valued consumer good in its own right and not merely the means to some other end; and that the consumption element is one of the principal reasons for the substantial state subsidy to this field of social activity). It is important also to say why waste in itself is a bad thing (although Hirsch to some extent implicitly does this when he rejects Galbraith's idea of the 'revised sequence' and defends growth in terms of consumer sovereignty, non-manipulated authentic desires and genuine non-satiety, thereby of course also closing the door to the argument that a viable alternative to increasing supply might be ascetically reducing demand, possibly via social control of advertising, on which he blames at least part of our contemporary commodity fetishism). Regarding frustration, it is important to stress that some mutual frustration is endemic to the human condition where the game is played for the fun of playing and the desire of winning; for he who enters a game attracted by jealous emulation and aggressive competitiveness must realise that he stands to lose as well as win, whatever the rules of the game and however low (or high) the stakes. Put in other terms, where positional goods are sought as status symbols rather than exclusively because of their own intrinsic physical properties (where we are speaking of diamond tiaras worn to charity galas rather than merely crowded railway-carriages), the commodities in question would by definition not be sought at all, were their consumption promiscuous rather than conspicuous; but other sources of distinction apart from earning and spending might then emerge (strength, beauty and intelligence are obvious candidates) which confer more prestige on some and, by implication, less prestige on others. Even in a classless society with identical incomes and no physically-positional goods, a sense of frustration might remain – if it is personal standing which men seek and if all are not equally placed (in terms of personal characteristics) to obtain it. In any discussion of status, since what all people want only some can by definition have, the only policy recommendation is a moral one: to accept that most men are risk-lovers rather than risk-averters, but to stress that each man regardless of his temporal estate still merits equal esteem because of his fundamental humanity and because of the function which he performs (whatever it is) within the framework of the social organism. A more accepting and more tolerant society is alone the precondition for the sharing of the nebulous and subjective benefits attached to positional goods sought primarily because of their status-giving properties. Goods positional in some more concrete and objective sense we have already dismissed as more of a footnote *curiosum* than a major social problem.

Consider now the policy-inferences which Hirsch draws from his conclusions (and which alongside the rigour and originality of his analysis appear surprisingly limited and modest). He is certainly right to imply that Rembrandt originals belong in museums and to assert that public transport should be provided publicly where it cannot be provided otherwise. He is, however, on shakier ground when he proposes zoning schemes to prevent over-building of country cottages in beauty spots. Such schemes would generate (as Hirsch himself reminds us) regressive windfall gains to owners already in possession of the scarce good (now artificially to be kept scarce), and who are presumably richer than the *nouveaux arrivés* further down the income scale; and yet Hirsch makes no proposals either for the expropriation of existing owners (so that, in a sense, they are to be allowed to pull up the drawbridge of privilege behind themselves, much as the residents of the Channel Islands can do at the present time) or for the transmission of their head start to be rendered more difficult over time (by the more intensive use, for example, of fiscal weapons such as death duties, capital-gains taxes and wealth taxes). Almost certainly aware of these difficulties, Hirsch does propose at one point that new entry is to be governed not by the price mechanism but by 'public allocation on a nonmarket basis' (p. 185). Almost certainly aware as well of the impossibility of securing any form of consensus for the idea of allocating country cottages as if they were council flats, or for the criteria which might in the present moral climate be applied, Hirsch then abandons his mysterious proposal for a collective view without further explanation.

Most controversial of all are the policy-inferences concerning top jobs (which stand, of course, at the very centre of the discussion, top jobs being both positional goods in their own right and the means, via high earning and spending power, to other positional goods). Here it is surely the liberal fallacy carried to its illogical extreme to assume that automaticity equals (and is perceived to equal) social justice; for even if it is true that deep-seated social tensions and resentments do exist and arise from a conviction that there is no 'conscious justification of the distribution of economic rewards' (p. 177), it is still not clear that supply and demand provide the necessary justification and popular legitimation. For one thing, this neglects the principle of need: an unintelligent but diligent workman with four children, an invalid wife and a heart of gold might maintain, when he compares himself with the bachelor whizz-kid on £20,000 a year, that justice is simply not seen to be done when the differentials he observes around him are set by market valuation rather than in accordance with some more absolute moral standard. Then too, this neglects the concept of class: displaying its roots in liberal individualism, the model speaks of rich and poor but makes no attempt to come to grips with the idea of inheritable status (status based, for instance, on informal education and familial expectations, on genetically-influenced endowments of brains and talents, and, of course, on ownership of non-human resources). Yet it could be maintained that these two omitted variables – the sovereignty of grab and the problem of social stratification – are by themselves, and without any reference to frenzied competition for increasing shares in fixed availabilities, adequate to explain present-day tensions with respect to income distribution. It could be maintained that militancy in the labour market reflects not the failures of capitalism in the positional but rather its outstanding success in the material sector; and that the accelerating free-for-all in a world of accelerating output really only mirrors the co-existence of unbridled greed in an antinomian culture (where the walk-out of ambulance men or power-workers at the height of a snowstorm bears the same relationship to textbook models of industrial relations as Sid Vicious bears to Beethoven) with resentment of anyone able to command two colour televisions while I have only one. If it is true, of course, that present-day tensions with respect to income distribution can adequately be explained in terms of the material sector alone (in terms, in other words, of the very massification of consumption rather than entry-barriers to participation in minority areas), and if it is true that the primary cause of those tensions is to be found in the breakdown of traditional (even if to the philosopher possibly, in terms of actual normative content, debatable) moral limitations, then Hirsch is in our view both right in seeking some 'conscious justification' for who gets what and wrong in thinking that he has found the justification in supply and demand. Supply and demand cannot be the solution, for they are in truth dimensions of the problem.

Hirsch's argument that differentials should be set by the unimpeded forces of the market is an attractive one; for it is clear that top jobs carry with them top status and top satisfaction as well as top pay, and that many incumbents are in consequence overcompensated relative to the natural reward which would just keep them in the trade. Yet reducing returns (either directly or via taxation of income earned) to an occupation up to the point at which the marginal supplier is just willing at that rate to supply his labour is an acceptable technique in economic terms only where lumps of labour are homogeneous. In so far as they are not, however, the danger exists that as incentives are reduced the best men might drop out of the market altogether, opting perhaps for less arduous employment, to start their own business, or to go abroad. There is no reason to suppose that the man just willing to accept a job for its own merits is also the man best able to perform it (although, naturally, there is also no reason to assume the opposite); and to the extent that human potential is widely differentiated rather than highly standardised, the choice the community may have to make is between the rich accountant and the second-rate accountant. Hirsch, presumably, would deny the existence of this choice, insisting instead that leadership positions alone, and not born leaders, are limited in supply. To the extent that the choice is a real one, however, then it has two important policy implications: first, if differential pay is an essential incentive to scarce meritocrats, then an economically rational community will remain obliged to pay a reward to the owner of inherited intelligence such as to put him well ahead in the race to buy country cottages; and secondly, if all children expect to grow up equal in all respects, then some are doomed to have their expectations frustrated precisely because their ambitions are unrealistic and their hopes false.

What a realignment of differentials will mean for social cohesion depends naturally upon one's personal assessment of the stigma associated with what Hirsch anticipates will be *de facto* reverse discrimination; and Hirsch himself, generally optimistic about the future ('The functional need for a change in the social ethic can be expected, over time, to promote it' (p. 179), predicts that the rich will in the last analysis come to accept diminution of privilege and narrowing of differentials because of some realisation that they 'are much farther from the incomes they could rely on if society broke down than are the labourer and the craftsman' (p. 185). Yet such an argument is unconvincing: society, to be frank, is not about to break down, and long before it does citizens with a vested interest in the *status quo* are more likely to press for law and order to defend the freedom of individual enterprise than they are to call for more equal pay and an extension of collective action. Nor are trade unions likely to welcome with any real enthusiasm social reforms which challenge the privileges of their members and also, by implication, the power of giant organisations to defend those privileges in the face of the social interest. The administered labour market is a highly imperfect one, and there are surely few members of the community who would find 'conscious justification' for pay structures in present-day modes of collective bargaining (favouring as they do the strong and the avaricious to the detriment of the weak, the moderate and the unrepresented). It must be noted, moreover, that even if measures were to be taken to substitute the *tâtonnement* and the auctioneer for the disruptive strike and the powerful union, more perfect competition need not upon closer inspection necessarily generate greater equality in remuneration; for it might simply reshuffle existing inequalities in favour of dustmen and away from doctors (although in view of the present-day surplus of workers prepared to supply their labour for low pay and the present-day shortage of certain key professionals, redistribution via the market mechanism might not in practice work to the net advantage of the poor) and thus not solve the problem of command over positional goods (for even supposing that rude mechanicals were actually to be compensated by high incomes for dirty jobs, there is still no reason to think that they would be any more successful than are today's managing directors in winning the caucus-race for a limited supply of country cottages).

The re-establishment (on the side of demand as well as of supply) of a perfectly-competitive labour market is impractical in terms of economic realities and democratic politics; and Hirsch's second-best solution of redistribution via taxation is not only bound to be an unpopular one but, in so far as it attempts to set differentials at the level they would have attained had the market been free, doomed to failure (since technocrats and administrators simply cannot know the equilibrium values that would have been set by some non-existent allocative process). Yet if neither solution provides the requisite 'conscious justification' for income distribution (the conception of incomes policies and quotas designed in accordance with information collected via attitude surveys might have been introduced here but was not), and if neither solution is in addition capable of implementation, then it is difficult to think of convincing reasons why unions should, so long as popular norms so strongly emphasise the individualistic as against the communitarian, willingly benefit unknown strangers at the expense (in direct contradiction to the dictates of self-interest) of their members. Unions are, incidentally, likely to be unusually reluctant to show voluntary restraint or accept less than they can get when the economy is growing slowly and their members are experiencing stagnating standards of living combined with diminished promotion prospects; and this reminds us of the fact that alongside social limits to economic growth there also exist economic limits to social growth. But even in the most favourable of material environments, philosophical arguments are still lacking which would explain why, in the current climate of moral attitudes, unions would or should accept less than maximum possible benefits on the grounds that the full use of their potential power to disrupt would be 'inimical to the general welfare' (p. 145): no one, after all, would demand of the peasant farmer or the manufacturer of soap that he should altruistically charge less than the traffic will bear, and even politicians and civil servants might turn out to have goals of their own such that Watergate is the rule rather than the exception and disinterested devotion to duty is too often subordinated to the values and principles of the wider society. Should the collective consciousness truly place a premium on individual success, then it is by no means easy to share Hirsch's optimism concerning the future of voluntary co-operation and internalised moral absolutes. Perhaps it is true, as he says, that 'in a fair game, I obey the spirit as well as the letter of the rules' (p. 145). What remains to be defined, however, is the precise nature of a fair game; and the essence of the critique in this chapter has been that Hirsch's proposals for a more just and co-ordinated society are by themselves not capable of bringing about either the popular perception of playing a fair game or the moral reformation necessary to ensure affectual commitment to its rules as valued ends in their own right. Nor, indeed, can his recommendations by themselves be expected to do so, for this would imply that perceptions of equity and morality are drawn from an ongoing consensual pool of ideals and essences; and in a society characterised by a decay of the moral nexus it is precisely this pool which would appear to be lacking.

The real social limit is the moral one; and the greatest contribution of Hirsch's book is surely the recognition that an exchange society is in unstable equilibrium so long as it is deficient in built-in restraint of a quasi-religious or ethical nature. As Hirsch puts it, 'in the absence of a "private" sanction such as that furnished by religious belief, co-operation can be expected only on the basis of some directly "felt" sense of duty or obligation' (p. 145). Yet in a large-scale national society one does not have at all times a vested interest in a good reputation or feel vulnerable to informal sanctions; one does have a vested interest in wherever possible being a free rider; and one is continually confronted with the widespread opinion that anything goes so long as the constable does not object.

It is *anomie* rather than the rush hour that presents the greatest threat to late utilitarianism, and Hirsch's justification of increased altruism in terms of *as if* is in a sense as depressing as the disease he identifies: it speaks the language of the enemy in so far as it focuses on right conduct rather than moral intent (I am asked not to litter lest I be littered upon, not because the act of littering is illegitimate in itself), it seeks to derive normative constraint from self-interest (I am asked to assist a stranger in distress as a form of social insurance against the risk that I should myself one day be in a similar situation), and it leaves much of human conduct suspended in the limbo of an ethical void (as where I push my way to the front of a queue comprised entirely of old ladies I am never likely to see again in the knowledge that the rejection of expediency bears no positive return and my selfishness attracts no punitive sanction).

As Hirsch makes abundantly clear, the decay of internalised moral norms only leads to additional waste in enforcing the rules, coupled with a widespread sense of disillusionment associated with the failure successfully to do so. The crucial social limit, one suspects, is not the existence of positional goods but a weakening of those collective ties which alone can give what the calculation of individual costs and benefits as supervised by laws and policemen are incapable of providing: the external moral constraint and perception of purpose that are essential for the process of social intercourse itself. We are truly, as Hirsch stresses, living off the internalised values of our common cultural childhood; and still avoid activities such as burglary, shoplifting, fare-dodging, bullying and deceit (despite the fact that they do in certain circumstances constitute the most rational means to attain a particular end) not simply out of fear but because of the inner voice of a man within who came to dwell long before we learned the art of buying cheap and selling dear. To the extent that his voice is now becoming muted, to the extent that the sitting tenant of ethics is being evicted so that his empty room may be converted into a counting-house, it may indeed be excessively optimistic to talk of social limits to growth. The real problem is surely how long we can continue, as we are at present increasingly seeking to do, to make progress through an ethical vacuum, to dance on the graves of dead philosophers and half-forgotten prophets. The real problem, in short, is not social limits to growth. It is social limits to tolerable survival.

Note

All page references in this chapter are to F. Hirsch, *Social Limits to Growth* (Routledge & Kegan Paul, London, 1977).

PART TWO

ISSUES OF TOLERABLE SURVIVAL

4 THE POLITICAL ECONOMY OF INFLATION

Colin Crouch

To draw attention to the social and political forces behind the economic process of inflation is usually to embark on a criticism of monetarist approaches to that phenomenon. However, it needs to be noted that monetarists are not as blind to political questions as some other kinds of economists; it is in fact to the Chicago school of primarily monetarist economists that we owe much of the recent revival of interest in the political economy of inflation. The problem is that they grossly over-simplify the role of the polity (e.g. Parkin, 1975). While the factor which they consider to be wholly responsible for inflation – excessive expansion of the money supply – is an economic one, it is controlled by a political agency, the government. Indeed, it is ironically monetarists who stress (many would argue exaggerate) the extent to which governments can actually control the money base. The monetarist explanation of inflation therefore lies beyond the economy and is therefore a political one, and yet, with a few honourable exceptions (e.g. Brittan, 1978), monetarists have been curiously willing to make do with some very simplistic and unexamined theories as to why governments are apparently so often willing to allow inflation to take place.[1]

There is in fact some disagreement among them on this. Some stress that responsibility for inflation rests solely with governments themselves, the most prominent representative of this school being Friedman (1963, 1975). Governments are so foolish, irrational, badly advised or 'woolly minded' that they insist on pursuing impossibly high levels of employment or on maintaining under-financed levels of public spending. But why should governments, institutions which have more access to expert advice than most, be so prone to error and folly? Either the evidence that full employment policies necessarily create inflation is not as overwhelming as proponents of the theory claim, or there are reasons why governments pursue policies which create inflation, reasons which deserve greater analysis.

Somewhat more sophisticated theories focus on the politics of public expenditure. Some years ago some American social scientists developed arguments which suggested public services were always likely to be *under*-provided (Downs, 1957; Olson, 1965). While people make a distinct and individual contribution to financing public services through taxation, their return in the form of enjoying services is indistinct, uncertain and not dependent on the fact or the size of their own contribution. Electors will therefore be unwilling to give adequate support to these services and will prefer to keep more of their money for private consumption. However, more recently this debate has been joined by those who have tried to stand the argument on its head and show that public services are *over*-provided. They point out that governments, unlike private persons, do not have to ensure that their spending is balanced by income. If there is public pressure for improved services alongside public resistance to taxation, then governments can go on spending by the simple expedient of printing more money (Buchanan and Wagner, 1977; Brittan, 1977). Further, public spending is here seen as constituting little more than electoral 'bribes'; if governments spend money they do so merely in order to win the electoral support of specific sections of the population. From this has been derived the recently popular thesis of the political trade-cycle: politicians increase public spending before an election and reduce it (or raise taxes) afterwards, thereby distorting the rhythm of the true economic trade-cycle in an inflationary way and at the same time producing unwanted goods.

These are not arguments to dismiss out of hand. (There are plenty of examples of targeted expenditure in the recent political histories of, for example, the USA, France and Italy; it is not too far-fetched to regard the EEC Common Agricultural Policy as being, in part, a mechanism whereby the whole of Western Europe subsidised the hold of the Gaullist Party on the loyalty of French farmers.) But they are grossly exaggerated: public spending is not just a matter of electoral bribes, but the means by which societies provide an infrastructure of education, health, roads, etc. on which the productive economy depends, provide such services as defence, police and environmental protection which cannot be privately financed, and support both industries and individuals temporarily or permanently unable to support themselves on the market and thus liable to become a threat to social stability. It is therefore not surprising that attempts to test the thesis of the political trade-cycle have been unimpressive (Nordhaus, 1975). The important point for our purposes is to note that the sources of pressure for government spending are more deeply rooted than these simple arguments about government folly or wickedness allow.

Another weakness of these arguments on public spending is their assumption that, while there is public resistance to increasing taxation, there are no forces inducing governments to control inflation. Not only does this disregard the enormous power of holders of a currency and investors to express their lack of confidence in an economy with high inflation (Hirsch, 1978, pp. 266–9), but even within the realm of electoral politics it assumes either that the electorate is not concerned about the price level or that it does not hold governments responsible for it – both highly unlikely propositions.[2]

If these monetarist arguments were correct one would expect to find some relationship between different countries' levels of public spending and their inflation rates. The same should follow from the argument of Minford (in this volume) that inflation by raising tax revenue, makes possible rises in public spending (see also Brittan, 1978). It is therefore highly significant that attempts at relating high levels of public spending to high levels of inflation in international comparisons have been unsuccessful (Peacock and Ricketts, 1978) or have even produced the opposite result (Panić, 1976, 1978). It may well be that there are occasions when a government is incapable of raising the revenue for a sudden massive increase in spending on an unpopular cause, with the resulting budgetary deficit contributing to inflation – the most famous and highly important example being the US Government's expenditure on the Vietnam War (Johnson, 1975; Soskice, 1978). But it would be wrong to assume that all dilemmas over public spending can be reduced to such a simple paradigm, or that governments have inadequate disincentives to allow inflation to occur. At the very least it has to be conceded that governments may have made a reasonable and intelligible trade-off when accepting a rise in the price level.

Trade Unions and Other 'Social Forces'

Some monetarists are prepared to go further in their acceptance that deeper social forces may lie behind inflationary policies (Hayek, 1958; Haberler, 1966). For example, Hayek argues that governments may increase the money supply in order to preserve full employment after successful wage claims have forced up the price of labour beyond that justified by higher productivity. This raises the whole question of the ways in which the actions of trade unions and other organised groups are relevant to inflation, which need to be understood more broadly than Hayek here concedes.

First, many monetarists discount the possibility of a constant union influence on inflation on the grounds that an existing level of 'monopoly power' cannot explain a constantly *rising* price level (Friedman, 1966). The problem with this argument is its attempt to assimilate union activity to simple monopoly theory, treating expansions in union membership as equivalent to the growth in market share of a commercial monopoly. But organisations of labour are not like orthodox monopolies. A business monopoly occurs when a firm reaches a certain degree of market dominance. It then adjusts its pricing and supply policies as a result of known parameters of its environment, and simply implements the decision to do this through its internal hierarchy. The position of a union is very different. Members do not just have to be recruited (the equivalent of the firm's growing market share), but they have to be sufficiently well-organised and confident of their own organisation to be able to put the fact of their membership to test in negotiations with the employer. A labour monopoly has to be *mobilised* in order to convince both employers *and* the union and workers themselves that it is viable. This process is both gradual and cumulative, as workers learn through their own experience, and that of others, the extent of their bargaining power and the strength of their solidarity. Studies of shop-floor bargaining have demonstrated this accretive process (Brown, 1973).

During the latter 1950s and 1960s, the years of creeping inflation, workers in many sectors of employment were gradually exploiting the possibilities opened up by full employment and trade union organisation; the 'labour monopoly' did *not* exist as a relatively constant fact, capable of no more than a once-and-for-all effect on the price level, but was growing in a manner compatible with the requirements of a cause of inflation. When we come to the period of much higher inflation, from the late 1960s onwards, we find a considerable increase in labour mobilisation. Indeed, in Britain and elsewhere, even the fact which would be acknowledged by monetarists as constituting a rise in labour's monopoly power, membership, was rising steadily. But alongside this there were developments in willingness to strike and in a shift in the organisational base to the shop floor (Barkin, 1975; Crouch and Pizzorno, 1978). The effect of some of these institutional variables on wage increases has been demonstrated in quantitative tests (e.g. Layard, Metcalf and Nickell, 1978). I am not necessarily arguing here that labour action is the autonomous source of upward pressure on prices, though it may be in certain circumstances, if a number of unions independently increase their strength over a short period of time (Flemming, 1978). In fact, there is some evidence that recent British wage explosions have been, at least in part, the result of workers trying to recoup losses in disposable real incomes following increases in taxation (Wilkinson and Turner, 1975). The point is that the organisation of labour makes it possible for workers to make fairly successful attempts at such a recouping, intensifying and perpetuating an initially exogenous inflationary shock. If their ability to do this has been increasing, then there will be a tendency to inflation.

Another objection raised to the role of unions in generating or perpetuating inflation rests on the observations that inflation must result from the simultaneous wage demands of large numbers of workers, and that workers do not actually choose inflation. Therefore, if unions found that their actions were contributing to inflation they would desist from the action concerned. This again rests on the analogy with the business monopoly, which has the capacity to take self-interested action in the face of its market environment. But again the analogy is inappropriate. In an industrial relations system of the British or North American type, union movements do not have that kind of overall co-ordination. Unlike the business monopoly such a union movement consists of a large number of actors, sufficiently organised to resist the immediate consequences of market forces, but not capable of cohesion across a broad front in order to steer the most rational overall path through those forces. Any one group of workers or individual union may realise that the effect of a general increase in wages will be inflation; but by definition no one group of workers can by its own actions affect general behaviour. Indeed, to stand aside in some perceived general interest while the rest of that generality presses its claims is simply to ensure that the group concerned loses out. Centralised union movements of the German, Austrian or Scandinavian type are in a different position – they are capable of overall co-ordination in the face of macro-economic variables; but, to anticipate a later argument, these are precisely the union movements which have been associated with low rates of wage-led inflation. A union movement which is growing in strength, confidence and efficiency of organisation, but growing in an unco-ordinated, decentralised way is capable of adding to inflationary pressure, and that is precisely the kind of union movement Britain (and, more recently, Italy) have known. But to grasp that point requires a wider sociological appreciation of the nature of trade union strength than is provided by the extension of simple monopoly analysis.

A second set of arguments which has been deployed against the more simplistic notions of some monetarists about the nature of wages pressure goes far deeper than the above organisational account. The central claim here is that, over the past decades, a series of status barriers which formerly inhibited the ambitions of ordinary people have been eroded. At the same time, full employment and civil liberties have made it possible for them to press successfully their demands for a share in the good life, trade unionism being one but not the only form taken by this drive. Society has not been able to resist this pressure, but existing privileged groups have also been able to protect their position, and the resulting strain on resources has been borne by the price level.

This argument has appeared in a variety of forms and from the most heterogeneous political positions. Arguments that the libertarian climate of the 1960s bred a 'cult of symbolic and temporary but forceful action' which spread from the students' movement to collective bargaining (Wiles, 1973, p. 378); that pop culture and black immigrants corrupted traditional Western values (Mishan, 1974); or that democracy itself is likely to threaten economic sense (Brittan, 1975) are clearly voices from the right. On the other hand arguments that a mature working class has gradually thrown off the artificial status restraints of an irrational traditional deference (Goldthorpe, 1978); that inadequate public spending leads to people satisfying their increased expectations through inflationary demands and industrial conflict (Panić, 1978; Hibbs, 1978); or that capitalism is caught in the contradictions wrought by its own incitement of an acquisitiveness which it cannot accommodate (Hirsch, 1977, 1978) are those of the left.

However varied, these arguments have a common root which derives ultimately from the far-sighted observations of Schumpeter (1942) – who was, fittingly, a Marxist turned conservative! The argument, which has been developed most originally and most recently by the late Fred Hirsch (1977) is that the viability of a capitalist economy depends on a certain pre-capitalist moral legacy: while entrepreneurs are expected to be vigorous, thrusting, innovative, the mass of workers is meant to be obedient and docile, respecting the authority of the employer just as their rural predecessors deferred to their feudal lord. Early capitalism inherited that kind of deference. But by its nature capitalism cannot itself generate it (though there have been some very important attempts to do so (Bendix, 1956)), and as the pre-capitalist residue eventually declines, capitalism's own acquisitive ethic passes on to the working class.

These themes are broad, and it is difficult to find evidence for them.

One piece of possible *counter*-evidence has been the finding that, despite the upheavals in the United Kingdom over the past decade, reference groups remain very much what they were in the early 1960s (Daniel, 1975; Runciman, 1966). Working people still have little perception of how the truly rich fare, and fix their ambitions in terms of people around them with similar but slightly higher standards of living. It should be remembered that when the leaders of the National Union of Mineworkers declared in the winter of 1973/4 that miners should be 'top of the tree', they were referring explicitly to the league tables of earnings of *manual* workers. However, it may be that, while objectives themselves have not changed radically, people's determination to pursue existing objectives or willingness to use militant means to secure them, has changed. This would then be consistent with our earlier discussion of changes in trade union organisation, though these last points suggest far deeper currents of change. Further, while it may be difficult to find evidence that links a decline in deference to inflation-producing behaviour, there is considerable evidence that deference as such has declined (McKenzie and Silver, 1968; Goldthorpe and Lockwood, 1968–9; Jessop, 1973; Crouch, 1975).

Some of the proponents of the arguments discussed here would regard themselves as monetarists on economic policy – e.g. Brittan. These show a greater interest in social variables than many of their colleagues. But these arguments have important implications for monetarist accounts of and remedies for inflation. If the Hirschian version is correct, that capitalism destroys the legacy of pre-capitalist values on which it depends though which it contradicts, then a monetarist economic regime is likely to make matters worse rather than better by hastening the decline of that legacy and inhibiting the emergence of any modern equivalents. This is because the policies which accompany monetarism – a full-blooded return to the free market and the reduction of publicly-provided welfare – are the embodiment of that acquisitiveness which is considered to produce the incessant drive for higher income.

A third set of arguments puts the growth of trade-union power in another wider context: that of developments in the structure of the economy. If the values of capitalism have been spreading, its structures have not. Rather, a whole range of forces serve, if not to destroy competition and market disciplines, at least to make their operation 'sticky' and subject to heavy interference by the economic actors involved. Given that the actors able to do this are almost without exception those on the supply side, an important consequence is a steady upward pressure on the price level. The phenomenon concerned is one which Hilferding (1910) identified in Austria and Germany as 'organised capitalism'. He saw the main mechanism as the protective cartelisation of that period, which was perhaps inaccurate, but he correctly identified the direction of change in modern capitalism.

Partly because of the natural consequence of competition itself, which by punishing the unsuccessful reduces the number of producers, partly because of the scale of modern technology, and partly because of the nature of contemporary commercial and promotional techniques, there is a tendency towards oligopoly in most sectors of modern industry. The costs of establishing capital-intensive plant, of maintaining a large research and development facility and of setting up advertising and marketing outlets impose enormous barriers to new entrants into a market, unless of course they are existing large companies extending their activities to new fields (Sylos-Labini, 1974). Further, the scale of investment required for important new projects in several leading sectors means that private firms are unable to bear the risks usually attendant on market activities, and the government has to intervene to underwrite many of those risks (Galbraith, 1967). Large companies also want to insulate themselves from the vagaries of the labour market; they develop pay structures and career patterns that pursue their own internal rationale rather than one dictated by external market forces (Crouch, 1974; Dore, 1973). Further again, for a variety of motives governments themselves intervene in the market to sustain employment levels and to provide certain goods and services, and while these sometimes follow market principles, they do not do so rigorously. Finally, countries with sizeable agricultural populations develop farm-support policies to guarantee rural incomes which insulate farming operations from much of the fluctuation of the agricultural market.

In other words, at many points the modern economy is liable to manipulation by primarily producer interests. This generates a constant tendency towards inflation of a kind that has previously only been known in wartime. Those aspects of this phenomenon which relate to government activity alone are of course well known to monetarists, but those stemming from the structure of private industry itself are less often discussed by them. The most important, because most deeply rooted, aspect of the whole process is the trend to oligopoly. It is not that there is no competition in such sectors; in a sense all goods and services compete with each other, and in some sectors there is fierce international competition. But oligopolistic firms are not subject to the market in the same way as those in perfect competition; they have some capacity for strategy, for planning prices and output, and of course for collusion, even if of a tacit kind. They are able to act, not just as units governed solely by the market, but as organisations; their price behaviour has some degree of autonomy from overall levels of demand, and a capacity for strategic decisions is not compatible with the concept of a free market. As Sylos-Labini has expressed the point (1976, p. 227):

> The fact is that in competition, when demand falls, price falls, since firms cannot do anything to prevent that fall. In oligopoly, firms, and particularly the leading firms, which control sizeable shares of the market and must be concerned with the behaviour of total demand, can avoid a price fall by reducing their output; they can also avoid a price rise when demand increases.

A similar relative autonomy from demand levels is also true, through a somewhat different process, in the public sector – which has in most countries also increased in size. Now, it is within the oligopolies and the public sector that unionisation in most countries is strongest; and because of the relative autonomy of prices, it is within these sectors that unions are able to bid up wages, not entirely independently of overall levels of employment, but with considerably less dependence than in a perfectly competitive system, especially where the firms are developing their own internal labour markets. However much union leaders may complain about the trend to oligopoly and monopoly in their public political statements, trade unions and corporate giants thrive together. Unions have been able to pre-empt for labour at least some of the fruits of market power produced by the concentration of industry, leading to either a profits squeeze or, as prices eventually rise, inflation – probably a combination of both.

An important implication of this argument is that, given the relative autonomy of the wage-price fixing process from overall levels of demand in the economy, the level of unemployment necessary to eliminate the inflationary thrust will be considerably higher than in a competitive system; and it is the big oligopolies who, even in times of monetary contraction, will have continued access to credit from financial institutions and their own overseas operations. To return to Sylos-Labini (1976, p. 227):

> under contemporary conditions, a considerable price fall can take place only during a severe slump in output and employment, whereas

> in the past century a price fall was a normal occurrence and only exceptionally accompanied by an interruption of the process of economic growth.

If a rise in unemployment is large enough it must eventually have an impact on union wage pressure, but that rise may be very large and prolonged, far more intense than a frictional adjustment of economic variables. During that process it will be the more competitive, market-exposed sectors which will suffer first, ironically leaving the economy more characterised by oligopoly than before.

There is a final set of arguments concerning socio-political developments in the economy that can best be summarised by saying that in modern economies we have eaten of the tree of knowledge, a position from which there is no return. By this I mean that we have learned that the rules of the economy are man-made and can be interfered with when they press too hard. We no longer believe that the level of unemployment is something beyond the reach of government policy, or that the gold standard has to be maintained at all costs, because in the past we have disobeyed the taboo and survived. As Brittan reluctantly concedes: 'For myths have social value only when people do not realise they are myths' (1978, p. 179).

And yet it is an important plank of much monetarist thinking to try to devise institutions that will somehow put the stability of money out of the reach of politics, to ensure that whatever other goals of policy are sacrificed, this one will never be tampered with. The constitutional neutrality of Central Banks is proposed, or constitutional amendments which will impose permanent ceilings on the level of public expenditure. But as Hirsch has argued (1978, pp. 9, 268) both business and government are likely to use the extraordinary complexity of the international monetary system to find ways round such constraints, while such measures would still lack the binding force of a widely-believed myth. Since it would be known that the constitutional provision had been introduced as a specific political choice, it would always be open to scrutiny in the light of alternative political choices. In pointing this out I do not of course mean that politics can ignore the constraints of the market indefinitely; these constraints can only be diverted, rechannelled, postponed. But it is on modifying action of that kind that everyday politics thrives, and there is no way that an issue once acknowledged to be politically manipulable can then suddenly be placed beyond bounds. Current proposals by Milton Friedman and others to have public spending limits incorporated in the

Constitution of the USA are likely to go the same way as the last attempt to prescribe substantive behaviour in that document: prohibition.

Policy Conclusions

Inflation should therefore be seen as an expression of an economy which cannot work as a perfect market economy with a suppressed working class, for reasons which include but go far beyond simple questions of the autonomous behaviour of governments. It is important to note that such an account does not of itself dictate any particular policy conclusions. It is possible to concede all the above and still maintain a monetarist stance. It can be argued that, if such is the state of the economy, then it is even more important to impose a stern monetary drag on its inflationary tendencies. If the supply of money is pressed down far enough it must eventually reduce inflation, whatever its original source. As Friedman has said (1953, p. 266):

> Suppose the Federal Reserve were to sell $10 billion worth of government securities and thereby roughly halve the reserve balances of member-banks. Could inflation nonetheless proceed? If so, then what if it sold $15 billion? $20 billion? Clearly a sufficiently drastic reduction in the supply of money could bring economic activity almost to a halt.

However, as this implies, there may be high costs to such a strategy, especially if the initial monetary expansion was a response to pre-existing and durable social forces. Some of the main problems which need to be borne in mind are the following:

(1) If the forces which impart inflationary tendencies to the economy are more deeply rooted than government manipulation of the money supply, then attempts to control inflation through that weapon alone are likely to involve savage distortions. At the same time monetary policy cannot of itself rid the economy of those inflationary forces, which will re-appear after the period of contraction – unless the contraction is of such severity that it induces a level of unemployment so high that both organised labour and large-scale industry are virtually destroyed.

(2) Inflation is not necessarily the worst disaster which can befall an

economy, and within certain levels it may serve as a useful defuser of otherwise uncontainable conflicts. In saying this I am not pretending that we can afford to be complacent about inflation or that nasty and unpopular measures need never be taken in order to reduce it. I am also aware of the strength of the monetarist argument that it is difficult for inflation to be sustained indefinitely at modest levels without accelerating, as a result of inflationary expectations. However, it is as well to recognise some of inflation's positive contributions, if only to become aware of the likely adverse consequences of elevating price stability to the one supreme goal of economic policy. As a succession of observers has acknowledged, and as has been implicit throughout the above analysis, inflation is a means of easing distributional conflicts between social groups. Where different groups of workers, entrepreneurs, and the recipients of public spending are all competing for income shares, and all have the freedom to push for their interests, inflation is an albeit temporary means of softening the outcome.[3] Rather than the conflict being resolved directly and openly, with victories and defeats definite, they all receive money gains but see these eroded by subsequent rises in the price level. One can of course object to this. Marxists will reasonably complain that workers' money wage gains become a mere mystification and that it will be the workers who eventually lose from rising prices. Conservatives will equally reasonably complain that it would be better to have the conflict out and cut back directly on the shares of workers and public spending rather than go through the charade of an inflation which makes arbitrary redistributions and renders the whole economy less competitive. Nevertheless, it remains a rational option to prefer conflicts to be terminated before the point where one side has to destroy the other, and to prefer them to be deflected into less violent channels, of which inflation may sometimes be an example. A temporary burst of inflation such as that undergone in the UK and elsewhere in the mid-1970s may enable a society to turn an awkward economic corner with conflicts and violence more contained than by some alternative policies. In the longer term, continuous but modest levels of inflation may permit the co-existence of social interests which would otherwise become incompatible.

(3) Following from this, we can try to place in some perspective the experience of the Keynesian period of Western economies, which ran broadly from World War II to the mid-1970s. It has become fashionable to regard those years as wrong-headed and disastrous,[4] primarily because they led to more or less constant increases in public social

spending and persistent inflation. But were they such disastrous years? Coupled admittedly with the post-war surge of technical development, the Keynesian period of full employment created confidence in industry that expansion would be sustained, which meant that it was sustained. Economies grew and the great majority of people led more prosperous and secure lives than ever before in recorded history.[5] But more than that, Keynesian policies, again assisted by technical progress, enabled resolution of a social conundrum that had previously been feared to be impossible: the co-existence of a primarily capitalist economy with full employment and widespread liberties for a fully enfranchised working class. One of the reasons it was possible was that inflation bore some of the strains of the distributional conflict which was able to express itself. The new monetarism, which is so impatient of Keynesian permissiveness, has yet to show that it can maintain a similar subtle balance of freedoms; some might say that it has yet to show that it intends to try – a view which is lent considerable credence by the aversion for democracy openly displayed by many monetarists (e.g. Minford in this volume; Brittan, 1975). But what alternative counter-inflation policies might flow from an account of the socio-political roots of inflation?

A first suggestion follows from the observation that an oligopolistic economy gives considerable discretion in price fixing to producer interests, making prices 'sticky downwards'. We need agencies which will provide spurs to efficiency and keen pricing in the absence of effective market forces. Something of this kind was attempted by the National Board for Prices and Incomes (established by a Labour government and abolished by a Conservative one) and more recently by the Price Commission (established by a Conservative government, expanded by a Labour government, but abolished by another Conservative one). There is room for debate and amendment over the particular criteria applied by such agencies and over the nature of their powers, but there can be little doubt that an economy both as concentrated and as inefficient as the British needs something of this kind. The effectiveness of these agencies cannot be judged simply from their imputed effect on the retail price index during a particular year. Their value will be seen as, over a period of years, firms get to know which issues the agency members are likely to probe, and on which matters they will expect action to have been taken before the firm appears before them on a future occasion. These agencies therefore need to become established and accepted in order to do their work, and it is most unfortunate that the Conservative Party cannot be persuaded to adopt a more consistent positive line on what could easily become a useful part of the political consensus. Policies to counter inefficiency and inflationary pricing through the stimulation of competition alone are unlikely to succeed, because in so many leading sectors oligopoly is inherent to the technological and commercial process.

Investigations into pricing can also have some effect on wage fixing, but, to move to a second area of policy, the inflationary implications of union behaviour need separate attention. British trade unionism has been characterised here as extensive but unco-ordinated, and it is this combination which is inflationary. It is not enough to tackle this by a formal incomes policy, because this builds up tensions which, given the structure of collective bargaining, burst the banks of the policy after only short intervals (Brittan and Lilley, 1977; Tarling and Wilkinson, 1977). One problem is that incomes policy is not just trying to control autonomous wage pressure, but to restrain money wage growth to protect employment and public spending. Full employment is potentially inflationary in that it increases workers' capacity for wages pressure.[6] Conscious restraint by labour may therefore increase the level of employment which is compatible with price stability. Similarly, attempts by labour to recoup through wage rises taxation raised to finance public spending will also be an inflationary pressure, which conscious restraint can contain, raising the level of public spending which is compatible with price stability.

Full employment, high public spending and price stability are all in unions' interests – indeed the first two are high among their priorities. And yet their bargaining actions so often act counter to these priorities. This is partly because the decentralised, fragmented nature of collective bargaining enables each group to pursue its own immediate wage goals, but does not permit it to take account of macro-economic consequences or general goals, as has been discussed above. At moments of temporary centralisation, as in 1948–50 or 1975–7, the union movement has been capable of co-ordination; so, over far longer periods, have the considerably more cohesive union movements of West Germany, Sweden, Norway, the Netherlands and Austria.

What will make the British movement more co-ordinated? The subject is a detailed one in itself and cannot be discussed fully here; all we can do is put some themes on the agenda of debate. First, there should be positive gains from giving the Trades Union Congress and the national union leaderships a greater stake in national economic planning. This *both* clarifies the economy-wide implications of wage behaviour *and* by enhancing the importance and capability of the national structure strengthens the role of the leaderships within the movement as a whole. Processes of this kind preceded the spells of union co-operation mentioned above. But on both these occasions the effects were temporary. One reason has been the ineffectiveness of the forums in which the unions were involved in actually affecting the course of economic policy – a problem touching wider issues of British economic structure, in particular the relationship between the industrial and financial sectors (Blank, 1977; Crouch, 1980). Another concerns the fragmented nature of shop-floor power. Can this be harnessed to activities other than constant wage pressure without losing its valuable role in defending workers' day-to-day interests – something that might have been secured by the various abortive proposals of the mid-1970s for worker participation in management (Bullock, 1977) or in the operation of planning agreements?

These points discussed so far concern adjustments to institutional relations. Their central rationale is this: a modern economy is characterised by organisations, on the sides of both capital and labour, which have some power to interfere with market forces. Organisations cannot be regulated solely by economic means, because they are political phenomena. We therefore have to look for initiatives at the political level, and not just the economic (Crouch, 1978). However, having stressed that, it is finally important to remind ourselves that inflationary strain can be eased, though not cured, by a high level of economic growth. If inflation is a means of absorbing distributional conflicts, economic growth can achieve the same end far more satisfactorily. As the late Anthony Crosland never tired of pointing out, if there is growth everyone can have something more, even if their interests conflict.[7]

This is not a very helpful point to make unless we can go on to show how a declining economy can grow in the teeth of a prolonged world recession, but it is worth saying for two reasons. First, it points to the possibility of more constructive solutions than institutional rejigging. Secondly, at a time when expansionary policies are under attack and being avoided on account of their inflationary implications, it is well to be reminded that expansion can, by reducing important sources of inflation, offset some of these; and *vice versa*, a strategy of deflation and cut-back as advocated by monetarist theory – especially when it is used as a political weapon rather than an economic tool – may carry its own paradoxical inflationary momentum by sharpening the intensity of distributional struggles and by reducing the ability of the public sector to soften those struggles by making available universal goods.

Acknowledgement

I have been greatly helped in preparing this chapter by my participation in the discussions of the Brookings Institution project on the politics and sociology of global inflation, convened by Leon Lindberg and Charles Maier. I have also drawn greatly on the papers in Hirsch and Goldthorpe (1978). The tragic early death of Fred Hirsch early in 1978 robbed the study of political economy of one of its most brilliant exponents at a time when his contribution to both the academic and the practical issues of that field is greatly needed.

Notes

1. Much of the following argument implies, for the sake of debate, acceptance of the *economic* argument linking money supply and inflation. This is of course fiercely contested by other economic schools – see for example Cripps (1977), who ends his account with a conclusion similar to that of the present chapter: 'The two main routes to abatement of inflation are, therefore, improved economic performance, which will bring real wages more nearly in line with norms, and institutional agreements to moderate wage targets. Both are more likely to be achieved in conditions of full employment than in times of low output and high unemployment' (p. 111).

2. It was neglect of these factors which led Michael Parkin to predict, in 1975, that by 1977 inflation would be running at around 30 per cent (quoted in Brittan, 1978, p. 184).

3. These are the interests which seem most relevant in the political economy of contemporary Western societies. At other times and places the configurations may be different (Maier, 1975 and 1978; Jackson and Turner, 1975). Others who have noted the conflict-softening role of inflation are Aujac (1950) and Crouch (1978).

4. See Buchanan and Wagner (1977); also the speech by Sir Geoffrey Howe, Chancellor of the Exchequer, to a *Financial Times* conference, 23 July 1979.

5. West Germany is sometimes regarded as an important exception, in that its growth rate has been extraordinarily good, while it did not formally adopt Keynesian politics until 1967. However, this overlooks the fact that German economic growth was very heavily export-dependent – that is, dependent on demand in other countries which were pursuing Keynesian policies. It was a clever strategy, but by definition one which could not be imitated by all economies; to that extent it is not unfair to regard Germany as having been a 'free rider' on international Keynesianism (Crouch, 1980). In addition, German tight-money policies never extended to credit available to industry; and for several years German public spending has taken a bigger proportion of gross domestic product than that of Britain.

6. In saying this, one should not forget that high wage claims can make a positive contribution to productivity by forcing companies to improve efficiency in order to meet the cost of the claims. This has long been the basis of union wage policy in Sweden (Robinson, 1974).

7. This point is also made by Marquand in this volume. It is subject to the important limitation pointed out by Hirsch (1977), that some goods are

'positional'; that is, people desire them because they put their possessors in front of everyone else and not for their intrinsic quality. A rich society can provide everyone with comfortable seats at the football ground, but only a few can sit in the front row. However, for a critique of Hirsch on positional goods, see Reisman in this volume (Chapter 3).

References

Aujac, H. (1950), 'L'Influence du Comportement des Groupes Sociaux sur le Développement d'une Inflation', *Economic Appliqué*, 4

Barkin, S. (ed.) (1975), *Worker Militancy and its Consequences, 1965–75* (New York: Praeger)

Bendix, R. (1956), *Work and Authority in Industry* (New York: Wiley)

Blank, S. (1977), 'Britain: The Politics of Foreign Economic Policy, the Domestic Economy and the Problem of Pluralistic Stagnation', *International Organisation*, vol. 31, no. 4

Brittan, S. (1975), 'The Economic Contradictions of Democracy', *British Journal of Political Science* (April)

——— (1977), *The Economic Consequences of Democracy* (London: Temple Smith)

——— (1978), 'Inflation and Democracy' in Hirsch and Goldthorpe

Brittan, S. and Lilley, P. (1977), *The Delusion of Incomes Policy* (London: Temple Smith)

Brown, W. (1973), *Piecework Bargaining* (London: Heinemann)

Buchanan, J. M. and Wagner, R. E. (1977), *Democracy in Deficit: The Political Legacy of Lord Keynes* (New York: Academic Press)

Bullock, Lord (1977), *Industrial Democracy: Report of the Committee of Inquiry into Industrial Democracy*, Cmnd. 6706 (London: HMSO)

Cripps, F. (1977), 'The Money Supply, Wages and Inflation', *Cambridge Journal of Economics,* 1

Crouch, C. J. (1974), 'The Ideology of a Managerial Elite: The National Board for Prices and Incomes 1965–70' in Crewe, I. (ed.), *British Political Sociology Yearbook, Volume I: Elites in Western Democracy* (London: Croom Helm)

——— (1975), 'The Drive for Equality?' in Lindberg, L. *et al.* (eds.), *Stress and Contradiction in Modern Capitalism* (Lexington: D. C. Heath)

——— (1978), 'Inflation and the Political Organisation of Economic Interests' in Hirsch and Goldthorpe

——— (1980), 'Varieties of Trade Union Weakness: Organised Labour and Capital Formation in Britain, Federal Germany and Sweden', *West European Politics* (January) vol. 3, no. 1

Crouch, C. J. and Pizzorno, A. (eds.) (1978), *The Resurgence of Class Conflict in Western Europe Since 1968*, two volumes (London: Macmillan)

Daniel, W. W. (1975), *The PEP Survey of Inflation* (London: PEP)

Dore, R. P. (1973), *British Factory – Japanese Factory* (London: Allen & Unwin)

Downs, A. (1957), *An Economic Theory of Democracy* (New York: Harper & Row)

Flemming, J. (1978), 'The Economic Explanation of Inflation' in Hirsch and Goldthorpe

Friedman, M. (1953), *Essays in Positive Economics* (Chicago: Chicago University Press)

——— (1963), *Inflation: Causes and Consequences* (Bombay: Council for Economic Education)

——— (1966), 'Comment' in Schultz, E. P. and Aliber, R. Z. (eds.), *Guidelines* (Chicago: Chicago University Press)

——— (1975), *Unemployment versus Inflation?* (London: Institute of Economic Affairs)

Galbraith, J. K. (1967), *The New Industrial State* (Harmondsworth: Penguin)

Goldthorpe, J. H. (1978), 'The Current Inflation: Towards a Sociological Account' in Hirsch and Goldthorpe

Goldthorpe, J. H. and Lockwood, D. (1968–9), *The Affluent Worker: Three Monographs* (Cambridge: Cambridge University Press)

Haberler, G. (1966), *Inflation: Its Causes and Cures* (Washington, D.C.: American Enterprise Institute)

Hayek, F. A. (1958), 'Unions, Inflation and Profits' in Bradley, P. D. (ed.), *The Public Stake in Union Power* (Charlottesville: University of Virginia Press)

Hibbs, D. A. (1978), 'On the Political Economy of Long-Run Trends in Strike Activity', *British Journal of Political Science* (April)

Hilferding, R. (1910), *Finanzkapital* (Berlin)

Hirsch, F. (1977), *Social Limits to Growth* (London: Routledge & Kegan Paul)

——— (1978), 'The Ideological Underlay of Inflation' in Hirsch and Goldthorpe

Hirsch, F. and Goldthorpe, J. H. (eds.) (1978), *The Political Economy of Inflation* (London: Martin Robertson)

Jackson, D. and Turner, H. A. (1975), 'Inflation, Strato-Inflation and Social Conflict' in Jackson, Turner and Wilkinson

Jackson, D., Turner, H. A. and Wilkinson, F. (1975), *Do Trade Unions Cause Inflation?*, 2nd edn (Cambridge: Cambridge University Press)

Jessop, B. (1973), *Tradition, Conservatism and Political Change* (Cambridge: Cambridge University Press)

Johnson, H. G. (1975), 'World Inflation and the International Monetary System', *The Three Banks Review* (September)

Layard, R., Metcalf, D. and Nickell, S. (1978), 'The Effect of Collective Bargaining on Relative and Absolute Wages', *British Journal of Industrial Relations* (November)

McKenzie, R. T. and Silver, A. (1968), *Angels in Marble* (London: Macmillan)

Maier, C. S. (1975), *Recasting Bourgeois Europe* (Princeton: Princeton University Press)

——— (1978), 'The Politics of Inflation in the Twentieth Century' in Hirsch and Goldthorpe

Mishan, E. (1974), 'The New Inflation', *Encounter*, 42

Nordhaus, W. D. (1975), 'The Political Business Cycle', *Review of Economic Studies* (April)

Olson, M. (1965), *The Logic of Collective Action* (Cambridge, Mass.: Harvard University Press)

Panić, M. (1976), 'The Inevitable Inflation', *Lloyds Bank Review* (July)

——— (1978), 'The Origin of Increasing Inflationary Tendencies in Contemporary Society' in Hirsch and Goldthorpe

Parkin, M. (1975), 'The Politics of Inflation', *Government and Opposition* (Spring)

Peacock, A. T. and Ricketts, M. (1978), 'The Growth of the Public Sector and Inflation' in Hirsch and Goldthorpe

Robinson, D. (1974), *Solidaristic Wages Policy in Sweden* (Paris: OECD)

Runciman, W. G. (1966), *Relative Deprivation and Social Justice* (London: Routledge & Kegan Paul)

Schumpeter, J. A. (1942), *Capitalism, Socialism and Democracy* (London: Allen & Unwin)

Soskice, D. (1978), 'Strike Waves and Wage Explosions, 1968–1970: An Economic Interpretation' in Crouch and Pizzorno (1978), vol. 2

Sylos-Labini, P. (1974), *Trade Unions, Inflation and Productivity* (Farnborough: Saxon House)

——— (1976), 'Competition: the Product Markets' in Wilson, T. and Skinner, A. S. (eds.), *The Market and the State* (Oxford: Clarendon Press)

Tarling, R. and Wilkinson, F. (1977), 'The Social Contract: Post-War Incomes Policies and Their Inflationary Impact', *Cambridge Journal of Economics*, 1

Wiles, P. (1973), 'Cost Inflation and the State of Economic Theory', *Economic Journal* (June)

Wilkinson, F. and Turner, H. A. (1975), 'The Wage-Tax Spiral and Labour Militancy' in Jackson, Turner and Wilkinson

5 NORTH SEA OIL: A CHANCE TO CHANGE?

Colin Robinson

Introduction

In March 1978 the then Labour Government published a White Paper entitled 'The Challenge of North Sea Oil'. It begins with a resounding statement: 'North Sea oil provides a unique opportunity for Britain to improve her economic performance, raise her living standards, move forward to full employment and develop as a socially just society.' It ends with the challenge which presumably justifies the White Paper's title,

> As a people we have been given the chance to harness our talents and energies to a programme of National Recovery, that will rebuild Britain's prosperity and greatness. It is in that spirit that the Government invites the nation to use the decade of opportunity presented by North Sea oil.

The sixty paragraphs which separate those two statements were generally dismissed by newspaper pundits as being essentially empty; it is indeed difficult to find substance in a document which appears to have been drafted by not just one but several committees. Nevertheless, although there are many statements in the White Paper with which one might take issue and the hectoring tone of such documents is always rather distasteful, the reactions of those who wrote dismissive notices are perhaps more revealing than the White Paper itself. They demonstrate in striking fashion how deeply embedded in our society is a belief in government-prescribed instant solutions to economic and social problems. Evidently, many people seriously believe that a government is capable of defining for many years ahead what the benefits of North Sea oil will be and setting out a precise programme of how those benefits should be channelled in desirable directions. In economists' language, they want the government to specify a social welfare function and to find means of maximising it. The rest of us presumably remain passive, following sheep-like the writing on the tablets handed down from above.

This chapter puts forward a different view of the impact of North

Sea oil. It is different principally in two respects. First, it stresses something which government statements tend to conceal but which a number of us at the University of Surrey have been trying to explain for several years – the considerable uncertainties which still surround both the future development of the North Sea and its impact on the British economy. Secondly, it emphasises that, just as the rapid development of the North Sea has up to now been due mainly to privately-owned companies, so the extent to which North Sea benefits are actually realised is likely to depend primarily on private sector response. The government's role seems to me principally to be to pursue a macro-economic policy which makes it possible for North Sea gains to be reaped and to provide a more competitive climate in which enterprise can flourish.

The chapter begins with a very brief explanation of the likely scale of North Sea oil and the major related uncertainties; it then moves on to discuss possible effects on the economy.

The Scale of British Offshore Oil

Exploration offshore Britain began about fifteen years ago[1] and there was considerable excitement when, late in 1965, BP made a gas find (the West Sole field) off the coast of East Anglia, which was followed in 1966 and 1967 by the discovery of several larger fields. The natural gas finds of those years were large enough for the nationalised gas distribution industry (then the Gas Council and Area Boards) to undertake a major expansion programme. During this programme, virtually all gas appliances were converted to burn natural gas, gas sales approximately quadrupled between the mid-1960s and mid-1970s and gas distribution was transformed into one of the fastest growing industries in Britain.

The oil companies which had made the discoveries were less happy with their experience. They had to attempt negotiations with the Gas Council, which was effectively sole buyer of North Sea gas, and a government dedicated to achieving a low price (see Robinson and Morgan, 1978, Ch. 9; Robinson, 1978). The result was that the Council (now the British Gas Corporation) obtained its gas at little more than one penny per therm, or about two-thirds the going price of imported crude oil. Subsequently, the oil companies greatly reduced their exploration effort in the southern North Sea and moved north – offshore mainland Scotland, Orkney and Shetland – where the

Table 5.1: Estimated United Kingdom Continental Shelf Oil and Gas Reserves at End 1978

	Million tonnes oil equivalent		
	Oil	Natural gas	Total
Remaining recoverable reserves in present discoveries			
Proven[a]	1397	592	1989
Probable[b]	509	273	782
Possible[c]	605	376	981
Total	2511	1241	3752
Possible recoverable reserves in future discoveries	900–1800	0–461	900–2261
Total (rounded)	2300–4300	600–1700	2900–6000

Notes:
a. Virtually certain to be producible.
b. Better than 50% chance of being producible.
c. Significant but less than 50% chance of being producible.
Source: Department of Energy (1979), ***The Development of the Oil and Gas Resources of the United Kingdom*** (London: HMSO). The figures of gas reserves have been converted to oil equivalent.

expectation was that any finds would be of oil (which did not have to be sold to BGC) rather than gas. The success rate was remarkable in the early years. From 1969 to 1976, about every fifth well drilled struck oil, and in the best period (1970 to 1975) about half of those strikes appeared to be economically exploitable: that is, about one well in ten made an apparently 'commercial' find. It is, in practice, difficult to define 'commercial' since the expected rate of return on a field depends on changing expectations about oil prices, technology, tax rates and other government policies; however, since 1975 the proportion of commercial strikes appears to have fallen sharply to around one in fifty wells drilled.

As a consequence of the drilling activity of the last fifteen years Britain appears to have the recoverable reserves of oil and natural gas shown in Table 5.1. To place these reserves in context one can attempt a comparison with world reserves. Estimated British proven oil reserves are nearly two per cent of estimated world proven oil reserves. Of course, British reserves may well increase since exploration in the area is at a relatively early stage, but world reserves are also likely to rise. An estimate by Moody (1975) of ultimately-recoverable world oil

Table 5.2: World Oil Production, 1978, Selected Countries

	Million tonnes
USSR	572
USA	512
Saudi Arabia	411
Iran	260
Iraq	131
Venezuela	107
Kuwait	104
Libya	98
Nigeria	95
Indonesia	81
Canada	78
Abu Dhabi	72
Algeria	61

Source: *The Petroleum Economist* (April 1979). Figures in barrels have been converted to tonnes at 7.35 barrels per tonne.

resources by area suggests that total North Sea oil resources (including the Norwegian sector) may turn out to be in the range of two to three per cent of the oil ultimately recovered from the world. As an approximation we can say that present evidence indicates British North Sea reserves to be in the region of one to two per cent of the world total.

Rather than struggling with such heroic concepts as world oil resources, it is simpler to demonstrate the relative size of North Sea oil in a world context by comparing likely British oil output in the 1980s – 100 to 150 million tonnes a year – with output from other oil-producing countries. It is clear from Table 5.2 that Britain should be firmly in the middle league of world oil producers, along with such countries as Iraq, Venezuela and Kuwait, although our output will be substantially less than production from each of the world's three biggest oil suppliers (USSR, USA and Saudi Arabia).

More parochially, we can appreciate the impact of offshore oil, and the somewhat smaller impact of offshore gas, on Britain's energy market by examining Table 5.3. Up to the early 1970s, despite the growth of natural gas production and a limited increase in output of nuclear electricity, the United Kingdom was becoming steadily more dependent on imported oil as the indigenous coal industry declined. Since 1973, energy trends have changed. Consumption in total has fallen and oil consumption has fallen faster under the influence of rising oil and other fuel prices and economic recession. At the same

Table 5.3: United Kingdom Fuel Production and Consumption

	1960		1973		1978		1980 FORECAST	
	m.t.c.e.*	% of total	m.t.c.e.	% of total	m.t.c.e.	% of total	m.t.c.e.	% of total
FUEL PRODUCTION								
Coal	198	98.5	132	70.2	124	43.4	116	31.8
Oil	–	–	1	0.5	90	31.5	165	45.2
Natural Gas	–	–	43	22.9	57	19.9	64	17.5
Nuclear	1	0.5	10	5.3	13	4.5	18	5.0
Hydro	2	1.0	2	1.1	2	0.7	2	0.5
Total	201	100.0	188	100.0	286	100.0	365	100.0
FUEL CONSUMPTION								
Coal	199	69.6	133	34.8	120	33.5	118	31.6
Oil (Energy uses)	68	23.8	164	42.9	139	38.8	138	37.0
Natural Gas	–	–	44	11.5	64	17.9	75	20.1
Nuclear	1	0.3	10	2.6	13	3.6	17	4.6
Hydro	2	0.7	2	0.5	2	0.6	2	0.5
Non energy uses	7	2.5	20	5.2	16	4.5	18	4.8
Bunkers	9	3.1	9	2.5	4	1.1	5	1.4
Total	286	100.0	382	100.0	358	100.0	373	100.0
PRODUCTION AS % OF CONSUMPTION	70		49		80		98	

*m.t.c.e. = million tonnes coal equivalent.
Sources for 1960–78 calculations: Department of Energy, *Digest of Energy Statistics; Energy Trends.*

time, import dependence has dropped very sharply from about 50 per cent in 1973 to 20 per cent in 1978 and will very likely be only a few per cent in 1980 when the only significant net imports of fuel should be pipeline gas from the Frigg field which is partly in the Norwegian sector. There are good prospects for an export surplus of fuel for a period in the 1980s. We return later to a discussion of the extent to which energy self-sufficiency is in itself a 'good thing'.

So far we have examined the short-term prospects for offshore oil and gas. What of the later 1980s and 1990s? One of the main criticisms of the 'official' view[2] is that it tends to be expressed in old-fashioned point forecast terms, so that, for example, oil revenues or the balance of payments effects of North Sea oil for some future year are expressed as single numbers against the given year, with only passing reference to error margins and their sources. In reality, there is so much uncertainty about the North Sea that it makes no sense to attach such apparent precision to the future. The uncertainties can be classified into two broad areas. First, there is *uncertainty relating to the future of the offshore area itself* – what will happen to such variables as costs, prices, technology, taxes and government policy. Secondly, there is *doubt about the effects on the economy of given developments on the Continental Shelf.* The latter is left to the last part of this chapter; we deal first with the problem of forecasting events in the offshore area.

When an oil company is considering investment in exploration or in developing a find which has already been made it goes through a complex exercise which is not easily simulated and may well not fully be articulated by the company (see Robinson, 1979). Since most offshore oil projects are likely to have very long lives – exploration money spent successfully in the late-1960s will probably result in the production of oil from the mid-1970s to the early years of the next century – companies have to make long-term guesses at a number of critical variables. Among the most important will be behaviour of any reservoir which has been found, technological changes in oil production methods, specific and general cost inflation, oil prices, alternative investment opportunities, tax rates and other government policy instruments. How companies behave at any given time depends on their expectations about such factors. Therefore, if for example one wishes to forecast production from the British offshore area, strictly speaking one can do so only on specified assumptions about these critical variables. More precisely, it is necessary to make assumptions about company *expectations* (which may or may not be realised) of such variables.

Faced with this awkward problem, we have taken refuge in a device used by Herman Kahn – the 'surprise-free scenario'. The idea is that, in anticipation of a very uncertain future, one begins by specifying a yardstick or basing point which is how some given variable would be expected to change if there were no 'surprises'. Everyone knows of course from past experience that the unexpected will happen; consequently the most surprising outcome would be for the surprise-free projection to be realised! However, the surprise-free trend is no more than a crude benchmark: the interesting part of the analysis is to carry out sensitivity analyses by altering key variables (introducing 'surprises') to determine to what extent they disturb the outcome.

Our surprise-free scenario for British North Sea oil (Robinson and Morgan, 1978, Ch. 3; Robinson and Rowland, 1978a) assumes that there are no geological surprises, no major changes in exploration and production methods, the ratio between oil prices and extraction costs remains as it was at the end of 1978, tax rates and the tax structure remain unchanged, and there are no substantial alterations in government policy. On these assumptions and applying some subjective judgements my colleague Chris Rowland has produced Figure 5.1 which relates to the United Kingdom North Sea south of the 62nd Parallel. The lowest line shows how North Sea oil production might change if the only fields developed were the 23 which are either already producing oil or for which there are firm development plans ('established commercial fields'). The middle line incorporates another 19 fields which we describe as 'potentially commercial' since they have already been found but have, as yet, no firm development programmes; on our surprise-free assumptions these fields would most likely be developed so that, in the absence of further discoveries, British North Sea production would peak at 130 to 140 million tonnes in the late 1980s. Since it would be surprising if no further discoveries were made, logic compels us to include some more finds, albeit of smaller average size and in remoter areas than discoveries made earlier. Thus our complete surprise-free projection suggests oil output rising from 53 million tonnes in 1978 to a peak of around 140 million tonnes at the end of the 1980s, declining steadily thereafter to 60 to 80 million tonnes at the end of the century. Since United Kingdom oil consumption is likely to be in the range 100 to 120 million tonnes a year in the 1980s, the surprise-free projection suggests ten years or so of self-sufficiency in oil.

It must be stressed that Figure 5.1 is no more than a benchmark or a peg on which to hang an argument. We have found it difficult, for

Figure 5.1: Possible North Sea Oil Output, 1975–2000

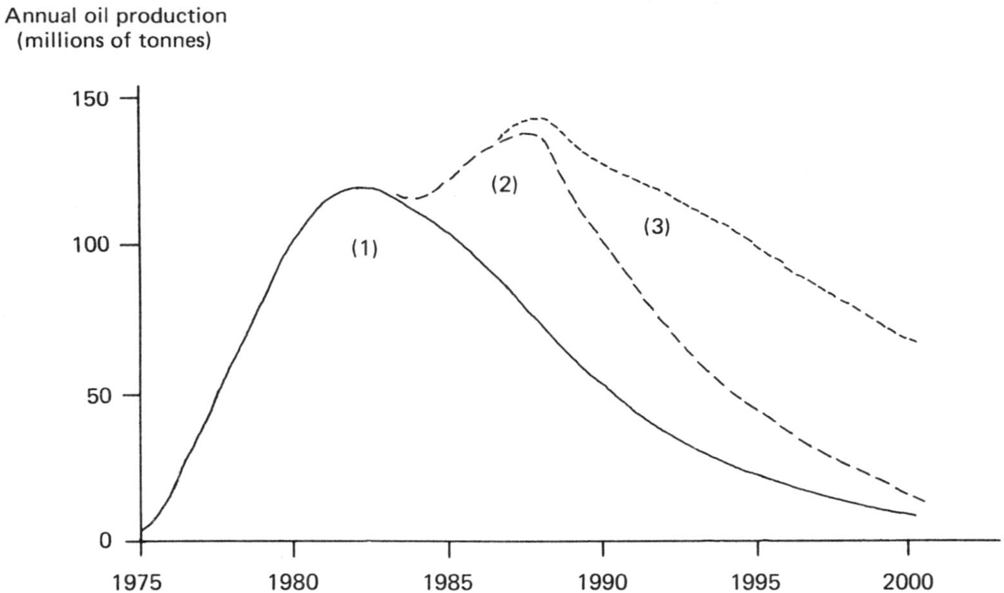

Key: (1) Output from established commercial oilfields.
(2) Additional output from potentially commercial reserves.
(3) Additional output from assumed new discoveries.
Note: For assumptions underlying these graphs see text.

example, to take into account the impact of possible further delays in field development programmes; it is quite conceivable that such delays will smooth out the peak shown in Figure 5.1. However, if the diagram is accepted as a yardstick one can carry out numerous sensitivity analyses to try to calculate what would happen if the key variables were to change, as some if not all of them almost certainly will. Some brief comments on the effects of the more important factors are given below; in each case the other key variables are assumed to remain constant when the one under discussion changes.

(1) Geological Surprises

Oil production areas, particularly those which are in the early stages of exploration, have a habit of producing surprises. If all our other surprise-free assumptions were to be realised, there would still be a good chance of finding more oil than Figure 5.1 implies – possibly in the relatively unexplored areas to the west of the United Kingdom or north of the 62nd Parallel. Our surprise-free projection in Figure 5.1 is, in fact, deliberately specified only for the North Sea south of 62° North: even in this area one must expect surprises (pleasant or unpleasant).

(2) Price Variations

The effect of price changes (with other variables constant) is complicated. Offshore fields already in production or on which large amounts of capital have been spent are rather insensitive to price variations because a high proportion of their costs is unavoidable (Robinson and Morgan, 1978, Ch. 6; Robinson and Rowland, 1978a). A forward-looking producer who calculates his return on avoidable costs and revenues is likely to be willing to produce oil at any price level we can reasonably imagine although there might be some fairly small increase or decrease in the amount he recovers from a reservoir if prices rise or fall substantially compared to his expectations. Exploration expenditure (all of which is avoidable) and capital spending on fields for which there are so far no firm development plans are, however, much more sensitive to price variations. Thus, curves (2) and (3) could be displaced substantially upwards or downwards by large price changes of the sort we have seen in 1979 and associated alterations in expectations.

(3) Tax Changes

The tax system for British North Sea oil is peculiar, even by the standards of the rest of what we call the tax 'system' in this country. Its oddest feature is the Petroleum Revenue Tax (PRT) the incidence of which by field is arbitrary and the rate of which can be varied within wide limits without having any significant effect on the government's percentage tax 'take' (Robinson and Morgan, 1978, Ch. 5; Robinson and Rowland, 1978b; Rowland, 1979; Kemp, 1979). Changes to the rate and the structure of PRT were proposed by the Labour government in August 1978 and implemented by the Conservatives in the 1979 Finance Act. Tax changes and expectations of changes might well affect company after-tax returns and thereby indirectly affect supplies in the future. By analogy with other oil-producing areas, one can only assume that any likely changes in taxes will be upwards. To that extent, the surprise-free scenario may somewhat exaggerate supplies.

(4) Other Government Policy Changes[3]

There are numerous ways in which government policy might affect future offshore oil supplies, for instance through depletion controls designed to flatten and extend the peak of oil production. Such a policy would probably have the intentional or unintentional effect of reducing production below the surprise-free projection (other things equal). Even if the objective were merely to spread the production peak, the effect would most probably be to reduce ultimate oil and gas recovery from the North Sea by reducing its attractiveness as a home for investment. On the other hand, if present and future governments adopt less interventionist policies in the North Sea and reduce the role of BNOC, supplies might well be greater than Figure 5.1 suggests.

The general message is that the future of British North Sea oil is very uncertain and is especially sensitive to changes in the variables just mentioned. In previous work (Robinson and Morgan, 1978, Chs. 5, 6 and 7) we have estimated the effects on profitability (and therefore, indirectly, on output) of prices, taxes and depletion controls. Here it is worth combining some of these effects to show how the likely profitability of North Sea fields may have been changed by recent events in the energy market. In Table 5.4, which relates only to 'potentially commercial' fields where all but exploration costs are avoidable, two cases are illustrated. The first column shows the orders of magnitude of real internal rates of return which might have been expected for these fields about a year ago, assuming a gradual increase in oil prices (referred to as the CPI price scenario in our earlier work),

Table 5.4: Estimated After Tax Real Internal Rates of Return on Selected 'Potentially Commercial' Oilfields (per cent)

	Expected late 1978*	Expected late 1979**
Alwyn	12	20
Andrew	15	28
Beryl West	12	27
Crawford	12	19
Lyell	17	27
Renee	14	28
Tern	15	26
Toni/Thelma	11	18

*Assuming North Sea oil prices increase at 5 to 7 per cent per annum from 1979 onwards; the exchange rate is $2 = £1; and the PRT rate and allowances are those in force before the 1979 Finance Act.
**Assuming North Sea oil prices increase 40 per cent in 1979, 23 per cent in 1980 and 15 per cent in 1981, thereafter rising at 7 per cent per annum except for another 25 per cent jump in the mid 1980s; the exchange rate is $2.2 = £1; and the PRT rate and allowances are as altered by the 1979 Finance Act.

the original rate of Petroleum Revenue Tax and a $2 exchange rate. Column 2 demonstrates the apparent sharp rise in real IRRs which might be expected from much higher oil prices in 1979 and the future (described as the UMP price scenario in our previous papers) even when dampened by the increased Petroleum Revenue Tax and sterling/dollar exchange rate. It is, of course, impossible to know how returns on North Sea fields will actually turn out; the table is not a prediction but rather an attempt to simulate what company expectations might be since it is expectations which determine the willingness to invest. It is particularly hard to know how expectations about costs may have changed now that the prospects for inflation have worsened. Although we have built into column 2 faster rates of general and specific inflation than in column 1, the specific rate of inflation for North Sea equipment and services may well rise more than we have assumed, so cancelling out part of the effect of higher oil prices. Nevertheless, it seems certain that recent oil price increases – and the expectations they have stimulated, whether rightly or wrongly, of further rises – have significantly increased the attractiveness of investment in the North Sea.

Given all the uncertainties, there are obvious problems in summarising what the future range of output variation might be. For illustrative purposes we can use the range between curves (2) and (3) in Figure 5.1, although there is a significant probability that if there are further big oil price increases, a less interventionist government policy and geological surprises of the pleasant kind, production from the United Kingdom offshore area as a whole may be above curve (3).

Direct Effect on the Economy

The Continental Shelf Region, as it is now described in the official statistics, is a very fast-growing sector of the British economy. Some measures of its present size relative to the economy as a whole are given in the Department of Energy's latest 'Brown Book' (1979) and in the Economic Progress Report for August 1979. In 1978 GNP derived from oil and natural gas was apparently of the order of £2,200 million which is about 1.5 per cent of GNP at market prices. The identified favourable balance of payments effect of oil and gas combined is officially estimated as about £4,600 million in 1978 (including long-term capital) and government tax revenues from the offshore area were just over £500 million in 1978/9. One of the most striking measures of the size of North Sea activity is a comparison of investment in the area with total investment in the United Kingdom: North Sea investment, about two-thirds of which has been carried out by foreign companies, has been about £2,000 million a year for the last few years which is about eight to nine per cent of all United Kingdom investment.

In interpreting such estimates one should remember that they merely measure the more obvious impact of the North Sea. They are not designed to show the *net* effect of offshore oil and gas on the economy. To assess this net effect one would have to include spin-off effects to other industries (most obviously oil equipment and service suppliers) and make a deduction for the output, exports, imports and tax revenues which resources now employed in oil and gas might have produced in the absence of the North Sea.

Some estimates of future North Sea direct effects are also given in the Economic Progress Report article referred to but, as already implied, they are insufficiently explicit about the uncertainties of the future. Consequently, our own University of Surrey estimates are used to summarise the likely future tax revenue and balance of payments effects of the North Sea (Robinson and Morgan, 1978, Chs. 8 and 9; Robinson and Rowland, 1978a; Hirst and Rowland, 1979). The estimates relate to *oil* alone. Gas is omitted, partly because we have less information on gas than on oil and partly because most of the benefits from natural gas production have already accrued. The ranges used are defined in terms of two of the key variables:

(1) *Oil output* where the lower end of the range is curve (2) in Figure 5.1 and the upper end is curve (3).
(2) *North Sea oil prices*, where the lower end of the range assumes steadily-increasing oil prices, whereas the upper end assumes further sharp increases. The two scenarios are explained in the footnote to Table 5.5.

Table 5.5: Estimated Government Revenues from North Sea Oil* Expressed in 1979 Prices

	Possible range** £000 million
1978	0.6
1980	2.0
1985	4.1–5.2
1990	4.2–6.4

*Corporation Tax, PRT and royalty.
**The lower end of the range assumes production as in curve (2), Figure 5.1 and the upper end of the range assumes production as in curve (3). North Sea oil price assumptions are in $/barrel and current prices:

	Lower	Upper
1980	24	24
1985	31	42
1990	44	59

and the assumed exchange rate is $2.2 = £1. The upper end of the price range is the same as the price assumption specified in the second footnote, Table 5.4. The lower end is higher than the assumption in the first footnote, Table 5.4, because it includes the upward step in oil prices in 1979.

To avoid too many figures the range used takes as its lower limit curve (2) and the lower price assumption, and as its upper limit curve (3) and the higher price figures. An exchange rate of $2.2 = £1 is assumed in both cases.

First, we can examine government tax revenues, which arise from Corporation Tax and two taxes specific to North Sea output – PRT and royalty. For North Sea fields in total, if we assume the PRT changes implemented in the 1979 Finance Act and a steady rise in oil prices, the government's 'take' from all three taxes is likely on average to be around 70 per cent of company revenues net of costs (although tax take actually varies from about 60 per cent for some fields to about 75 per cent for others).

Table 5.5 shows how tax revenues from the North Sea might be expected to change in future, using the range already defined. Two features stand out. One is the sensitivity of future tax take to the assumptions made about oil output and prices: in 1985, the top end of our range of tax revenues is about 25 per cent higher than the lower end, and in 1990 the difference is around 50 per cent. The other is the large size of revenues from North Sea oil. For comparison, in 1978/9 VAT yielded nearly £5,000 million a year and the taxes on alcohol, tobacco and oil each yield some £2,000 million to £2,500 million. So North Sea revenues are likely to form an important part of total government receipts in the 1980s. It should be repeated that the tax effect measured in the table is not the true net impact of North Sea oil for two reasons. Some of the resources used in oil would probably have been employed in other activities had there been no North Sea and so would have yielded some tax revenues; to that extent the figures may exaggerate the North Sea tax effect. On the other hand, the table is confined strictly to oil taxation and takes no account of possible extra taxation paid by some North Sea related activities (platform and pipeline construction, helicopters, supply boats, catering services and so on). In general, the official estimates of future tax revenues are near the top of our range, although they include gas whereas our figures are for oil alone: Economic Progress Report, August 1979, puts government revenues from the North Sea at £4,750 million (in 1978 prices) by the mid-1980s.

Next, the balance of payments effects need examination. The potentially favourable effect of North Sea oil on the balance of payments is its most obvious economic impact. Instead of importing oil we are now substituting indigenous output, valued at over £3,000 million in 1978, thus directly improving the trade balance. We can also expect some exports of oil-related goods and services as the North Sea supply industries grow. At the same time, there has been a substantial capital inflow (about £1,000 million net *per annum* in the last few years) from the overseas companies investing in the North Sea, which has improved the long-term capital account. Against these benefits must be set imports of North Sea goods and services such as pipelines and platforms which have also been about £1,000 million *per annum* in recent years, and an increasing invisible outflow of interest and profits (roughly £800 million in 1978) which have been earned by overseas companies. These gains and losses give an apparent net total gain of over £2,500 million in 1978 from North Sea oil alone.

As in the case of tax revenue estimates, one has to be careful in estimating net North Sea balance of payments benefits because resources used in the North Sea might otherwise have been used in different employments and would therefore have had balance of payments effects. We have tried to include rough estimates of such effects in our calculations which are intended to show the difference between two states of the British economy – one with North Sea oil (NS) and the other without the North Sea (nNS). The gain is measured in terms of the balance on current and long-term capital account; in practice, some or all of it could appear as sterling appreciation of the kind we have seen in 1979.

There are many complications in making such estimates which it is not appropriate to explore here: some summarised results are presented in Table 5.6. As in Table 5.5, two features stand out. First, there is considerable sensitivity to price and output assumptions. For example in 1990 the top end of our range is nearly 1.7 times the bottom end. Secondly, the calculated gains are very large. The biggest deficit for official financing which the United Kingdom has incurred in recent times was about £3,600 million, in 1976; although our estimates in Table 5.6 are in current prices (not adjusted for inflation) they are obviously very substantial relative to recent deficits.

Table 5.6: Estimated Impact of North Sea Oil on the United Kingdom Balance of Payments (NS minus nNS)*: Current and Long-term Capital Account

	Possible range** £000 million (current prices)
1978	2.7
1980	5.0
1985	10–13
1990	12–20

*See text for definition.
**Defined as in Table 5.5.

Many people will be surprised at the size of the possible gains set out in Table 5.6 and one may also feel uncomfortable at the notion implicit in the table and consequent on our use of a state without North Sea oil (nNS) as a standard of comparison, that the faster oil prices rise the more Britain gains from the North Sea. I can only sympathise with such thoughts. One can only calculate *potential* gains; there is no guarantee that all or even any of such benefits will actually be realised. We now turn to some of the deeper issues which underlie the question of the realisation of North Sea benefits.

Impact and Secondary Effects of North Sea Oil

Although at the University of Surrey we were probably the first people to publish detailed estimates of North Sea costs and profitability, effects of the oil tax regime and the balance of payments impact of oil, we have always tried to encourage a healthy scepticism about such calculations. There are truly daunting uncertainties associated with the future development of the British offshore area which mean that one can only make informed guesses about what will happen to prices, costs, extraction technology, taxes and other important variables. Furthermore, in assessing the impact of oil on the economy an extra layer of uncertainty is added.

In a recent book (Robinson and Morgan, 1978, Ch. 9) we said that many people seem to believe that North Sea oil is a crock of gold presented to the British nation by a grateful Almighty: on this view, the only real issue is how to distribute the unexpected blessing. Election campaigns tend to encourage such ideas. From the statements of some politicians one might imagine that they had actually been out in the North Sea exploring for and producing oil – without any aid from the multinational oil companies they appear to dislike so much – and that they know precisely how to use 'our oil' to save the economy. Let us turn from such nonsense to consider to what extent an apparent windfall such as North Sea oil with its arrival almost coinciding with massive increases in world oil prices, can benefit the economy.

Any industrialist knows that, when he is seeking new investment opportunities, what he most wants are markets where likely prices substantially exceed likely costs. That is not to suggest anything so crude as that companies are merely profit-maximisers, but simply that desire for profit is one of their principal motivating forces, or in technical terms, one of the elements in the managerial utility function is profit. Now, one of the distinguishing features of North Sea oil is that, for most of the fields so far discovered, there is a significant positive margin between price and cost (excluding taxes). Thus it is potentially very profitable. The price of North Sea oil is determined primarily in the world energy market, with some premium for proximity to market and the relatively high quality of British oil, so that the companies in our offshore region are price-takers. As a consequence of fears of future oil scarcity and the presence in the market of a powerful semi-monopolistic grouping in the form of OPEC, the world oil price now is of the order of 15 times what it was in 1970. Even though areas such as the North Sea are high-cost as compared with the Middle East and even though costs have risen in the wake of price increases, the remaining price-cost margin means that North Sea oil presents a good investment opportunity. From the viewpoint of the country as a whole, there are few places where we might expect to get such a return as can be obtained by investing resources in exploiting offshore oil.

The impact effect of the North Sea is therefore favourable. Instead of using resources in relatively unprofitable industries or possibly leaving them idle altogether, a new and profitable investment opportunity has appeared. An initial GNP gain is therefore to be expected since productive factors will probably earn more than they would otherwise have done; tax revenues should rise, as we have seen; and the balance of payments should initially improve as oil imports diminish. Under certain assumptions, the gains to GNP, tax revenues and the balance of payments can be shown to be identical (see Robinson and Morgan, 1978, Ch. 8). The common source of gain is more efficient use of resources, and possibly some utilisation of resources which would have been unemployed had there been no North Sea.

But these are all impact effects which can fairly readily be seen. How can we determine what will happen to the British economy after the initial favourable impact of the North Sea? To be honest, economists do not really know how to answer such a question in any detail, although many of them pretend to do so. All we can do is to explore some of the main determinants of the long-term effects on the economy of North Sea oil and pass some general judgements on which kind of system is likely to produce most long-term benefits.

First, since any gains will be relative, let us be clear to what they relate. Just before the big oil price increases of 1973–4 Britain could import crude oil at just under £9 per tonne (the equivalent of $3 per barrel).[4] After allowing for inflation since 1973 – British prices (both retail and wholesale) have more than doubled in the last six years – it is clear that the costs of most North Sea fields are higher than the resource costs of importing OPEC oil before 1973. Consequently, the chances of significant gains in British economic performance *relative to the past* seem remote. The fact that North Sea oil is indigenous may bring us some small improvement in the security of our energy supplies, but it is expensive oil in terms of the resources we need to employ to extract it. If, magically, we could return to the days of cheap OPEC oil, we would obtain our oil more cheaply than from the North Sea.

Where we may expect to benefit is because, as the only large West European country with indigenous oil, that oil is less expensive in resource terms than are imports from OPEC. In other words, any gain is likely to be not in comparison with our own performance in the past but relative to other countries' performance in the future. This relative future change is a mixed blessing, however. Although Britain's competitive position should improve via a kind of price effect (if we use the North Sea opportunity wisely, of which more in a moment), the rising cost of energy may well have an adverse effect on world economic growth. Consequently, offsetting the potentially favourable change in our competitive position will be an adverse income effect causing some reduction in the rate of growth of world GNP and world trade. It is very hard to assess the relative strengths of the two effects even if we take a simple indicator such as the rate of increase of real GNP. Quite probably in the 1980s we shall see a convergence of economic growth rates in Western Europe – indeed it is already happening – so that Britain's growth rate will be nearer the European average than it has been in the past. However, it would be surprising if Britain's rate of increase in real GNP in the 1980s were higher than the 2.5 per cent *per annum* we managed between the mid-1950s and mid-1970s.

A second problem in assessing the economic impact of offshore oil concerns a familiar difficulty in economic analysis – the variability of human behaviour. No matter how we refine our computer models, in the end we depend on information about past behaviour to make predictions (though we do not have to assume the mechanical repetition of past events). The initial effects of North Sea oil have already shown up in an improved trade balance. However, just because the oil we consume is indigenous instead of imported there is no reason to believe that the principal gains will go to the balance of payments. The influence of offshore oil will spread through the economy in ways which are difficult to envisage because they depend on the behaviour of millions of people. There is no reason to believe that the eventual effect will be of similar size to the impact effect; it is even possible for a favourable impact to be translated into an adverse final effect.

Consider North Sea oil as follows. As the trade balance improves and extra tax revenues begin to flow, does people's behaviour remain unchanged? That is, can we assume that the only difference between a state with North Sea oil and a state without North Sea oil is the presence of oil and its directly associated effects? Of course we cannot make such an assumption. As the oil flows and the initial favourable effects appear, the behaviour of consumers, investors and government becomes different from what it would have been without the oil. It is this behavioural change which it is so difficult to capture quantitatively. Even the direction of change is not clear. On the one hand, governments might relax their efforts to control inflation so that all or most of the apparent benefits of the North Sea are dissipated in a faster rate of price increase than we would otherwise have had. On the other hand, companies might become more optimistic and the initial gains might somehow be channelled into profitable investment projects, thus improving the United Kingdom's international competitiveness and multiplying the early benefits.

Consequently, though we can assess the magnitude of the potential gain from North Sea oil (approximated by what we described earlier as a balance of payments benefit) we are in great difficulty in trying to estimate how much of that potential gain will be realised. The only recent precedent is not very encouraging. If one carries out the kind of figuring for North Sea natural gas which we have done for oil, the conclusion is that in the last few years gas has been providing substantial benefits to the economy – possibly of the order of £2,000 million of GNP in 1978. Whilst it is hard to see what would have happened in the absence of natural gas, few of us will readily accept the notion that a *net* gain of this size has actually accrued. Admittedly, governments pursued especially foolish policies towards gas, handing most of the 'rent' over to the British Gas Corporation (Robinson, 1978, pp. 289–91) but they can hardly be given higher marks for their oil policy where again, until recently, the operations of a nationalised corporation (BNOC) have naïvely been regarded as synonymous with the 'national interest'.

Realising the Benefits

So far this chapter has tried to explain the problems in assessing to what extent the potential gains from offshore oil, which are undoubtedly considerable, may be translated into actual benefits. To summarise, it has suggested that the principal difficulties in estimating actual gains are first, that they will occur in a future significantly different from the past and secondly, that the advent of indigenous oil may itself alter behaviour in ways it is difficult to predict. Let me now give some personal views on how the potential benefits may be captured.

Most people would agree that if there are to be long-term gains from North Sea oil some of the initial proceeds should be invested. Otherwise we shall merely enjoy a short-lived boom in private and public consumption. There, however, agreement stops. How much of the initial gains should be invested? Should the investment be at home or abroad? How can resources be channelled into investment? We ought to admit that, as with all important issues, there are large elements of faith and judgement in answers to such questions.

In recent times the conventional view has been that the prime responsibility for ensuring the proper use of North Sea oil lies with the government, aided by the nationalised oil and gas corporations. According to this line of argument, strong central control in the 'national interest' is needed both of activity in the North Sea and of the distribution of the benefits thereof. This chapter is not primarily concerned with government policy towards company North Sea activities. Some ideas on such policy have been expressed in detail elsewhere (Robinson, 1979; Robinson and Morgan, 1978, Ch. 8) where I have tried to explain the dangers, distortions and inefficiencies which increasing state control seems to have brought, and also to specify some of the characteristics of a more market-related regime. In the recent past we have seen the early stages of a less interventionist policy by the Conservatives which seems to me to be more likely to succeed than the old regime. In the rest of this chapter, therefore, we can concentrate on government policy towards use of the initial benefits arising from the North Sea.

The state-control school's view is typified, though by no means in its most extreme form, by the last government's White Paper on 'The Challenge of North Sea Oil' (1978). As explained earlier in this chapter, newspaper comment on North Sea oil is even more revealing. The typical leader-writer's attitude to the use of North Sea revenues is that someone ought to produce what is usually labelled a 'clear-cut policy'; generally the writer has little or no idea what that policy should be but he wants to shift responsibility for providing it on to the government. Academics are often even worse. They tend to favour grand industrial strategies – which, no doubt quite incidentally, happen to provide excellent employment opportunities for academic economists! – in which governments pour money into certain favoured industries, usually of the 'high technology' variety.

There is a breathtaking naïveté about the grand-strategy approach. The belief that a group of politicians and civil servants, perhaps aided by the CBI, the TUC and some university economists, can provide a national strategy, presumably picking out 'winners' for the British economy, would be truly comic were it not so serious a matter. The experiences of recent years might suggest that the result is more likely to be hand-outs for the ailing than encouragement for the innovative and the efficient.

I have grave doubts about centralised decision-making, much of which seems to occur for reasons which have little to do with economic efficiency. One needs to look closely at why more and more decisions have been taken over by central government – at least until our latest administration appeared – before advocating still more state intervention.

The ostensible reason for increasing government control, in the North Sea as elsewhere in the economy, has often been the hackneyed market-imperfection and market-failure argument. Those British economists who are still living in the 1930s continue to write *ad nauseam* about the imperfect results of markets; incredible as it may seem, they appear not to have awakened, as have their American brethren, to a realisation that governments too are imperfect. Of course, any intelligent person can see that the unfettered operation of market forces may have undesirable effects. Evidently it takes more sophistication to perceive the rather subtle virtues of allowing a significant place for the market to function, providing signals (imperfect though they may be) to producers and consumers. In Harry Johnson's words 'The defects of market organisation seem obvious to anyone, or can be made to seem so, whereas the socio-economic functions of the market are obscure and difficult to appreciate' (1962).

There is another most important point. Politicians, civil servants and academic advisers to government have a self-interest in increasing centralisation since it increases their power at the expense of the rest of the community. This is not to accuse them of malevolence but simply to say that their motivations are similar to those of people in the private sector. The significant difference is that in the private sector the pursuit of self-interest is bounded by competitive pressures which are largely absent from the public sector. Indeed, politicians and civil servants are in a strong position to fulfil their wishes since they can and do plead 'national interest' considerations in support of their proposals. Herein may lie one of the principal sources of the upsurge in government activity we have seen in the post-war period: big government seems to have been supplied rather than demanded.

This is hardly the place for a discourse on the errors of collectivism, but my own view is that the highly imperfect electoral, political and administrative processes we have in Britain, coupled with the strong self-interest of the government in building up its power, have led in many sectors of the British economy to excessive central intervention which has had results which, in both economic and political terms, are worse than workably competitive markets would have provided.[5] One does not have to be an advocate of completely free markets to believe that the self-generating nature of government activity has led governments to become far too involved in interference with the decisions of producers and consumers and that more use of markets is needed.

In so far as the use of initial North Sea gains is concerned it is difficult to see what the value would be of a plan. The advocates of planning have certainly not provided us with any evidence that it would help. Probably it would be both misleading and harmful, providing the populace with no more than the comfortable illusion that their leaders are terribly busy at solving the problems of the British economy. It is inappropriate to be dogmatic in such a difficult field, but a strategy which seems to me to have a higher probability of success is to eschew detailed planning, leaving people free to decide how the initial gains should be spent subject only to broad macro-economic constraints: for example, it is important that the government's macro-economic policy should leave room for investment of the initial benefits. Given the strictly limited foresight and wisdom with which most of us have been endowed, there is a better chance of success in most fields of economic activity if one relies on a system of broad ground-rules which provide incentives and penalties to producers and consumers rather than if an attempt is made to direct and coerce from the centre.

As the North Sea revenues accrue, the government might, for instance, embark on a gradual programme of tax reduction. A more imaginative idea, which would take the expenditure of North Sea revenues out of the hands of politicians, is the scheme for a people's stake in North Sea oil suggested by Samuel Brittan and Barry Riley (1978; also Brittan, 1979, postscript). Under this, each of us would receive (marketable) rights to a share in the income stream from the North Sea and it would be for individual decision what use is made of such rights.

Under such a regime of less detailed state intervention there would still be a significant place for government action although it would be different in nature from the neo-mercantilism we have seen in recent years. I am not suggesting a completely 'free market' in the sense of unrestrained capitalism on the basis of existing institutions. The objective would be for government to concentrate on working with market forces rather than trying to fight a perpetual battle against them, and to attempt to stimulate competition and, as far as possible, ensure that the social costs of decisions enter prices. In the energy market, for example, there is plenty of scope for promoting competition between nationalised and private corporations. In addition, it is possible that in some instances there is a case for limited government support, on the insurance policy principle, for research and development into new energy sources which are unlikely to be profitable until well into the next century and for long-term energy conservation projects. However, in all such cases one needs to be very wary that the schemes are not merely the pet ideas of those pressure groups which thrive on government patronage.

The view just suggested may seem unappealing in a society which is apparently searching for instant solutions. I make no concrete proposals for supporting this or that industry or for promoting some specific project. My whole purpose is indeed to say that such suggestions merely give the illusion that the author is being constructive. It seems to me better to provide a *system* in which enterprise has the opportunity to succeed than to engage in vain searches for 'national interest' solutions which so easily become the occasions for increasing state coercion. Of course if British industry is inherently unenterprising and uncompetitive a greater resort to market forces will not help – but nor will anything else in such circumstances.

Given a changed regime with more use of market forces, some of the major problems foreseen by would-be planners would be much less serious. For instance, there has been considerable discussion of the danger of 'Dutch disease' infecting Britain. This dread ailment is a tendency of the exchange rate to appreciate on account of mounting indigenous oil or gas production, leading to problems in exporting products other than oil and a decline in the non-oil sector of the economy. Alternatively, the symptoms may be a stable exchange rate with rapidly rising wages and salaries. It is clear from the very substantial potential balance of payments gains summarised in Table 5.6 that there is the possibility of further increases in the sterling exchange rate. Whether this would have adverse or beneficial effects on the economy is less obvious. It depends on the price elasticity of foreign demand for our exports and the elasticity of British demand for imports; one needs also to take into account the favourable effect on the rate of inflation of a rising exchange rate. In any case the risk of illness would be reduced under a more market-orientated regime. As is so frequently true, the disease the planners wish to cure is partly a consequence of past government action. The sterling exchange rate during 1979 has been inflated because governments have in recent years insisted on maintaining outward exchange controls (although the Conservatives have begun to dismantle those controls). It is retention of the relics of a siege economy rather than Dutch disease about which we should be most concerned. There is a good *prima facie* case for investing some of the proceeds of North Sea oil in profitable ventures outside Britain rather than trying to confine them to this country.

Another so-called problem which worries the would-be planners is 're-entry'. It is symptomatic of the central planners' mentality that, instead of rejoicing that there is an opportunity for Britain's economic performance to improve in the 1980s with the advent of North Sea oil, they wallow in self-induced anxiety about what may happen in the 1990s and beyond when the peak of oil output may be past. Re-entry is a problem many countries would dearly love to face. It is apparently feared that as output declines the economy will find difficulty in adjusting back from being a net exporter of oil to increasing import reliance. The economy may well have problems if it is forced into a rigid plan, but it is not clear to me why an economic system which relies to a greater extent that we now do on market forces should have serious re-adjustment difficulties. Probably by the 1990s we shall have to devote substantially more resources than we do at present to obtaining each barrel of oil we need but if the initial North Sea benefits have been well used we shall have more resources available.

Indeed, 're-entry', with its implication of a dramatic step change is a most misleading term. The course of events under a market-related regime would be roughly as follows, with all the changes occurring gradually. North Sea oil output would pass its peak, possibly in the 1990s, with a concomitant rise in imports, but well before then marginal resource costs of indigenous oil would have begun to rise – they are, in fact, increasing now – as higher-cost reserves came into use. Government tax revenues would therefore begin to decrease. By the time significant net oil imports resumed, the resource costs of marginal fields would probably be little below import prices. Furthermore, if British consumers always pay the world market price for their fuels, the resumption of imports should pass almost unnoticed by them. There is no reason why re-entry *per se* should raise prices, except to the very minor extent that extra British demand produces a slight shift to the right in the world demand curve for imported oil.

Conclusions

This chapter has covered a lot of ground in an attempt to summarise more complex arguments presented elsewhere. It has tried to illustrate the likely future scale of North Sea activity, to explain some of the determinants of the economic impact of such activity and finally to say what kinds of policies would and would not be likely to realise the potential benefits.

As regards policy, I have no confidence in the conventional wisdom as expressed by the last government's White Paper which is, in its words,

> A large part of the new resources and extra revenues must be consciously identified and allocated to the kind of long-term investment which we have not always been able to afford in the past. (1978)

Nor do I agree with many of the White Paper's critics who want still more centralised planning such as a North Sea oil fund which could be allocated to the worthy. I do not see how such decisions about allocation can be made efficiently from the centre although there is no shortage of people who would like the power to try.

Earlier I emphasised the large element of judgement there must be in any decision about how best to use the opportunity presented by North Sea oil: no amount of economic, political or sociological theorising will bring ready-made answers. My personal judgement, based largely on study of what I regard as past failures in British energy policy and industrial policy generally, is that the probability of failure is very high if we regard the prime responsibility for maximising North Sea benefits as a matter for government planning. The government needs to set the macro-economic framework. It needs also in my view to move away from the detailed interference in industry which has grown up in the post-war period, concentrating instead on a judicious use of the market system which, imperfect as it may be, is still the best device we have for efficient, decentralised and participatory decision-making.

Acknowledgement

I am grateful to Chris Rowland of the Department of Economics, University of Surrey, for providing the estimates in Tables 5.4, 5.5 and 5.6 and Figure 5.1.

Notes

1. The history of exploration is explained in more detail in Robinson and Morgan (1978) especially Chapters 1 and 2. See also Robinson and Rowland in P. S. Johnson (ed.) (1980).
2. As expressed, for example, in short articles on the economic effects of offshore oil and gas in *Economic Progress Report* (HMSO) in July 1976, August 1977 and October 1978.
3. Robinson (1978) describes and criticises government policy in the period 1964 to 1978.
4. Import prices are given in Department of Energy, *Annual Digest of Energy Statistics* (Table 28, 1978 issue).
5. For an excellent discussion of the dangers of collectivism see Rowley (1979).

References

Brittan, S. (1979), 'Giving National Assets to the People', postscript to *Participation without Politics*, Hobart Paper Special 62, Institute of Economic Affairs

Brittan, S. and Riley, B. (1978), 'A People's Stake in North Sea Oil', *Lloyds Bank Review* (April)

Department of Energy (1978), *The Challenge of North Sea Oil*, Cmnd. 7143 (London: HMSO)

——— (1979), *Annual Digest of Energy Statistics*

——— (1979), *Development of Oil and Gas Resources of the United Kingdom*

Economic Progress Reports, July 1976, August 1977, October 1978, August 1979

Hirst, N. and Rowland, C. (1979), 'Current Price Predicament Could Tip the Scales in Favour of Developing Marginal Oilfields', *Petroleum Review* (June)

Johnson, H. G. (1962), 'Planning and the Market in Economic Development' in Johnson, H. G., *Money, Trade and Economic Growth* (London: Allen & Unwin)

Johnson, P. S. (ed.) (1980), *The Structure of British Industry* (London: Granada)

Kemp, A. G. (1979), 'An Analysis of the Proposed Changes in Petroleum Revenue Tax', *Proceedings of the Institute of Fiscal Studies Conference on North Sea Taxation* (London)

Moody, J. D. (1975), 'An Estimate of the World's Recoverable Crude Oil Resource', *9th World Petroleum Congress* (Tokyo)

Robinson, C. (1978), 'A Review of North Sea Oil Policy', *Zeitschrift fur Energic Wirtschaft*, 4

——— (1979), 'North Sea Investment and Profitability', *Oil Now,* Den Norske Creditbank, 7

Robinson, C. and Morgan, J. (1978), *North Sea Oil in the Future: Economic Analysis and Government Policy* (London: Macmillan for Trade Policy Research Centre)

Robinson, C. and Rowland, C. (1978a), 'An Economic Analysis of British North Sea Oil Supplies', *OECD Workshops on Energy Supply and Demand* (Paris)
——— (1978b), 'Marginal Effect of PRT Changes', *The Petroleum Economist* (December)
——— (1980), 'North Sea Oil and Gas' in Johnson (1980)
Rowland, C. (1979), 'PRT: Objectives, Problems and Implications', *Proceedings of the Institute of Fiscal Studies Conference on North Sea Taxation* (London)
Rowley, C. K. (1979), 'Liberalism and Collective Choice', *National Westminster Bank Quarterly Review* (May)

Author's Note

This chapter was written in the summer of 1979 before the full extent of the oil price increases and the recession of 1979–80 had become clear. It has been left as first written, even though some of the statistics are dated, because the conclusions still stand.

6 LOCOMOTIVES, CONVOYS OR WHAT? – THE INTERNATIONAL ADJUSTMENT PROBLEM

Patrick Minford

The title of this chapter is pregnant with the words and ideas of post-war orthodoxy. First, the 'problem' of international adjustment. What problem? Why *international* adjustment, rather than *individual* adjustment? Why not – the mechanics of individual's adjustment to changing circumstances? Secondly, locomotives and convoys. This is the language of recent OECD bulletins, of 'economic summits' and so forth. The world economy has to be 'driven' like a locomotive or 'guided' like a convoy.

We will come back to precisely what these policy recommendations were and what 'problem' they were assumed to be solving. But at this stage simply notice that the language takes it for granted that governments must *act*, preferably in concert, to put and then keep the world economy on an appropriate path.

Contrast this with an alternative view which has been increasingly emphasised in recent years – though more at a theoretical level than in the arena of international policy – that the world economy, like the domestic economies that compose it, is moving along a path of adjustment to shocks of all sorts, including the infamous 'oil shock', in a manner determined by the decisions of a multitude of individuals, consumers, firms and governments. The role of world action is that of identifying institutional blockages and distortions along this path, of attempting to remove them, and of smoothing the process if they cannot be entirely removed at least in the short run. The role is *not* to try and put the world on a path to a different end-state.

The theme of this chapter will be to describe these opposing positions more fully, to set out a view of how adjustment does occur to international disturbances, with a review of some of the evidence bearing on this, and finally to consider the central issue of inflation and how Western governments can hope to return to sound domestic and international money.

The OECD View

The OECD view was most fully set out in the McCracken Report of June 1977. This view was subsequently endorsed with variations by the Carter administration. It set out various possible medium-term strategies for getting the world back to full employment by target dates in the early 1980s. These involved concerted action by Western economies to stimulate their economies. However, because certain economies – such as those of the UK and Italy – suffer from higher inflation and worse current account deficits than others – such as those of Germany, Switzerland and Japan – the greatest stimulatory action should be taken by the latter economies, which would thereby be acting as the 'locomotives' of world recovery. Later, when it was – reasonably – argued by these economies that they too would have difficulties, especially with inflation, were they to follow stimulatory policies, a compromise version of the strategy was put forward by the OECD, the 'convoy' approach, whereby all countries would stimulate their economies moderately, but some *rather* more than others. This compromise view was to some extent the basis of communiques by economic summits, though even further watered down by the insistence of Germany and Japan that inflation control must remain the highest priority.

Behind this OECD view there lay the argument that in the 'stronger' economies stimulatory action would not worsen inflation because wages were very largely institutionally determined by 'moderate' unions in these countries. In the 'weaker' economies, to the extent that they were expanding less rapidly, their exchange rate would appreciate and this would relieve the more militant union pressures for wage increases in them. This 'cost-push' analysis is supplemented by an analysis of world commodity prices, where it is argued that, since demand pressures in the world economy are low and output of commodities below capacity, therefore inflation from this source is not to be expected; it is safe for demand to be raised up to the point at which commodity output reaches capacity levels. Hence the reduction in the 'imbalance' of the world economy and so of exchange rate pressures would probably help anti-inflation policy, while the overall stimulation would raise output without worsening overall inflation pressures. In a nutshell, this is a traditional old-style Keynesian analysis that up to a certain level of world demand there is a 'deflationary gap', i.e. there is excess capacity, and above it there is an 'inflationary gap', i.e. demand pressure. So the appropriate policy is always to reflate until demand is up to capacity levels of output, and only worry about inflation once demand is above those levels. This analysis is supplemented with some exchange-rate theory based on the view that exchange rates depend on relative trade balances.

If we go back a few years to the 'oil crisis' of 1973/4, we heard the same arguments then in a slightly different form. We were told that, because the oil countries had levied a tax on the West, there was a transfer of income from high consumption economies to low consumption economies, in many cases sparsely populated desert kingdoms. This transfer would cause a recession because the oil countries would be unable to spend their extra revenues whereas the West would cut back their spending by virtually the whole of the lost revenues. Consequently, Western governments should run budget deficits to offset the cut in world demand; they should finance them by borrowing back the oil revenues – a process that was called 'recycling'.

The analysis then, as the later OECD analysis, ignored one obvious fact of the situation, a fact that could not be easily rationalised within the OECD theoretical framework – inflation.

If there was a 'deflationary gap' and a lot of spare output capacity, why was inflation worldwide running at ten per cent *per annum* or more? If the reason alleged was that unions were demanding ten per cent *per annum* or more in wage increases, why were they doing so, when the very same unions were demanding five per cent or less a decade and a half previously? Such a theory of inflation – whether termed 'institutional', or 'cost-push', or what you will – has failed all available tests against the data; no independent measure of 'institutional factors' has been constructed that can explain such an acceleration. Instead explanations that have been given have been narrative, of the type *post hoc ergo propter hoc* ('this happened first so it was the cause'). They amount to a confession of failure to explain.

It is an accepted point in the methodology of science that when a 'paradigm' is reaching the end of its life, embarrassing problems are first labelled special cases and embarrassing successes of the rival paradigms are adopted as important special qualifications; in time the paradigm is jettisoned in favour of the rival. So the OECD view eclectically recognises the dangers of 'going too fast' in stimulating the world economy, in case 'inflation is re-ignited'; money supply growth must be 'controlled', budget deficits must not be 'excessive', and yet both must be orientated towards 'expansion'. Such is the language of a school of thought in ragged retreat.

The New Classical Analysis

The alternative explanation[1] starts from the general assumption that markets are clearing within some relevant time period; supply is equal to demand in general. This equality is brought about by price flexibility. Individuals plan on the assumption that they will be able to sell their labour at some price; and their problem is to determine what that price and the prices of the goods they will buy may be, and given these expectations to decide how much labour to sell today and in future, and how much to save. Firms similarly must decide how much labour to hire and how much to invest. When unexpected events occur, they cause plans to be falsified; prices accordingly change, plans are remade, and the economy adjusts along a new path. If no shocks occur for long enough, the economy converges to an equilibrium growth path.

The major problem faced by an economy is the conveying of information about *relative* prices by means of absolute prices; absolute prices are of course the prices in terms of money, whether gold or silver or paper money. To say this at all is to minimise the complexity of the information involved; we should remember that prices are quoted today for not only the whole range of goods currently available but also for financial assets, and for a vast range of goods and financial assets available at all future dates; these latter 'futures' prices are not always explicit but can be derived from combinations of interest rates, storage costs and current prices (e.g. a bushel of corn for delivery in ten years would 'cost', if you asked for a quotation from a corn dealer, the current price $\times \left(\frac{1 + \text{storage cost p.a.}}{1 + \text{interest cost p.a.}}\right)^{10}$

Inflation and the accompanying uncertainty about what the general price level will be interferes with the efficiency of this information system. When a price rises today, the individual is uncertain whether it represents a rise in the relative or the absolute price. When interest rates rise, an investor is uncertain whether this rise will be compensated by inflation and so a rise in price of the goods he is investing in or not. This uncertainty and confusion causes costs, not merely economic but also social costs that we perceive in a variety of ways – increased bitterness in wage bargaining, general social unrest, and so on.

Furthermore, a sustained but unexpected rise in inflation causes the private sector considerable financial problems to which adjustment can only occur gradually; these financial problems arise essentially from the fall in the value of money assets which are used as backing for operations in goods markets.

Nevertheless, governments may gain from inflation since it is a way of raising revenue that does not involve going through Parliament or levying explicit taxation. One possible reason is that the particular supporters of the party in power may have an interest in this form of taxation. Inflation as a tax works as follows. The government runs a higher deficit, which it finances by creating credit for itself from the banking system. The faster rate of credit creation causes a faster rate of growth in money which causes a faster growth in prices. The higher inflation rate causes a rise in interest rates as borrowers require compensation for the loss of purchasing power on their loans. Consequently, those who suffer from the tax are those who hold money (now depreciating faster) and other financial assets (these both depreciate faster and fall in capital value with the rise in interest rates). Those who gain from the tax are those with few financial assets but who pay ordinary taxes.

A further reason would arise if a government was unable to raise ordinary taxation because of an unwilling legislature; then inflation is the only possible tax.

Inflations therefore are explicable in terms of governments' own aims, even though society as a whole is damaged by them.

Shocks of any substance that disturb economic equilibrium and lead through the adjustment processes to what we recognise as the 'business cycle', can perhaps be classified into three main categories:

(a) Shocks to consumer preferences.
(b) Shocks to technology.
(c) Shocks to government policies (i.e. voter preferences).

Forced to give a view of what set of shocks the world economy was experiencing in the period 1973–9, the classical economist would probably point to all three types:

Examples of (a)-type: increased concern for environmental matters (especially in the US and Japan).
of (b)-type: the slowing down of oil discovery (or equivalently the rising marginal extraction cost of oil); the rapid growth of LDC competition in manufactures.
of (c)-type: the inflationary policies pursued in the US, the UK, Italy, and to a lesser extent in many other European countries.

However, the main points that emerge are that:

(1) The idea of concerted world action by governments misses the point that these very governments are responsible for their policies for electoral/political reasons and are hardly likely to be persuaded to change them by diplomacy.
(2) The world economy is adjusting in the fashion determined as optimal by micro-agents subject to the policies being followed by governments; if governments *did* agree to concerted action to 'stabilise' this path, the relevant question – to which we do *not* know the answer – is what set of rules for such concerted action to follow year-in-year-out would give the best framework for individual choice.
(3) The principal long-term objective governments ought to have – and the international community to pressure them into – is the reversal of inflationary policies instigated for sectarian reasons but against the social welfare. However, these being an internal matter, it is clear that there are limits to the scope for international action.
(4) The use of measures like unemployment, capacity utilisation for purposes of macro-policy recommendations ignore the way in which the decisions by individuals and firms to choose these levels of unemployment and utilisation have been reached. The simple-minded assumption that there is a 'deficiency of demand' is quite misleading. The objective of 'bringing down unemployment' to some historical figure is a foolish and dangerous one.

The International Adjustment Process

This classical analysis appears to me to be capable of explaining the facts of post-war, and particularly recent, international experience in the macro field more coherently than the OECD alternative.

These facts are summarised in Tables 6.1 and 6.2, and Figure 6.1. Table 6.1 encapsulates the history of fixed rates. The US budget deficit rose to over one per cent of GDP in the late 1960s and over two per cent in 1971. This was accompanied by a dramatic rise in its balance of payments deficit which spread the resultant growth in the money supply, through the exchange market intervention of other central banks, across the rest of the world. World inflation accordingly

Table 6.1: Money Supply, Deficits and Inflation under Fixed Rates

Average	1953–9	1960–5	1966–71	1971
US budget deficit (% of GDP)	0.6	0.7	1.1	2.3
Other 'big 9' budget deficit (% of GDP)	1.6	0.9	1.15	1.3
US balance of payments deficit ($bn p.a.)	1.4	2.0	6.4	29.7
Other 'big 9' central bank rise in $ reserves ($bn p.a.)	0.9	1.0	5.8	27.4
World money supply growth (% p.a.)	5.5	7.8	8.6	11.8
World inflation (% p.a.)	2.8	3.8	5.1	5.9

Table 6.2: Money Supply, Deficits, Inflation and Unemployment under Floating Rates – Average 1972–7

	World	Germany	US	France	Japan	Italy	UK
Govt deficit (% of GDP)	2.4	1.6	2.3	0.5	2.9	10.8	4.4
Money supply growth (% p.a.)	13.4	10.3	5.9	11.5	15.5	17.3	12.3
Inflation (% p.a.)	11.2	5.6	7.0	9.6	11.6	14.4	14.8
Unemployment (millions)							
1972	8.46*	0.25	4.84	0.38	0.73	1.38	0.88
1978	12.4*	0.99	6.05	1.17	1.24	1.57	1.38

*Sum of six countries shown.

rose to reach six per cent in 1971. Table 6.2 extends the story to floating rates, showing the diversity of experience across different countries. Some, like Germany, chose to pursue a relatively conservative fiscal policy. Their exchange rate appreciated and their inflation rate was held down. Others, such as the UK and Italy, pursued expansionary fiscal policies, and achieved inflation rates well into double figures. *All*, regardless of their fiscal policies, experienced substantial rises in unemployment, as consumers and firms digested the shocks administered by the jump into double-figure inflation and interest rates, and as other changes – especially labour supply composition and energy-related changes – impacted on the labour market. Figure 6.1 shows the inflation history for the main industrial countries, including the UK (as the most extreme example of price acceleration since floating).

I wish to fill in some of the details of that part of the international adjustment process which deals with balance of payments disequilibrium and draw attention to some of the evidence on it.

We can distinguish two main sorts of disequilibrium in international payments of the sort that the OECD and others have worried about. One I shall call 'flow' disequilibrium, the other 'stock' disequilibrium.

Stock disequilibrium is of the type stressed most clearly in the 'monetary theory of the balance of payments' (Frenkel and Johnson, 1976). The 'oil crisis' exemplifies it beautifully. One set of countries' income is enhanced, and another set is reduced, but their spending does not immediately reflect the change in their income; consequently, the one runs a surplus and the other a deficit on the current account of their balance of payments. However, as the one's assets accumulate it spends more, while as the other's decrease it spends less. As asset stocks of each set of countries change, so the income and spending flows come into equilibrium, and so does the balance of payments. This is in fact precisely what happened between 1974 and 1978 to OPEC and the West, contrary to many doom-laden pronouncements in 1974 to the effect that world payments would be out of equilibrium indefinitely with the threat of an inevitable financial collapse of the oil-consuming countries. In 1974 OPEC current account surpluses were \$66 billion; already in 1975 they had fallen to \$33 billion, and in 1978 they were a mere \$5 billion. Their net foreign assets had risen from virtually nothing in 1974 to \$168 billion by the end of 1978. It turned out the desert kingdoms could spend quite easily – and massively!

Flow disequilibrium is of the type most usually stressed in the old-style 'elasticities' analysis of the balance of payments, practised in the pre-war and early post-war period. A good example is the rapid growth of LDCs' manufacturing output. This is cheaper quality for quality, than Western manufactures. If Western prices remain higher, then their markets will be captured; the less-developed countries (LDCs) will run a surplus on current account, and the developed countries (DCs) a deficit, as both economies spend at normal output levels but switch their spending patterns towards LDC output. This situation clearly calls for a movement in relative prices, or as it is sometimes put, the 'real exchange rate'. However, the extent of the movement is a matter of micro-choice; at its simplest, we could think of DC labourers finding their real wages falling – or not rising as rapidly as before – and deciding to produce less rather than take an extreme cut. A

Figure 6.1: Inflation in the UK and Main Industrial Countries, 1953–77

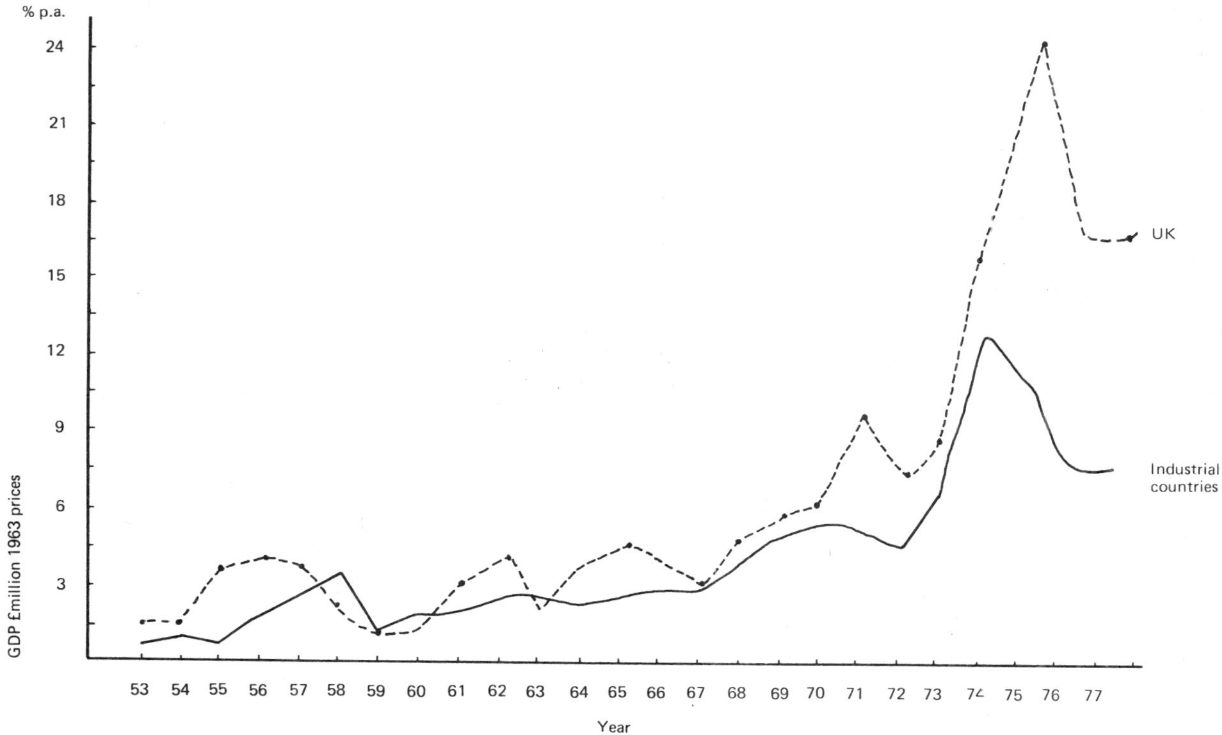

country – the UK springs to mind – can 'grow old gracefully'; its goods get relatively expensive, its markets contract, but its workers are content to let this happen and enjoy some modest real wage increase rather than change their attitudes, work practices and so forth or cut their real wages sufficiently to hold on to these markets. So flow disequilibrium in the balance of payments is partially eliminated by the fall in relative prices and wages, and the rest by the cut in incomes that follows from the cut in output as markets are lost.

Here it is of interest to look at the speeds with which different countries adjust their real wages and so their real exchange rates to changes in their circumstances. Estimates by Michael Brech and myself (Minford and Brech, forthcoming) across nine countries give the following for the period of time it takes for workers to adjust (95% of the way) towards a new equilibrium:

	Years
USA	2
Canada	2
Germany	3
Japan	5
France	5
Italy	6
Netherlands	5
Belgium	11
UK	14

So, quite apart from the new equilibrium chosen by workers faced with competition, we find that it takes them quite a lot of time to reach it, and a particularly long time in certain European countries where competition has over the centuries become less fierce.

This sluggish adjustment of relative prices in developed countries is to be contrasted strongly with the rapid adjustment to changing demand pressures that is found in LDCs. Thus in equations estimated for world agricultural raw materials and metals prices Michael Beenstock and I (1976) found that within two years the responses to a one per cent drop in world industrial production were respectively 0.4 per cent and a staggering 3.8 per cent.

So, to summarise the adjustment issue, we find that stock disequilibrium tends to be eliminated by the accumulation and decumulation of assets, while flow disequilibrium (due to changes in comparative advantage) requires relative price changes. The latter are more rapidly forthcoming in LDCs than DCs.

This adjustment aspect has two main implications for policy.

The first concerns recycling. The adjustment of spending in response to the oil transfer took place over about four years. Whether Western governments would have 'improved' this process by intervening to spend more in the initial years, is unclear but doubtful, since the evidence on lags in consumer adjustment suggests that Western consumers themselves unaided would have roughly offset the deflationary effect of the oil transfer in the early years. This implies that the world recession in 1975 should in no way be confused with the oil transfer (and indeed the major reason for that recession was the dramatic rise in inflation in 1974 and 1975, though this is not the place to document that assertion).

Secondly, the slowness of DC responses to relative price disequilibrium explains the steadily rising clamour in the West for protection. It also suggests that policy to defuse this clamour should be directed at providing the conditions for greater price adjustment. This means not subsidising the continuance of unviable firms, not providing social benefits at levels close to working wages (that therefore are made rigid downwards), and so forth – the opposite in effect of much recent policy at the micro-level in these economies. Western workers will simply have to get used to the idea that they do not have a prerogative to be rich relative to their LDC counterparts, and governments should not obstruct this process.

Re-entry to a World of Sound Money

So far we have been examining the properties of the international economy. We have conjured up a world finding its own path to equilibrium in response to a variety of shocks. This world will have cycles, and there may be some minor role in it for governments to set up fixed stabilising mechanisms – some already exist of course in the form of the automatic tax stabilisers; others could perhaps be designed. Governments should also eliminate those of their policies that interfere with and slow down adjustment; for example, levels of social security payments so high relative to potential wages at work that the incentive to work is attenuated, incomes and prices controls, high marginal tax rates, barriers to mobility in housing, and so on. But we have to recognise the constraint on governments posed by the democratic electoral system. We don't know a better system; but it is clear that many of the economic arrangements that democratic majorities set up are far from ideal for economic efficiency.

We have ridiculed the notion that governments, let alone any world collective action, could push the world economy towards some arbitrarily chosen 'full employment' state. Micro-agents choose the *equilibrium* condition towards which the world will tend. Governments' attempts to push for higher employment will be inflationary.

We have not yet however considered what government policies would be consistent with sound money (zero inflation) nor whether their espousal would entail a severe cost in unemployment as often argued by those of the OECD school.

The world of floating exchange rates that we now have is designed to accommodate the differing desires and tolerances of national governments for inflation. One country with high inflation is insulated from another with low inflation by the appreciation of the first's exchange rate with the second. Our question therefore relates to a single country. If all countries then behaved in the same way, we would have sound money internationally and in effect exchange rates would then be fixed *de facto* by the fixity of the relative values of domestic moneys.

The zero-inflation level of the budget deficit and of money supply growth can be computed from the rate at which the private sector would accumulate financial assets when the economy was growing at its equilibrium rate and there was no external deficit (external equilibrium). In this situation the budget deficit as the sole source of total financial assets for the private sector must be of just such a size as to generate what the private sector requires. Money supply growth must also match up with the growth required by private holders – remember that interest rates must be constant for this to be an equilibrium. For the UK, my calculations suggest that a public sector borrowing requirement (PSBR) not above one per cent of GDP and growth of sterling M3 in the range of three to five per cent *per annum*, are the orders of magnitude for the zero-inflation fiscal and monetary targets respectively.

Returning to sound money from current inflation rates of ten per cent *per annum* or more poses a re-entry problem for governments across the Western world; many fear massive unemployment would result from the immediate implementation of such low targets. This fear is based essentially on the view that wages and prices do not respond rapidly to changed government policies, because expectations of future inflation are based exclusively on some weighted average of past inflation rates, so called 'adaptive expectations'. Yet there is good reason to challenge this view on the grounds that agents are aware of other recent events, notably government policies, and use this information, as well as the history of inflation, to form their forecasts – this is the 'rational expectations' hypothesis. This view has considerable plausibility and it also appears to account well for wage formation across nine major economies (Minford and Brech, forthcoming).

To show its implications, in Figure 6.2 I set out two simulations from the Liverpool model of the UK which embodies rational expectations (these are detailed in Minford, 1980). These simulations can be considered to be typical in broad outline of any major Western economy. One assumes *gradual* reduction of money supply growth and PSBR sufficient to reduce inflation by eight per cent; the reductions are spread over four years in equal steps. The second assumes a sudden *immediate* cut of both, sufficient to reduce inflation at once by eight per cent.

It is obvious both from common sense and from the simulations that the shock treatment carries the greater risks. The difficulties of convincing people that the government truly means business are compounded if it all has to be done suddenly, overnight so to speak.

Nevertheless, the attractions of this second case are immense if conviction can be achieved. All the 'nasty medicine' is administered in one supreme effort of will. The effects on output are minimal. Once the shock is over, the economy can so to speak get back to normal at low inflation; no further sharp policy changes are needed. Government can take a back seat.

No doubt on balance governments will always go for the gradualist solution and indeed this has been eloquently and persistently advocated by monetarists as diverse as Milton Friedman, Karl Brunner and Alan Walters. The worry is that they will never actually go the whole way and we will never get rid of the inflation cancer that has crept up on Western economies and has sapped so much of their economic dynamism. Nevertheless, to revert to the central theme of this volume, such efforts, halting as they are likely to be, will no doubt ensure some sort of tolerable survival for the international economy of the West.

Figure 6.2: Gradualism and Immediacy Compared to Base Case, 1977–87

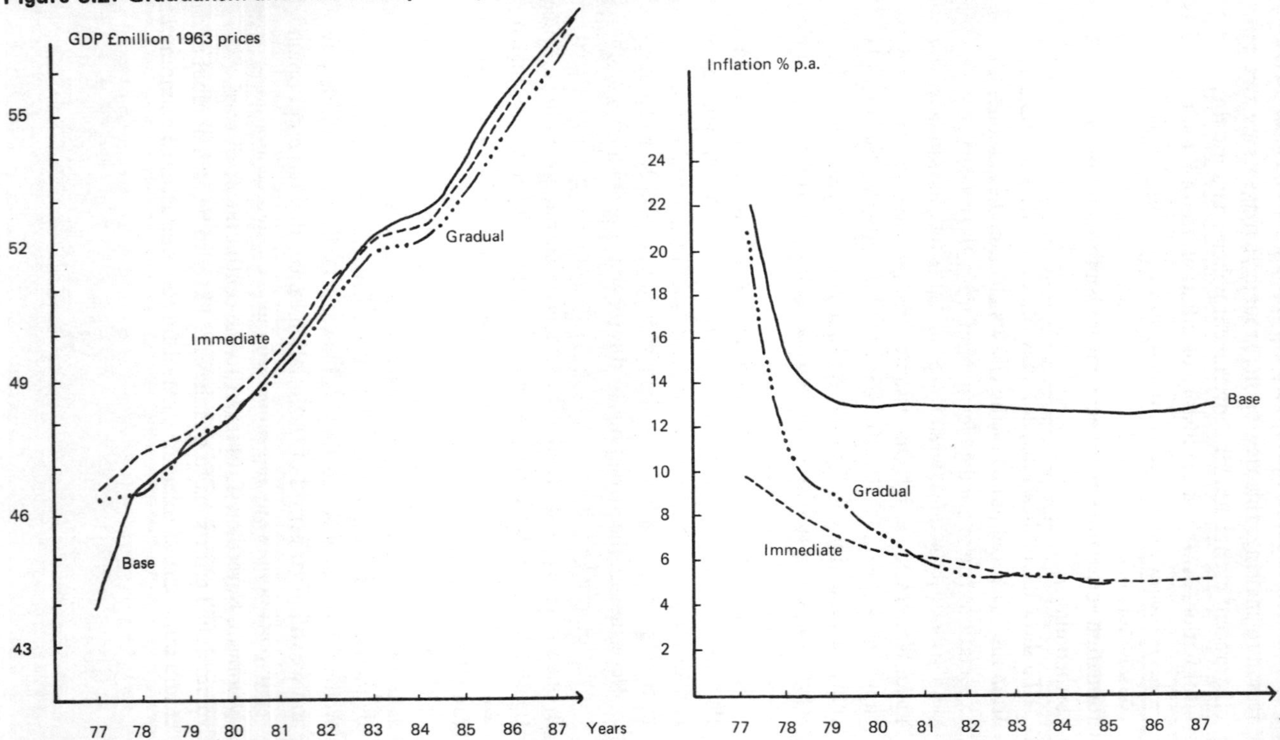

Note

1. This analysis owes much to the work of Milton Friedman and latterly to that of Robert Lucas, Jnr. and Thomas Sargent. See, for example Lucas and Sargent, 'After Keynesian Macroeconomics' in *After the Phillips Curve: Persistence of High Inflation and High Unemployment* (Proceedings of June 1978 Conference, Federal Reserve Bank of Boston).

References

Beenstock, M. C. and Minford, A. P. L. (1976), 'A Quarterly Econometric Model of World Trade and Prices, 1955–71' in Parkin, M. and Zis, G. (eds.), *Inflation in Open Economies* (Manchester: Manchester University Press)

Frenkel, J. and Johnson, H. G. (eds.) (1976), *The Monetary Approach to the Balance of Payments* (London: Allen & Unwin)

McCracken, P. *et al.* (1977), *Towards Full Employment and Price Stability: A Report to the OECD by a Group of Independent Experts* (Paris: OECD)

Minford, A. P. L. (1980), 'A Rational Expectations Model of the UK under Fixed and Floating Exchange Rates', *Carnegie-Rochester Conference Series on Public Policy*, vol. 12 ('On the State of Macro-economics')

Minford, A. P. L. and Brech, M. J. (forthcoming). 'The Wage Equation and Rational Expectations' in Proceedings of 1979 AUTE Conference (London: Croom Helm)

7 TECHNOLOGICAL CHANGE AND THE FUTURE

Tom Stonier

The decade which spanned the period roughly from the mid-1960s to the mid-1970s saw the emergence of a public concern over a constellation of problems, which were perceived to threaten human survival. These problems included pollution, impending shortages of critical resources, over-population, nuclear annihilation, and repression of personal liberties by increasingly centralised governments. It is the purpose of this chapter to point out that although these problems deserve continuing concern, their threat is declining under the impact of advances in science and technology. At the same time, a new set of problems is emerging, of which the most important is the accelerating displacement of labour by the new 'information' technology. Both the problem, and a potential solution, are considered here in greater detail.

Environmental Accounting

By the late 1960s, there had emerged in most of the Western (OECD) countries an environment movement able to articulate its concerns in three basic areas: pollution, potential resource shortages and over-population. Pollution was affecting the air, water and land with a variety of man-made, or man-caused products such as industrial wastes, chemicals and sewage, by excessive use of fertilisers and DDT, or just plain litter. On a global scale, DDT, nuclear proliferation, or atmospheric catastrophies threatened the world. Included among these were the destruction of the ozone layer, the possibility of an ice age from too much fine dust in the stratosphere, or conversely, too much carbon dioxide, creating a 'greenhouse effect' which would melt the polar ice caps, and a similar polar melt which could result if sufficient spills from oil tankers reached the polar caps. These concerns, representing a broader, global ecosystems approach, received much impetus by the publication of Rachel Carson's book *Silent Spring* in 1962. The second area of concern, shortages of critical resources, included minerals and fuel as well as clean air, water and good farmland. These concerns became systematised by the publication of *Limits to Growth* (Meadows *et al.*, 1972) and their potential danger was driven home dramatically by the Arab-imposed oil sanctions in late 1973. Finally, over-population as a threat was backed by statistics from the UN and other sources, brought forcefully to the public attention by Paul Ehrlich (1968).

Unlike the more traditional 'conservation movements', which date back to early in the Industrial Revolution, and which involved mainly the rich, the environment movement became broadly based, though still primarily middle-class. Its primary response to the combination of environmental threats, can be summed up by E. F. Schumacher's phrase 'small is beautiful' (1973), which served as a paradigm for a whole generation of students.

The environmental movement was vital in bringing awareness and public pressure to deal with these problems. As a result, increasingly stringent legislation reduced air and water pollution and severely restricted the use of DDT. Nuclear energy developments slowed and increasing sums of money became available for developing alternative energy sources. At the same time, industry, government and individuals were motivated to begin serious energy conservation schemes. In addition to these victories, the environment movement could not have foreseen the further technological developments such as computer-based control systems which reduced the requirements for energy and materials. Nor were they able to predict the technologically feasible exploitation of undersea oil reserves and deep ocean minerals. Under the impact of science and technology, the problems have receded in importance and the forecasted critical time span has been pushed back. The breathing space has been enhanced by the fact that a number of Western countries have achieved zero population growth.

This by no means implies that the problems are solved. Much work remains to be done. Along with the new knowledge of population dynamics and existing resources, technology needs to continue to explore alternative solutions such as solar, wave and fusion power. Technology now involves substituting information flows for energy and materials: one example involves the use of the telephone instead of the mail or making visits. Another involves reducing fuel consumption by microprocessor-controlled fuel injection systems in automobiles. A third which may develop significantly over the next two decades involves 'telecommuting' by means of home-based computer terminals, by which business can be conducted with the office or even with foreign offices, without leaving the home.

Creating substitutes, such as coal processed into oil and replacing copper cables with optical glass fibres should be considered as prototypes for solving shrinking materials-resource problems.

Technology can develop other new resources, including a vast expansion of food production in the form of coastal fish farming and making the deserts bloom. As a result of a massive expansion of productivity, sufficient wealth can be produced around the world to effect a demographic shift and permit the attainment of a stable population.

1984

The threat of over-population, of pollution and of resource shortage are not the only problems which face global society. Political repression and nuclear war must also be added to the list of concerns when dealing with the future. Paradoxically, inherent in the very technology which has created these threats lies the solution.

Societies which have undergone the 'electronic revolution' are emerging into a new era, the 'communicative era' (Stonier, 1976). One of the parameters for determining whether a country has moved into the communicative era is that the majority of its households possess radio, television and telephone. Modern transportation facilities, plus the combination of electronic communication and printed-word media, yield a highly efficient information network, which becomes very difficult to control from the centre. Add to this an increasingly complex society run by increasingly sophisticated information operatives, and it becomes apparent why an expanding, advanced information network presses one country after another into increased democratisation. As the communicative era overtakes the Soviet Union and Eastern bloc countries, corresponding changes in the political structure will be observed there as well.

The Institution of War

Perhaps the most important shift in the economy of communicative society is related to the increasing specialisation of the global economy, made possible by modern communications and transportation technologies, resulting in a trans-national web of production and services. The economies of communicative society are having the same impact on the political organisation of the globe today, as the rise of mercantilism a few hundred years ago had on the political organisation of Western Europe. The present shift from national polities to supranational polities, as exemplified by the European Community, reflects the fact that national economies are no longer primarily closed systems. The change is accelerated by the shifting military technology. Just as the shift from feudal- to nation-states a few hundred years ago was accelerated by gunpowder and other military inventions, so have the traditional defences of the contemporary nation-states been breached by the nuclear missile technology.

Associated with the replacement of the nation-state by larger political units is the decline of large-scale warfare as an institution. Here again, the situation is analogous to the decline of that other ancient institution, slavery, which disappeared with the advent of industrialisation. The primary social motivation for slavery involved the need for maintaining an extensive economic infrastructure through the use of coerced labour. That noxious social institution could not survive when society found an improved technology, namely, the combination of machines and wage labour. A comparable process is taking place today, as nations move from the national economies of the 'mechanical era' into the trans-national productive web characterising the 'communicative era'. Although it is often couched in ideological terms, the primary social motivation for war always has been the extension of resources (with secondary motivations involving such other factors as status, defence or revenge). In recorded historical times, whenever one group was sufficiently powerful to deprive another of valuable resources, it was merely a matter of time before that deprivation came to pass. This is no longer true. The vast productivity of technologically advanced societies makes the extension of resources through technological ingenuity not only possible, but much more reliable. It becomes easier to substitute synthetics for raw materials or to grow crops more efficiently than to enter into foreign conquests with the immense destructive risks associated with advanced military technology (Stonier, 1977).

The New Threat

The greatest threat to Western society at the moment is the rapid displacement of labour by technology. Present trends in unemployment do not represent a mere downturn in business activity or a temporary recession, which will in time correct itself. Jobs in the manufacturing sector are, and have been for some time, on the way out. What we see now is an acceleration of an historical process which can be traced back at least a couple of centuries, a process which involves a shift in the principal economic activities from manipulating land, to manipulating machines, to manipulating information (Stonier, 1978).

At the beginning of the eighteenth century, over 80 per cent of the workforce laboured on farms to feed the rest (Deane, 1965). Today, it takes less than three per cent in the US to feed not only the rest of the country, but much of the world as well (US Department of Commerce, 1977; US Department of Agriculture, 1970). This dramatic shift reflects the effective coupling of new technologies to better-informed farm operatives. The American farmer works no harder than his forefathers. He sits in an air-conditioned tractor or drives a combine harvester, listening to a transistor radio. However, he is doing as much work as 50 men breaking their backs using a sickle. He has at his disposal the use of fertilisers and pesticides, information on weather, hybrid seeds and world market conditions. The modern farmer is highly productive because he is a highly skilled operative who has available to him a wide variety of technological back-ups.

Over the past three centuries, largely as a result of this increased efficiency in agriculture, the bulk of the labour force shifted from farms to the manufacturing industries. The new job market was created by the Industrial Revolution. That revolution in turn was marked by the invention of the steam engine, not just another piece of technology but a 'meta-technology' (Stonier, 1979). Steam coupled to existing machinery made it many times more powerful. Coupled to a loom, it became a power-loom; coupled to a wagon, it became a locomotive. Ultimately, the increasing mechanisation in industry, largely over the last hundred years, brought about a further shift in labour from the manufacturing to the service industries. Today an even more dramatic shift is taking place as a result of a new technology.

The New Meta-technology

The appearance of the microprocessor is having a profound effect on labour patterns. The microprocessor does nothing radically different from its progenitor, the computer. But it does it faster, more reliably and cheaper. Coupled to existing machinery, it greatly increases productivity.

A new technology displaces an older one as a function of how much better it is. If a new technology is only ten per cent better, it displaces existing technology very slowly, if at all. If it is 50 per cent better, then it begins to make inroads, although the process may take decades. When it is many times better, as clearly the new microprocessor technology is, then it moves very rapidly indeed.

Among the new microprocessor-based technologies emerging are industrial and office robots. Industrial robots, once they become cheap enough, have enormous advantages. They can operate in dangerous situations and under inhuman conditions. Moreover, a welding robot, for example, can be 'shown' how to weld a wing onto a car in an assembly line by having the motions traced for it *once* by a master welder (the perfect apprentice). From that point on, it carries on the function 24 hours a day, 365 days a year, without going on strike, tea break or sick leave (unless designed badly). Investment costs can be recouped in a year and a half. Additional robots monitor lining-up procedures and are programmed to signal difficulties or shut down production. Indeed, there already exist entire sections of such plants in Western Europe and Japan, virtually devoid of human operatives. Other robots can monitor stocks and, by means of terminal links with suppliers, re-order parts. Specifications for cars can also be received directly from retailers, thus eliminating many middle-line managers as well as workers on the shop floor.

Equally startling will be the displacement in offices; as recent experience has shown, typing pools can be cut in half, and achieve an overall 300 per cent increase in output. The corporation's investment in this case may be zero, since the microprocessor can be bought on time, out of the savings on staff (Frankland and Jones, 1978).

The effect of these changes is evident in the statistics of, for example, the textile industry. In Bradford, an annual production of £200 million (approximate current prices) of wool one hundred years ago took 20,000 to 30,000 workers (Richardson, 1976). Compare this to the synthetic fibre plants at Teesside. The same volume can be produced by 600 to 1,000 workers, that is, it takes only about three per cent of the amount of labour to produce comparable amounts of wealth in manufacturing industries. That three per cent figure in terms of labour requirement is almost the identical figure which we have seen in the US in terms of farm labour. As the electronic revolution proceeds with the microprocessor at its core, comparable statistics will be attained throughout all the manufacturing industries. It is highly probable that by early in the next century it will require no more than ten per cent of the labour force to provide us with all our material needs, that is, all the food we eat, all the clothing we wear, all the textiles, appliances, etc. In the near future, the vast majority of labour will be engaged as information operatives, that is, workers who make their living by creating, organising, applying or transmitting information: scientists, managers, engineers, librarians, computer programmers, technical salesmen, all those in formal education and the mass media, etc. As a result of the burgeoning information technology, industrial labour is now shifting to adapt to the new productive systems, which require greater mental and less manual effort. This shift in labour is parallel to the historical one from farm to factory.

Modern productive systems are becoming less and less dependent on land, labour and capital for their primary input. Instead, they become increasingly dependent on organised information. The displacement of labour in the form of technology has already been referred to. Similarly, the requirement for land, both for agriculture and housing, becomes reduced by advancing technology such as skyscrapers, multi-storied chicken farms and mechanical farming. The advent of the tractor released millions of acres used for growing horse fodder. The acreage released will be even greater with the advent of single-cell protein to feed cattle. Finally, capital moves today not in terms of the transfer of large sums of gold or even money, but in the transmission of credit information. Post-industrial economies are run primarily on credit, rather than cash transactions.

In modern post-industrial society, where labour requirements are beginning to shrink in manufacturing as they did in industrial society for agriculture, the primary input is knowledge, and the most important single resource the post-industrial society has, is its human capital and the skills and knowledge it can harness. At the base of all technological skills and back-up is a history of education, and research and development. This trend will accelerate such that in the next century education will become the number one industry and employ about half the total workforce. The education industry will include far more than schools and universities.

The New Wealth Producers

The DES and its local partners and subsidiaries should begin planning now, how they can become the nation's number one employer. All government departments should begin to develop policies to aid in the shift from farm, and industrial and machine, operatives to information operatives by an expansion of the education system.

In order to effect such a change, we must understand that applied science and technology is *the* major producer of wealth. About a thousand years ago, northern Europe was a fairly barbaric part of the world. Compared to the Mediterranean, it was poor and backward, largely because it did not have the economic base the Mediterranean area did. Northern Europe did, of course, have enormous potential in terms of the fertile grasslands, but these could not become a major resource until the invention of the deep plough and ancillary technology (White, 1962). It was the so-called Agricultural Revolution of the ninth and tenth century which set the stage for wealth creation. This was followed by the rise of mercantilism and the beginning of the ascendancy of northern Europe over Mediterranean Europe. The emergence from the Dark Ages became a reality because technology made into a resource something which had not been a resource before, fertile land. We can say the same thing about North Sea oil. We all know that the British economy (as reflected by the value of sterling) turned around because of the presence of North Sea oil. That oil has been there a long time. It was there before the Battle of Hastings, it was there before there was a Europe, it was there long before there was a humanity. But it was not a resource. It became a resource only when a sophisticated consumer technology appeared and made oil a valuable commodity, then developed a whole technology for exploring and finally extracting oil from under the sea. Here again, technology based on knowledge (organised information) developed a new area of wealth. By the mid-1980s, we will see a similar phenomenon as we begin mining the deep oceans for manganese, nickel, copper and other elements. It was not very long ago when elements such as manganese and nickel were not considered particularly valuable, nor for that matter were aluminium and magnesium.

Technology is probably *the* most important single factor in increasing capital for any society. Yet the new knowledge is always based on previous knowledge transmitted from one generation to the next, principally by the education system. And that education system is maintained at public expense. The PhDs who develop a new chemical process or electronics system, the engineers who design the plant, the technicians who help in the construction, all will have had their education paid for only to a small extent by the industries which use them. We must understand that the government is not merely important as a political institution, or even as a social institution. It is also a major, perhaps *the* major economic institution. Much of what passes as profligacy, 'wasting the tax-payers' money by creating huge edifices of government', is really good economics: the government is the only institution able to co-ordinate modern post-industrial economies. In fact, in modern post-industrial systems, the national government may no longer be adequate. Thus, just as we see a drift of firms becoming multi-national, we see a similar drift of national governments becoming regional governments such as the EEC. By the next century, that process should lead to a global association and our children and our grandchildren will all be very grateful for it.

The answer to the unemployment problem is to accelerate the shift away from the manufacturing and into the information sector of the economy. The most sensible way to achieve that shift is by a massive expansion of the education system. We should seriously consider doubling the education budget by the mid-1980s and then redoubling it again by the mid-1990s. There are several reasons why this would be both practical and desirable. First, education is labour-intensive and can provide hundreds of thousands of jobs. It is one of the few areas in our society where it makes sense to be labour-intensive. A teacher responsible for only 20 students is at least twice as effective as one responsible for 40, and only ten pupils is twice as good again.

The second reason why a massive expenditure on education will solve the unemployment problem is that the bulk of the unemployed are youngsters. To give a specific figure, between early 1975 and late 1977, the under-26 unemployed in the EEC jumped from about 0.5 million to 2 million (Palmer, 1977). Many of those youngsters who are out of work have been turned off the education system, usually when they were at about middle-school level, some earlier, some later. They can't wait to get out. Simply forcing them to stay in for another year is probably of very little help to them, their classmates or the teachers. If we designed a truly attractive system, many, hopefully most, of the young people would stay in education perhaps right through university level. By expanding further and community education, we could attract more mature individuals back into education as well, thereby relieving the welfare rolls still further. Thus the bulk of the unemployed would be gainfully engaged, in accordance with a well-established historical tradition (over the last hundred years) in which the average educational level has been rising steadily. Relying solely on such a historical process is inadequate. We need to engage in a deliberate policy of accelerating the up-grading of education for all people, so that it matches the acceleration of labour displaced by technology. Such a policy is crucial for social and economic health.

In addition to expanding education, the government must also expand research and development. It is no good churning out a lot of

PhDs and then having no jobs for them. On the other hand, if research and development is coupled to an up-graded education system, then the country can begin to generate new technology and new sources of wealth which will pay for the whole system. Consider the following possibilities.

Current economic analyses are dominated by the assumption that Britain must export manufactured goods, because it must import food. That assumption is not valid if one were to develop technologies which could make Britain a net exporter of food. A combination of single-cell protein production and coastal fish farming could probably make Britain such a net exporter of food.

ICI has a plant in operation now, producing a single-cell protein for cattle feed supplement (MacLennan, Gow and Stringer, 1973). This technology is still in its early stages. The product is as good as, or better than, other feed supplements. However, the price of the single-cell protein is such that it is cheaper than fish meal or soya-bean meal when soya beans are expensive, but cannot compete when soya beans are cheap. A good deal of Britain's food imports involve food for cattle. More than half of all the cereal consumed in this country is eaten by cattle (MAFF, 1977). Perhaps even more important in the long run is the possibility of coastal fish farming. This is practised to a very limited extent now but could be expanded enormously once we know enough. The technology appears to require much greater inputs of basic knowledge in fields such as limnology, marine biology, ecology, etc.

North Sea oil is needed for both the production of energy and for the production of petrochemicals. Britain is an island on the leeward side of a highly energetic ocean. At the moment, the enormous energy provided by the waves hitting that island goes to waste. The energy is sufficient to provide about 50 megawatts per kilometre (Salter, Jeffrey and Taylor, 1976). This would be a major source of electrical energy if the existing technology could be made economic. Not only would it provide large amounts of energy, it would provide a large number of jobs in the shipyards, which would first have to fill a domestic market, and then, if Britain were first in the field, would be a major export item. Secondly, the technology which converts coal into oil is also quite advanced, but only marginally economic. There is no reason why, as the world runs out of oil, and the chemical processes converting the carbon of coal into hydrocarbon of oil becomes cheaper, that Britain's large coal reserves should not become an important source of wealth. Thus, there are substitutes which could have enormous economic benefit for Britain and the world after the oil runs out.

Imagine now that we have developed those four technologies and lo-and-behold, Britain becomes wealthy as it continues to be an energy exporter, and now also becomes a food exporter.

The function of developing new technologies and industries is not to produce jobs – some jobs will be produced – but the main function is to produce wealth. That wealth generates revenues for the government, which allows it to pay its employees. At present, more than one out of five of us work for the government (CSO, 1977). In the next century, perhaps half, possibly three-quarters will. The reason is that the labour required to operate the primary and secondary sectors of the economy (foodstuffs, raw materials and manufacture) will require no more than ten per cent of the labour force as the processes of mechanisation and automation accelerate. The other 90 per cent will be involved either in private entrepreneurial service sectors or (the bulk) working for the government. There is no contradiction in this economically, because what we are achieving in the post-industrial society is the creation of material wealth by robots. Boring work should be left to robots. Human beings should spend most of their time working with each other. Whether that is in the health services, in the education system, or in some other capacity is irrelevant. In any case, the post-industrial society will shift the labour force away from manufacturing, just as the industrial society shifted the labour force away from farming.

In conclusion, the biggest problem confronting British society at the moment is how to transfer labour from the manufacturing industries, where jobs are shrinking at an alarming rate, into the knowledge industries, which need to be subsidised by the government. The most sensible way to do this is through a massive expansion of the education system, which is first of all labour-intensive, producing ultimately millions of jobs; secondly, it would keep the young off the labour market; and, thirdly, it would create a more versatile labour pool. It would also encourage a more creative use of leisure time, and finally, it would help to develop the new industries, which would produce the wealth necessary for sustaining the process. The adroit use of technology could make Britain a net exporter of food and energy (even after the North Sea oil runs out). Thus a massive expansion in education, coupled to research and development, becomes a true investment in the future, not only in social terms, but also in pay-back economic terms.

References

Carson, R. (1962), *Silent Spring* (Boston: Houghton Mifflin)
CSO (Central Statistical Office) (1977), *National Income and Expenditure 1966–76* (London: HMSO)
Deane, P. (1965), *The First Industrial Revolution* (Cambridge: Cambridge University Press)
Ehrlich, P. R. (1968), *The Population Bomb* (New York: Ballantine)
Frankland, J. and Jones, F. M. (1978), 'Word Processing Takes Bradford into the Jet-Age', *Municipal and Public Services Journal* (18 August)
MacLennan, D. G., Gow, J. S. and Stringer, D. A. (1973), 'Methanol-bacterium Process for SCP', *Process Biochemistry* (June 1973)
MAFF (Ministry of Agriculture Fisheries & Food) (1977), *Output and Utilisation of Farm Produce in the United Kingdom 1969/70 to 1975/6* (London: HMSO)
Meadows, D. L., Meadows, D. H., Randers, J. and Behrens, W. W. (1972), *The Limits to Growth* (New York: Universe Books for Polomac Associates)
Palmer, J. (1977), 'Their Future Behind Them?', *The Guardian* (17 October)
Richardson, C. (1976), *A Geography of Bradford* (Bradford: University of Bradford)
Salter, S. H., Jeffrey, D. C. and Taylor, J. R. M. (1976), 'The Architecture of Nodding Duck Wave Power Generators', *Naval Architect* (January)
Schumacher, E. F. (1973), *Small is Beautiful* (New York: Harper & Row)
Stonier, T. (1976), *The Natural History of Humanity: Past, Present and Future*, Inaugural Lecture, University of Bradford (17 February)
——— (1977), 'Economic and Technological Prerequisites for Achieving Political and Military Stability' in Carlton, D. and Schaerf, C. (eds.), *Arms Control and Technological Innovation* (London: Croom Helm)
——— (1978), 'Materials Production Labour Requirements in Post-industrial Society', Central Policy Review Staff Working Paper, as reported by Owen, K., *The Times* (13 November)
——— (1979), 'Changes in Western Society: Educational Implications' in T. Schuller and Megarry, J. (eds.), *World Yearbook of Education 1979: Recurrent Education and Lifelong Learning* (London: Kogan Page)
US Department of Agriculture (1970), *Changes in Farm Production and Efficiency – A Summary Report 1970*, Statistical Bulletin no. 233 (Washington DC: US Government Printing Office)
US Department of Commerce (1977), *Statistical Abstract of the United States* (Washington DC: US Government Printing Office)
White, L. (1962), *Medieval Technology and Social Change* (Oxford: Clarendon Press)

8 REGIONAL DEVELOPMENT AND THE CHANGING ECONOMY

Edward Cunningham

Introduction

The title of this chapter has two components: the issues of regional development and the implications of the changing economy. 'Regional development' carries the connotation today of a problem or deprived area, although 70 to 80 years ago the term conveyed the exuberant growth of great industrial cities. There has always been unevenness of development within any one country and this has given rise to social and political conflict. I suppose it was the Depression that really brought into focus the problem of regional development as we talk about it today. Certainly regional policy as a conscious political act started to take on a specific form from that time with the Special Areas Act of 1934 being the first of varied efforts to offset decline in certain regions.

Economic change will inevitably set up forces that concentrate activity where the money is being made. Our problem today is that the process of change has been taking place far quicker than many members of our society can adjust to and indeed faster than our physical infrastructure can be made to respond. What has been true of the past with its resulting difficulties takes on added significance when we try to comprehend the scale and impact of future economic change.

The changing economy which confronts us comprises three powerful forces. The first and most obvious is the change in energy resources. The second is the change in technology. And the third is the shift in industrial power that is taking place between countries.

Against this background I will start by discussing the anatomy of a regional problem. Then I will comment on the impact of the changing economy, and I will conclude by examining if regional decline can be reversed in these circumstances.

The Anatomy of a Regional Problem

Predictably I will want to use Glasgow as an example which

exemplifies Scotland's problems and which illustrates general features of regional development in the broader UK context. But first it is worth reiterating that regional disparities are a universal phenomenon. Even Japan, customarily regarded as the paradigm of economic growth and success, has its sad coastal towns which were once the hives of shipbuilding and repairing; now these industries are in sharp decline as their centres of production have begun to shift towards less developed countries. There are of course also the problems of the American inner cities and the shift of industrial concentration from the old declining regions in the north-east to the growing new 'Sun Belt'. While unemployment is not the sole measure, it does provide a useful illustration of disparities. In Western Europe, all the major countries show ratios of a least two to one between their highest and lowest regional unemployment rates as Table 8.1 demonstrates.

Table 8.1: Comparisons of Unemployment Percentage Rates in Europe (Spring 1975)

Country	Highest regional rate	National rate	Lowest regional rate
Austria	5.0 (Carinthia)	2.1	1.2 (Vienna)
Belgium	4.1 (Wallonia)	3.2	2.7 (Flanders)
Britain	7.1 (N. Ireland)	3.6	2.4 (South-east)
France	5.5.(Mediterranean)	3.3	2.2 (East)
W. Germany	4.3 (Schleswig-H.)	2.9	2.1 (Baden-W.)
Holland	4.7 (South)	3.2	2.3 (West)
Italy	6.0 (Sardinia)	3.3	1.3 (Lombardy)
Spain	13.5 (Andalusia)	5.6	2.8 (Catalonia)
Sweden	4.4 (Mid-north)	1.6	0.8 (Stockholm)

Source: *The Economist* (1 April 1978).

In general terms, these differences have stemmed for the most part from either the absence of any industrial base, often as a result of poor natural resources, or as a consequence of the early start hypothesis leading to industrial stagnation. A further factor has been the loss of some earlier locational advantage. The main difference to be noted here is in fact that between countries and areas where the depressed regions were formerly thriving industrial centres – as, for example, in northern Britain and, outside Europe, the United States – and those where they have never been able to build up substantial industry, as in Italy, south-west England and Spain. If looked at in more detail, the regional problem has, of course, many variations. It is this diversity that serves as a reminder against too facile a diagnosis or assumptions on the remedy.

Indeed, the comfortable assumption that an economic balance could be reached between the various parts of an industrial or industrialising country on the basis of a widespread distribution of natural resources is no longer tenable. It may have provided a reasonable model for some countries in the early stages of industrialism, but it is no longer the recipe for distributing prosperity in a modern industrial nation. Today many industries, and most of those with strong growth prospects, are no longer closely tied geographically to sources of raw materials. Instead industry has become mobile, both nationally and internationally, and seeks areas with concentrations of key staff or with amenities capable of attracting such staff. Meanwhile traditional industries which were located where they are in the older industrial areas because of their original dependence upon certain local resources, have seen their advantage eroded by the growth of competitors elsewhere in the world who have been exploiting the fact that even traditional industries have ceased to be so geographically tied. Even so, the older and adversely affected industrial area can still offer a considerable reservoir of skills, supported by a good infrastructure of local universities and colleges, while a rural area, which may once have supported some industry, can still provide an immediately pleasant environment. However, the problem of these two main categories of area are still the same, namely that of having to counteract the process that leads to a concentration of people and wealth in areas elsewhere whilst they undergo a seemingly inexorable decline.

Regional disparities are inevitably associated with poor housing and education facilities, relatively high unemployment and other disadvantages which make for dissatisfaction. This in turn leads to emigration from which a bias then develops in the population towards the less employable groups. Also in many areas, and especially so in Scotland, the process of decline has been associated with vast tracts of industrial dereliction leaving ugly scars upon the landscape and urban areas. Thus, socially and environmentally, the process of decline becomes mutually reinforcing.

The process produces two important manifestations which infinitely complicate efforts to reverse the trend. The first is progressive social tensions reflected, in particular, in worker militancy. As industrial growth falters, workers seek to protect their jobs and all the more so if they cannot perceive alternative demand for their labour. Even though unemployment may be much lower in percentage terms now that it was during the Depression and much of the inter-war years, attitudes continue to be affected by the shadow of unemployment and are exacerbated by the higher expectations which prevail.

The second manifestation is that once decline becomes evident and hence widely recognised, it comes to be fixed as a general perception even when changes and effort towards revival are underway and in no context is this more true than in industrial relations. Indeed, it is the sweeping and glib assumptions based upon perceptions rather than facts that makes it difficult to reinstate the essential elements of confidence.

A Case Study of Regional Decline

But what are the characteristics of a regional problem? To take Glasgow as an example, the striking feature is the enormous and burgeoning success of the city in the latter part of the nineteenth century. It was the engineering centre of the world with a highly integrated industrial structure based primarily upon shipbuilding: our very own silicon valley of engineering. The population reflected industrial growth and rose from half a million in 1871 to over one million by the start of the First World War. Glasgow rejoiced in its success as we can see in its architecture and in the evidence of far-flung interests across the world. There was innovation and experiment. Indeed, Glasgow was early in the field of acquiring the car and airplane. But then the decline set in. The causes have been much examined and no doubt will continue to be and it is not my purpose to cover this particular ground. What I want to emphasise is that the regional problem has been conditioned by the contrast between yesterday and today.

The characteristics of today in Glasgow are epitomised by conditions in the Glasgow East Area Renewal Project (GEAR) where the Scottish Development Agency is working with other authorities to bring about a reversal of recent trends. Here the population has declined from 80,000 in 1971 to 45,000 or so today and unemployment is over 20 per cent compared with the UK average of five per cent and that of the south-east of England of four per cent. Of the unemployed, 50 per cent have had no employment for more than a year; for the UK the percentage is 22 per cent. There are other indicators; for example, car ownership is 0.15 per household while in the south-east it approaches 0.8. Furthermore ten per cent of the households in this area lack inside WCs (GEAR, 1978).

More broadly, Glasgow as a whole has experienced a low level of public and private investment and only obtained 14.7 per cent of total Scottish investment in 1977/8 against its population share of 16.4 per cent. In particular, private sector investment has been running at about only 65 per cent of the *per capita* level for Scotland. At the same time, employment is still dependent upon relatively few large firms, some of which are vulnerable to the changing economy. And the sparks of new enterprise appear to be noticeably fewer as the conurbation ranks low in that important indicator of entrepreneurship, the strength of the small firm sector. Only nine per cent of Glasgow manufacturing employment is in firms with fewer than 50 employees compared with levels of 15 per cent and 18 per cent in the more prosperous south-east and Greater London.

Glasgow's problems predominate in the region but in the context of Scotland, similar characteristics prevail elsewhere, albeit in some cases at a lower level of intensity. For instance, in manufacturing, Scotland as a whole has experienced larger percentage declines than the rest of Britain. In only one sector, electrical engineering, has Scotland experienced a growth in employment and, interestingly enough, has done so in stark contrast to the experience of the rest of the country in this sector which has seen employment decline. And although there has been some narrowing of disparities in terms of GDP per head and wages, unemployment remains well above the country's average.

In these conditions people's attitudes are affected. Kay Carmichael, who sought to assess the extent of poverty said, after living in a deprived part of Glasgow, 'I had to make an effort to talk differently, to hold my body differently, to look a little bit defeated. I deliberately learned to look rather worried most of the time.' (Reported in *The Listener*, 17 November 1977.) This is the human dimension of deprivation.

To summarise at this stage in the discussion, regional problems originate in a shift in comparative advantage. Some regions have been able to adjust and prosper and it was interesting to see a comment in *The Economist* (14 July 1979) that in growth terms the East Midlands was rapidly overtaking the West Midlands, hitherto the industrial heartland. In other regions, failures of judgement and inadequate foresight led into a downward spiral. The question before those caught in this situation is whether or not it is possible to reverse the trend in the face of the changing economy. But, first, it is necessary to look at the changing economy.

The Changing Economy

Futurology is a hazardous game and I cannot pretend to provide a comprehensive survey of this aspect. But, to my mind, the changes we are going to face are likely to be dominated by energy, technology and the shift in industrial power and, without question, these are changes that could have a very direct impact upon regional development. In addition, especially in the light of present experience, a further feature of the changing economy could be inflation with all the effects that Max Gaskin has already described in Chapter 1 of this book.

On energy, the implications of rising oil prices and constraints upon supply have been vigorously debated but, in general terms, there is some consensus over the impact upon oil-using activities and manufacturing. Whereas industrial growth over the past thirty years or so has been spurred on by the ready and cheap availability of oil, future growth will rely upon more efficient use of oil resources and the development of other energy sources. Without major breakthroughs in both of these areas, the prospect is that worldwide economic growth will be severely constrained with, obviously, a severe impact upon oil dependent activities. Conversely, areas with oil resources can look forward to substantial investment opportunities and therefore growth in employment and income prospects.

A specific point arises in connection with transport costs, as high fuel costs are bound to compound present geographical disadvantages of distance from the main markets. On the other hand, the more efficient use of fuel in transport systems may well be able to offset much of these costs which can be vital for the competitive position of regions. Certainly the price effect should stimulate efforts in this direction but results will need to be produced soon.

In technology, the implications of change are most unclear and while microelectronics is the subject of immediate concern, the seeds of yet other new revolutions appear to be emerging in fields such as biotechnology and medical science.

But to concentrate on microelectronics, confusion reigns over their likely impact. We read in one newspaper heading, 'Microelectronics threaten up to 250,000 office jobs', and in another, 'microelectronics may create 1 million or more jobs'. What is so striking is that both headings happened to come from the same newspaper on the same day (*Financial Times*, 20 March 1978) which only serves to exemplify the dilemma we face. This is that microelectronics will both create jobs and destroy them.

The more sanguine amongst commentators emphasise the alarms that were raised over automation after World War II and point now to the growth of new industries and products that has taken place since then. They go on to predict fewer workers on the factory floor and more in white-collar jobs including many concerned with software. It is interesting to note that the National Westminster Bank has reported a seven per cent increase in its staff during the 1970s despite the computerisation of many activities which has permitted a productivity increase of about seven per cent. The reason has been an expansion of demand resulting from more efficient services. The pessimists on the other hand have a little optimistic twist of their own when they start to talk about the emergence of a leisure society. However, we cannot assume that any balance, least of all an obviously favourable one, will be struck and in regional development terms this prospect is profoundly disturbing.

And to turn to the shift in industrial power, this has two dimensions. First, a profound change has occurred amongst the advance industrialised countries. For instance, in 1955 UK productivity was 15 per cent above that in France and Germany and 40 per cent above Italy. By 1961, France and Germany had passed the UK and now stand at about 30 per cent higher, while Italy may be marginally ahead (Jones, 1976). These shifts are the product of intensified competition in which the UK has lost out and it follows that those regions which originally placed the UK in the forefront are likely to have suffered disproportionately from this shift. With the prospect that world trade will be constrained over the next few years, the competition will be all the more severe and will again add to adverse pressures on the development of many regions depending upon old industries. The situation will be compounded by the rising competitiveness of certain third world countries, which is the second dimension in this shift in power. For example, West Germany has assessed that this could result in a net displacement effect of about 450,000 jobs up to 1985 or around six per cent of manufacturing employment (Kiel, 1976). If this proves true for Germany, the implications for the UK are highly disturbing and again it is those regions with a significant number of the old industries and technologies that will bear the brunt of the impact. On top of all this, there is inflation. In Chapter 1 Professor Gaskin has already referred to the social effects and inevitably those regions already under stress will be faced with an intensification of conflict.

Thus when one looks at the changing economy, there is little to suggest that regional problems might be resolved through overall economic growth. On the contrary, everything points to regional problems having to be solved within constrained circumstances. We certainly cannot expect a re-occurrence of the favourable combination of features that produced the early stimulus for development in these areas. This does beg of the question whether we can, or even should try to, reverse the trend.

Taking Scotland again, let us consider the pattern of emigration from the old urban areas to the hinterland especially to the 'new towns' which have played an important role in this regard, and that out of Scotland altogether. Recently, net emigration from Scotland has declined sharply, but within this overall result, the outflow from Glasgow has continued to be high. It was argued after the war that some depopulation of Glasgow was needed in order to permit rehabilitation of the inner city and this was a central recommendation of the Clyde Valley Report in 1946. But continued net emigration, and for 1977 it was as much as 21,000, could lead to stresses that would be difficult and costly to handle. So there is a compelling argument to recreate centres of economic growth.

Reversing the Trend

Notwithstanding the difficulties which the changing economy presents, I believe that it is possible for new economic growth and an improved social environment to be generated in Scotland. As Professor Gaskin said, 'the fundamental choice offered us is between a paralysing pessimism and taking action which is bound to be based on a mixture of faith and arguments that can be as easily refuted as supported' (above, p. 24). His context differs from mine but the choice is similar and that action is necessary is irrefutable. The pattern of action will vary from region to region, and for each there will be elements of potential to be exploited. The elements appearing in Scotland may not be applicable in all respects but certainly some should be relevant to regional development elsewhere.

But before describing these elements, so as not to create any false impression I should emphasise that, in economic and physical terms, change has actually already begun. Many of the disparities between Scotland and the rest of the UK have narrowed; North Sea oil has created jobs and the foundation for new industries; the shape of Glasgow is changing, and industrial dereliction is now beginning to be removed by the bulldozer.

The first and most significant element is the educational system and its links with industry which is an important legacy from the past. As a result Scotland has a higher proportion of students studying technical subjects, and of craft apprentices, than other regions. But even so, there is a need for a considerable expansion in output if available opportunities in new technological industries are to be exploited. In this context, for instance, action is already being taken to increase training in electronic-related subjects to support the development strategy for the industry prepared by the Scottish Development Agency.

Another element to which I referred to earlier is worker militancy. This has another perspective, since in aggregate terms, Scotland's industrial relations compare unfavourably with the rest of the UK. Strike activity in Scotland has been worse than in most other parts of the UK in terms of industrial stoppages, which are commonly taken to be a key indicator of the state of industrial relations. For instance, in Scotland, working days lost per 1,000 employees as a result of stoppages have run at about 50 per cent above the level for the rest of the UK since 1967: for manufacturing industries it was worse still (87 per cent above), whilst for engineering Scotland has lost about three times as many. Strikes also tend to be longer and to affect a larger proportion of the total workforce. Internationally, too, the Scottish record is poor. Out of 19 major industrial countries only Italy and Canada lost more working days per 1,000 employees in 1970–6. Perhaps most significant was that the US had a better record than Scotland during this period, whereas compared with the whole of the UK it did not. But strong qualifications need to be placed upon these aggregate data, and to get the industrial relations picture into perspective it should be noted that less than four per cent of manufacturing establishments have been affected over recent years. In fact stoppages have been concentrated in a few industries, and amongst the larger units. And, as with the UK as a whole, units of less than 500 employees have a very low incidence of work stoppages. Also, certain sectors, especially those involving high technology and most notably electronics, have enjoyed a good record.

The other key indicators of industrial relations are productivity, turnover and absenteeism. Starting with productivity, this is very difficult to measure, but the performance of Scotland compared with the rest of the UK has traditionally been lower. During recent years however, productivity growth in the manufacturing sector has been rather faster north of the border, so that the gap has been narrowed, possibly eliminated. In particular, this faster growth in productivity has occurred in food, chemicals, coal and petroleum products, electrical engineering and textiles and clothing. Poorer relative performance for Scotland has by-and-large been confined to the traditional and declining industries, namely coal, metal manufacture, mechanical engineering and shipbuilding. On turnover, the only evidence available for Scottish industry refers to 1973–4, which showed that Scotland had a higher turnover for males than any other region of Great Britain (20.8 per cent of the workforce with less than twelve months service in their current job). For females, on the other hand, it had one of the lowest turnover rates. Absenteeism, through which far more production can be lost than through industrial disputes, also appears to be higher in Scotland than in the UK overall.

But as I have already indicated, it is not valid to move from these aggregate figures to presumptions concerning industry or worker attitudes. There are industries with fully competitive productivity, and if this were not so there would not be the success rates achieved by, for example, many US companies and growing numbers of small Scottish companies. These successes are closely related to enlightened management and personnel policies. But the perceptions of those on the outside, relying solely on the aggregates, can be very different and can inhibit prospective investors.

A further element is that technology is favouring smaller units in a variety of sectors and so the future points towards promoting new starts of small units amongst the higher technology industries. This is having the effect that for some of the growth industries, particularly software and consultancy services, the barriers to entry by the small entrepreneur are minimal. Even in the traditional industries, new technologies will create new opportunities for the small firm as microelectronics will enable more products to be manufactured profitably to individual specifications in small runs, whilst the advance in communications systems will permit dispersal of activities into small units.

All of this presupposes that entrepreneurship is at hand to promote these starts. Unfortunately, a feature of decline is the progressive elimination of small firms and a corresponding reluctance to start new ventures as evidenced by the low proportion of employment in small firms to be found in declining regions. To rectify this deficiency must, therefore, be central to any regional development programme, because it offers an organic and self-sustaining approach to growth. Support for such an emphasis comes not from the 'small is beautiful' syndrome, but from the results of the massive MIT study on *The Job Generation*

Process published in 1979, which concluded that employment gains in the US over the past few years have come predominantly from small firms, even after allowing for the greater incidence of business failure amongst them. Another feature which also has to be taken into account is that regions tend to have a high proportion of branch factories. Much employment is dependent on these and they can play a key role in job generation. The MIT study found that branch factories generated 65 per cent of new jobs. But branch factories are subject to corporate decision-making located elsewhere and hence can be vulnerable to cutbacks. The remedy lies in encouraging research and development amongst branch units within the region, thereby achieving locally greater product authority and from this greater strength allowing branches to determine their own future. Thus, programmes to encourage establishment of research and development are an essential ingredient.

The potential that these elements offer in the Scottish context have to be set against the superior forces of the changing economy and especially the three particular factors I have identified. Each of these, as it happens, holds out opportunities and Scotland has certain advantages of its own. First, in energy, North Sea oil has already created around 60,000 jobs, a significant contribution. But more than this, it offers the basis for downstream development, which could begin with the proposed petrochemicals complex at Moss Morran. And the more difficult to exploit, but nonetheless substantial, coal resources that Scotland possesses will almost certainly become economic as the price for energy rises.

Secondly, in technology, the opportunities are clearly associated with serious threats. Scotland already has a substantial electronics industry which must be kept in the forefront of developments whilst parallel actions must also be taken to speed the adoption of microprocessors in manufacturing and service industries, so that international competitiveness can thereby be safeguarded. Initiatives are in fact already being undertaken as part of the electronics strategy for Scotland. But there are other technologies and the requirement for any region of an industrialised country must be to ensure that it keeps up and can adapt flexibly and speedily to changing requirements.

Thirdly, in international competition, traditional industries are obviously most vulnerable as we have been too painfully aware for some time in Scotland, and most immediately in respect of shipbuilding. But notwithstanding the impact of competition, there can still be opportunities to exploit. To take textiles as an example, presently 15 per cent of manufacturing employment in Scotland is still in this sector and the challenge is to modernise and strengthen competitiveness after having first established where future comparative advantage can be established. Advantages will be created in moving up-market and exploiting production processes utilising advanced technology, primarily microprocessors, which can offset higher labour costs and introduce consistent quality. To do otherwise than accept the challenge, certainly over the medium term, will only compound the problems of adjustment within the region. In newer industries, the future will rest exclusively with new technologies, and thereby demand constant and rapid adjustments to change.

Against this background, efforts to reverse the trend of regional decline must move from identification of all the elements with potential to action based upon a new sense of purpose and dynamism. And for this, strong individuals and progressive institutions are required. Unfortunately, there is no one formula to make the chemistry work and despite the effort of well co-ordinated and motivated forces, reversal of trends may still remain elusive.

In the Scottish context, the prospect for successful adjustment exists. There are skills; there is entrepreneurial talent as the expanding programme of the Small Business Division of the Scottish Development Agency has found; there is a well-developed local banking service; and the region is considered a favourable location by foreign investors, thereby introducing a new stimulus towards technology-based industries and competitive management. There are many profitable companies to give reality to these prospects. The best testament of all comes from the success of US companies in Scotland, of which there are nearly 200 in manufacturing accounting for 15 per cent of manufacturing employment. In electronics, 40 per cent of employment is in US companies.

These prospects imply a revival of private sector confidence and there are private and government institutions that have supporting aims in this process. Amongst the government institutions, the Scottish Development Agency has been given a wide remit to promote industrial development in association with the private sector and improve the environment. It is directly concerned in industrial investment especially with smaller firms, in providing industrial infrastructure such as factories and sites, in promoting inward investment from the US and elsewhere abroad, in rehabilitation of industrial dereliction and in some urban renewal, most notably as co-ordinator of the Glasgow East Area Renewal Project (GEAR). Almost more important than this list of functions is the flexibility it has to be innovative. As innovation, irrespective of scale, is an essential ingredient of any development process, there is plenty of scope for it to make a specialised contribution towards Scotland's own overall efforts.

The chemistry is beginning to work. While the prescription will not necessarily be feasible or work in other regions, certain basic elements are likely to be the same and include:

(1) the development of technical and management skills;
(2) an emphasis on entrepreneurship and small units;
(3) encouragement of research and development facilities;
(4) the constant assessment of shifts in comparative advantage;
(5) promotion of advanced technology industries and upgrading products;
(6) a willingness on the part of individuals and institutions to take risks in order to force the pace of change.

Above all, there should be effective promotion of the region to amend the perceptions of outsiders, especially prospective investors, and most importantly towards the details of industrial relations and the areas of success. Promotion should also be used to create a better understanding amongst residents of their achievements and thereby renew confidence and create positive attitudes.

References

GEAR (Glasgow East Area Renewal Project) (1978), Household Survey, Scottish Development Agency (unpublished)

Institut für Weltwirschaft, Kiel (1976), 'Analysis of the Determinants and Consequences of a Selective as Compared with an Unselective Research and Development Strategy' (April)

Jones, D. T. (1976), 'Output and Labour Productivity in Europe since 1955', *National Institute Economic Review* (August)

9 TOLERABLE SURVIVAL IN THE CITY: THE REALITIES FOR URBAN POLICY

Duncan Maclennan

Tolerable Survival: An Urban Perspective

The purpose of this chapter is to examine, in somewhat broad fashion, the recent experience of and immediate prospects for the core areas of British cities and conurbations. In particular, it is intended to focus on policy initiatives and viewpoints which have developed during the last five years. In this way the theme of 'tolerable survival' may be given some specific context and direction.[1] The concern of the chapter is with 'where' and for 'whom' the quality of life is, and will be, under the greatest pressure.[2]

An urban approach to the problems of tolerable survival or quality of life should really require no justification. The United Kingdom is a highly urbanised economy and society, with one-third of the population in conurbations and more than four-fifths in urban places with populations in excess of 10,000 persons. Thus the major origin and incidence of social and economic phenomena in the United Kingdom, including the prospects for growth as well as the problems of decline, is in an urban or inner-urban context. With respect to tolerable survival the major problems of poverty, and as a result the most direct threats to tolerable survival for individuals and society as a whole, require to be identified, defined and analysed in an urban context.

The identification and analysis of the threats to the attainment of tolerable survival, particularly with policy formulation as an objective, is not a straightforward task. The problems of households and environments observed in cities are complex and often difficult to measure, and they generally do not solely reflect the incidence of 'national' trends or events in the economy or society. A 'top-down' view of urban problems which has certain characterised economic models and policies in the UK, is an almost metaphysical view. For in discussing 'national' events the researcher is principally analysing the sum of events relating to a limited number of major urban places. Thus it may be misleading to confine attention to the urban impacts of 'national'growth' or 'national economic policy'. A 'top-down' view may be excusable, if not entirely appropriate, in the early stages of the development of a complex of problems. For instance, rising urban unemployment has generally been perceived to constitute a demand management difficulty. Thereafter, generically 'urban' processes and effects, both social and economic, may condition change at the local level and, by summation, at the national level. For example, if urban economic decline results in reduced real incomes or increased unemployment, urban housing market effects (and indeed non-market processes) may concentrate the impacts of decline into particular neighbourhoods. This concentration effect can then influence the dynamics of development, which differ from urban to rural contexts, and which may differ between large and small cities. For instance, in large cities a real differentiation may result in juxtaposed high and low income areas, and this may result in expressions of envy, apathy, altruism or political intent, which differ in kind and intensity from those arising with a spatially-dispersed pattern of poverty. At the same time, there may be generically urban-level characteristics of labour and housing markets and systems of service financing, which complicate the solution of intra-urban problems.

The essential thesis of this chapter is that economic change is invariably reflected in the uneven or unbalanced growth or decline of existing cities and settlements, and that internal geographical restructuring is generally a concomitant of economic development.[3] In addition, government policy, due to differences in ideas, information or objectives may run counter to or be supportive of underlying economic changes. For a period of 50 years, from 1926 to 1976, spatial policies in the United Kingdom were primarily specified at the regional level. These policies were often justified on the assumption that with sustained economic growth, increments in output and employment could be diverted from a uniformly-congested region to a uniformly-depressed peripheral region. In this approach, which emphasised the costs and benefits of economic growth at the regional level, scant attention was paid to the co-existence of growth and decline or the juxtaposition of affluence and poverty within the same region. Emphasis on the benefits of economic growth has been a commonplace strategy for British governments, to avoid making difficult distributional judgements (either spatial or functional); but here they may have contributed to a disregard for intra-urban disparities, these disparities implying that, in both relative and absolute senses, poverty and deprivation are already a major concern for perhaps more than one-fifth of British households in cities. Now, changing economic and political circumstances have forced government to contemplate the possibility of national, regional and local economic decline. Changes in industrial, occupational and spatial structures are now inducing severe localised decline – that is, processes of economic change are 'unbalanced' at both the *inter-* and *intra-*urban levels.

Such changes can generate problems or costs of spatial or structural adjustment in the short term, or they may generate long-run solutions which are not considered to be optimal. A variety of policies can be introduced to tackle such difficulties; these may be initiated and financed either by central or local governments and they may be functional in nature (with a concentrated urban incidence) or they may be specifically directed to particular urban functions or areas. Accepting that it is difficult to identify the extent of urban policy in Britain,[4] it is argued here that existing urban policies in Britain are badly defined and designed, and that present commitments to policy, research and monitoring are unlikely to forestall further decline let alone permanently improve the condition of urban areas. Instead, a commitment to understanding the impacts and raising the efficiency of existing policies would have been essential even without the present public expenditure restrictions. Thus, whilst an urban level view of existing policies is a possibility, it is unlikely that the next decade will see the development of an explicit urban programme.

Urban Change and Policy Change

The attention of urban policy makers and urban analysts is now firmly fixed upon the problems of the metropolitan core areas, or more particularly in the UK, on the inner-city areas.[5] These areas are rarely precisely defined but largely consist of the areas of land and older housing which lie outside the central business district but within two to three miles of the city centre. They contain stocks of old, poor quality, low-value private housing along with modern public sector renewal schemes and with industrial establishments in old properties. The inhabitants are relatively immobile, old, poor and unskilled in labour-market terms, with some concentrations of ethnic groups and with some young, upwardly-mobile households in the early phases of a life cycle of housing consumption. The focus of policy is now asserted to be on the causes and consequences of economic decline in the core urban areas. This approach is somewhat removed from, indeed contrary to, the analytical and policy standpoints of not more than a decade ago and it is a shift in governmental viewpoint which has occurred in a variety of countries outside the UK. For instance, in the USA, Berry has argued that a congested-depressed, cumulative causation view of urban development underpinned the 1970 Housing Act which encouraged and sustained population decentralisation. Yet, 'Barely a decade later beliefs about the nature of change appear to have reversed, however, and along with them the opinions on apparent growth directions to be promoted and the corrective reactions to be taken' (Berry, 1980). In the UK a similar shift in perspective, with policy apparently changing more rapidly than reality, is significant as it suggests some important hypotheses regarding urban policy formulation.

To assess the pre-inner areas standpoint, it is interesting to reflect on how urban problems and policies in Britain were perceived by the late Donald Robertson in a seminal essay 'The City' which was delivered to the British Association in Aberdeen in 1963. In that essay (Robertson, 1964) were developed two themes which are pertinent here. First, Robertson stressed the absence of economic inputs into the process of town planning and urban policy formation. This issue is discussed further below. Secondly, he stressed the need for urban and regional policies to be constructed and integrated to deal with the problems of core area congestion. Adopting a 'top-down' or 'national growth to local impact' standpoint, he argued that regional (or in the UK case largely inter-urban) policies were necessary to divert growth from the congested core areas of southern Britain to the relatively depressed regions of the north, Scotland, Wales and Northern Ireland. (The allocative efficiency 'arguments' for this policy are discussed in Maclennan and Parr, 1979.) At the same time, it was argued that problems of traffic circulation in core areas, and the adverse externalities of population living in older housing at high densities in the core city, necessitated a substantial and planned reduction in the population of core cities.[6]

Due to changing demographic structure and net emigration, this process had already begun and population dispersal, facilitated by cheaper public and private transport, had already commenced. However, policies of slum clearance, comprehensive redevelopment, public estate building, overspill and 'new town' development all accelerated the outflow from the city. Throughout the 1960s, and indeed until the mid-1970s, infrastructural development, transport system changes and housing developments were all geared to altering the spatial structure of employment and housing in metropolitan areas so that the periphery, within and beyond green belts, would develop at the expense of the core. Industrial location policies, at least in subsidy terms, although regionally differentiated, were generally locally neutral, though the provision of advance factories usually favoured the urban periphery. Indeed, some of the remnants of this strategy are still operating at the present time. In addition, it is pertinent that present urban population levels, now causing concern because of their low level or rate of decline, are often in excess of early post-war population intentions. For instance, the City of Glasgow now is a major focus of policies to arrest decline but its present population exceeds post-war targets of 650,000 by more than 150,000. In approving the strategy of regional diversion and intra-urban dispersal Robertson was effectively drawing to the attention of economists and planners the fact that the spatial structure of a region or conurbation may have a critical influence on the economic well-being or growth of the area. This principle is still valid and important, but is still ignored by the majority of economists (for an important and lucid exception, see Parr, 1979). The question has to be asked as to why policy perceptions and positions of what is a desirable structure have changed so markedly and contrarily to those held only a decade ago, particularly when physical and structure planning are well developed activities in the UK.

A variety of hypotheses to explain the shift may be advanced. The first is that the underlying economic situation has changed. In the period discussed by Robertson the assumptions common to most economic policy analysts were that there would be modest national growth, near-full employment could be maintained and that the 'congested-depressed region' model was appropriate. The subsequent reality is somewhat different. Increasing real incomes have been accompanied by rising unemployment and this growth in unemployment has had marked sectoral and spatial effects. Unemployment differentials have moved against both previously prosperous regions and urban core areas, whilst rising real incomes (for those in employment) have been reflected in income-elastic expenditures on transportation, housing and environment. That is, economic change has concentrated poverty and unemployment, and real income changes may have stimulated suburban decentralisation. This 'rediscovery' of urban poverty, or as it became known, 'multiple deprivation' (Norris, 1979), was particularly critical in shifting part of the focus of policy from a regional to an urban perspective. The core areas of the south (although they had always contained substantial pockets of unemployment: Holmans, 1964) consistently stressed the emergence of urban unemployment and advocated a shift in the spatial dimensions of employment policy (Stone, 1979).

In addition, it could be argued that the quality of inner-city housing had progressively deteriorated after another 15 years of neglect. However, by the 1970s rehabilitation as opposed to redevelopment strategies had begun to permeate policy thought. Further, the blight effects and adverse externalities produced by the planning process *per se* had further contributed to inner-area decline, and some of the early post-war policies designed to deal with difficulties of the city had now come to constitute problems in their own right. For instance, it has been argued in Glasgow that policies towards public housing had resulted in differentiation of and within the public housing stock which were associated with quality deterioration and incentives to decentralise. Further, throughout the 1960s pressures to switch from renting to owning housing could have exacerbated decentralisation due to supply, demand and finance considerations. More importantly, perhaps, policies of overspill and new town development had been numerically successful, but migration streams within and between centres had been quite selective. In the private sector, in the absence of any substantial gentrification movement, decentralisation was selective by income. In the public sector, again in Glasgow where some 50 per cent of the flow into the periphery was into public housing, there were two obviously selective streams. Within the city, inner-area or slum-clearance residents with families were transferred to larger, low-rise public housing estates on the edge of the city, leaving a population of older and smaller households in the public and private sector of the core. At the same time, movement out of the city into new towns and overspill areas was also selective with younger, higher-income, and more skilled households having higher probabilities of movement. Thus the socio-economic structures of city core, peripheral estates and new towns/overspill sites were quite deliberately and adversely altered by government policies, (Farmer and Smith, 1975; GEAR, 1978).

It would be correct, therefore, to conclude that the underlying situation has changed. These changes reflect new influences on the economy, an extrapolation of previously existing decentralisation processes and, of course, the effects of policies actually pursued in the 1960s. Clearly physical and economic planners of the 1960s could not forecast the changes in economic conditions which we have experienced in the 1970s. But it is at least arguable that they should have been aware of the existence of the consequences of decentralisation and its co-existence with increasing deprivation in urban areas. This implies that the theoretical and policy perspectives of urban economics were shortsighted and imperfectly developed. Since almost all policies will be imperfect, this difficulty could have been lessened if the policies implemented had been monitored and researched, and the relationships between economic change and spatial development carefully scrutinised. But this is not the British way of preparing and monitoring policies.[7] The issue of spatial structure was seldom discussed with any seriousness, and despite Donald Robertson's plea for economists to become involved in the physical planning process, at the national level physical and town planning were administered quite separately from industrial location and housing policies. At the same time, as in many areas of social and economic policy, policies have been designed and implemented on what appears to be an essentially mythological basis. That is to say, policies tend to respond to political pressures, are formulated on the basis of scant research, and are rarely if ever monitored for progress. For instance, with respect to the Inner Area Policy, the call for research post-dated the policy commitment and, on the same point, the 1968 Urban Programme was only given any, and unresearched, direction after political commitments were made (Mackay and Cox, 1979; for comments on the mythological basis of large segments of housing policy see Maclennan, 1978). One consequence of this essentially political and uninformed approach to policy-making is that policy is more unstable than reality. That is, perceptions of problems can change more rapidly, and more often than, reality itself. Clearly underlying realities can change, or governments' weightings of a given problem may differ. It is difficult to believe that it is these factors which have led to the sudden shifts in British urban policy by governments of the same political complexion within the period of less than a decade. It is somewhat worrying that the present minister responsible for urban policies and the environment has publicly questioned the value of research and intends, perhaps as a substitute, to listen to the arguments of interested parties.

There is no doubt that when government intervention was designed to influence broad aggregate economic targets such as the exchange rate or the interest rate, or even the overall level of demand in the economy, then central policies with limited information inputs could be attempted with a fair probability of success. However, since the Second World War, governments have increasingly tried to influence the operation or well-being of specific parts of the system. They have unfortunately tried to do so with a 'top-down' approach and a minor commitment to research and analysis. Until this cavalier 'top-down' approach is altered we shall never have an efficient urban policy, nor shall economists have an appropriate contribution to make to policy. Unfortunately, it must be added that economic science has been slow to develop suitable analytical frameworks for the discussion and assessment of spatial development. If policy-makers in the 1960s and 1970s had had available a reasonable model of spatial development then past policy might not have been pursued and the Inner Areas Strategy would be substantially different; and facts rather than fashions or fads could have shaped policy. In the remainder of this chapter, therefore, a broad model of spatial development is outlined and the Inner Areas Strategy is then evaluated against the model.

Spatial Development – A Long-term View

Both in encouraging peripheral growth in the 1960s and in focusing on inner areas subsequent to 1976, government was implicitly adopting a view regarding desirable or optimal spatial structures, although the relationship between economic growth and spatial growth was rarely carefully considered. It seems appropriate, therefore, to present a stylised picture of the economic growth/metropolitan structure relationship as experienced in the United Kingdom. Here a long-term view is presented as major structures only alter slowly: in the urban economy, history as well as geography is always important, and current economic and social processes are required to operate in structures which are largely inherited from the past.

Despite increased analytical attention to questions of location theory and urban/regional income and growth theories there has not yet been a satisfactory integration of both these research areas. Location theories, concerned with the investment and consumption decisions of firms and households, have been largely developed from a static, neo-classical, equilibrium standpoint. Location theories of two kinds can be identified. First, with an orientation towards general equilibrium modelling, there are location models which assume a simple, uniform structure of space and a simple competitive economy in which individuals pursue deterministic, optimising solutions. These models, illustrated by the work of Lösch and Alonso, can generate an equilibrium structure of space. For such models it is possible to develop comparative static or dynamic adjustments to take account of changes in goods produced, the technology of production, income and price changes, and changes in transport costs and technologies (Parr and

Denike, 1970; Evans, 1973). A second class of models deals with an existing anisotropic space in which resources or inputs or centres of demand are not uniformly dispersed but are unevenly distributed in space. Here initial underlying spatial structures are taken as given and optimal locations derived – Weber's model of industrial location is the most important example. Quite clearly neither type of location theory can provide the basis for a deductive model of long-term spatial development. In the deductive models, this would require a theory of product change, a theory of technological progress (including a theory of transport and energy development) etc. Clearly, further deductive theorising from this basis is not helpful to the present purpose, and this is also the case with Weberian theories where a dynamic model would also require a predictive theory of resource discovery and development.

Regional and urban growth theories, as they presently exist, have also been unable to model deductively the 'causes' of economic growth, although they have begun to examine the economic mechanisms and linkages which relate cities, regions and national economies. In addition, regional and urban growth models have been formulated which transform an initial change into 'cumulative causal' growth models (Richardson, 1973). However, these models have been developed in the Keynesian income-expenditure tradition and regions have been generally viewed as being points. The work of Richardson (1973) expected, regional/urban macro-economic models are merely multi-sector Keynesian models. The neglect of the dynamic effects of the spatial structure of cities, regions or individual markets not only disregards a potentially significant stimulus or hindrance to economic growth but has also de-emphasised the influence of space on economic systems. In general, economists have examined the effects of space as being the effect of transport costs in an equilibrium framework. But space is a fundamental dimension in urban and intra-urban markets. Apart from transport costs, space distorts information flows, makes searching costly and gives scope for differentiation. Individuals, householders and firms alike, may have spatial uncertainties and expectations. Space may fracture markets and make disequilibrium a normal rather than an abnormal state of affairs. It is interesting to note that the economics of Keynes has been re-evaluated with respect to the existence of the effects of time on uncertainty, confidence and expectations (Clower, 1965; Leijonhufvud, 1968; Weintraub, 1979). Such an approach to spatial processes may now be not only a desirable but a respectable activity for economists. This is not merely a theoretical point, though a theory of investment incorporating temporal and spatial expectations would be one way of beginning to link location theory and the theory of spatial growth. But the idea has policy significance in so far as industrial and residential disinvestment from the urban core may be exacerbated by inelastic expectations. The arguments are most commonly advanced in relation to the process of neighbourhood decline (Segal, 1979), but they may also apply to firms in so far as they have expectations regarding available labour, access to linked plants etc. Indeed falling area confidence, as much as inherent locational obsolescence, may be the key to inner-area problems – at least in the UK. In the absence of a well-developed and tested theory of urban growth a simply-structured, stage model of urban development constitutes the theoretical reality for urban policy[8] (Hall, 1974). The spatial development pattern of British cities can be broadly fitted to a typology of four major phases, which will now be described.

(1) The Pre-industrial City. In the early phases of economic development the size and growth of cities would be related to the productivity of the agricultural and transport systems. Apart from major points of defence, religious sites or coastal ports, settlements would be broadly distributed in a spatial structure consistent with structures deducible from central-place theory. Internally the city would be small in area with a dense population. Generally the urban place would be undifferentiated in land-use terms with industry and high- and low-value residences juxtaposed. There would be major problems associated with externalities of congestion such as overcrowding, epidemics of disease and noxious externalities. Public intervention and finance would be limited. This form of urban settlement has disappeared in the UK.

(2) The Walking Industrial City. The relationship between the generation of agricultural surpluses and industrial development is not pursued here, but it is clear that industrialisation transformed urban settlements – that is, a major and enduring change in the spatial structure of the economy took place and in a very limited time period (Hall, 1974). Cities, in the major phases of industrialisation, may have grown because they were 'central places', but primarily they grew as Weberian nodes for the production of capital goods and 'heavy' products close to the sites of raw materials. That is, in the 1800s, the transportation of raw materials or finished products was relatively costly and both inputs and outputs had a high bulk or weight to value ratio (Cameron, Firn and Maclennan, 1974). Thus major British cities,

particularly Glasgow, Newcastle, Manchester and Liverpool grew at sites close to port and raw material sources. At that time a global, near-monopoly on processes and colonial markets protected these cities from effective competition and this generated a dense and distorted structure of large cities based on a large and growing 'export base'. Throughout the second half of the nineteenth century the populations of these cities expanded more rapidly than their compact surface areas. That is, intra-urban transport of the working population was largely restricted to walking. As a result, bid-rent functions were extremely steep and residents lived at high densities, in small dwellings constructed within two or three miles of the urban centre. Again residential structure was relatively undifferentiated, and there were appalling problems of overcrowding and disease induced by pressure on houses and other facilities for living – for instance, water supply and sewage and garbage disposal. Once again there was an admixture of housing and externality-generating industries. Industry tended to be located at or near major break-of-bulk points in the transport system. Inter-urban or inter-regional forms of transport such as ship or canal, then later railways, were considerably more efficient than intra-urban forms of movement such as horses or hand-carts. Therefore, industries tended to be located at rail terminals on or near the edge of the central business district – in essence, the bid-rent functions for industries and their demands for centrality were steeper and more pressing than those of households.

Local authorities at this time had minimal expenditure commitments, although regulatory functions, such as building and land-use controls were not uncommon, and the functional city was generally contained within the administrative unit. Seeing that the quality of life for many urban households was appallingly bad, why did this change in spatial structure take place? The major reason is that spatial structures can change more rapidly the more rapidly population chooses or is forced to alter location. Undoubtedly rural poverty, the clearance of rural populations, the lack of a politicised workforce and the absence of welfare provisions all forced the rural-urban change. Such conditions, which are inherently undesirable, do not of course now pertain, so adjustments will always be less rapid if they occur at all (see Hirschorn, 1979).

(3) The Public Transport City. In the UK, the 'walking city' was in the process of transformation up until the Second World War. Although problems of the economic base were cyclically, and often severely,

encountered, industrial expansion, with some diversification into lighter products, continued and the growth of large cities began to be viewed as 'a problem'. In this period, changes in spatial structure were probably more important than industrial structure. The gradual development of tramways allowed an arterial, stellar extension of the older core, and suburban railway developments spread housing in a 'tentacular' fashion into the wider metropolitan periphery. The results of this process were of fundamental importance. Suburbanisation not only allowed functional cities to grow in size but permitted residential differentiation and allowed some small-scale (and then seemingly unimportant) fiscal decentralisation to take place.

The stylised description presented so far is quite consistent with the development of older industrial cities not only in Britain but also overseas, particularly the north-east of the United States. However, after the First World War, Britain developed in a different direction in so far as central and local governments developed policies with urban effects. For instance, the 1915 Rent Acts and the commitment of resources to a major public housing programme set a distinctive and long-lasting framework for urban housing policy in Britain. The scale and operational details of public housing were particularly striking and their existence has an important bearing on our subsequent critique of present Inner Area Policies. Similarly, the scale and financing of local urban service provision, by local authorities, was important and impressive. But these issues were only to become crucial in the period after 1945.

(4) The Private Transport City. It is worth considering this stage of development in more detail as it is against this background that the policy changes noted earlier were implemented. In the period after 1945, and with accelerating significance in the 1950s and 1960s, trends developed which, even in the absence of perverse policies, have almost inevitably resulted in the present plight of the inner cities. In the post-war period, there was a persistent fall in the real price of public and private transport (at least until the end of the 1970s), and a continued programme of investment in urban motorways, ring routes etc. has led to a reduction in travel times within and around cities and between central core and suburban periphery. The significance of the frictions of distance have been continually eroded, at least in terms of transport costs. Naturally, there have been dramatic effects on the spatial structure of urban areas. The population of the core cities continued to grow, largely due to high rates of natural increase outweighing net

migration losses, into the 1950s. At the same time there was a steady accretion of population growth in the surrounding metropolitan zone, particularly in-filling areas between arterial developments. Gradually increasing car ownership and more flexible public transport route systems made households relatively footloose, and encouraged them to leave the core city and to consume larger housing units and more environmental 'goods' in the suburban fringe. By the late 1950s and 1960s core-area populations in most British conurbations were already decreasing.

It may be useful to subdivide decentralising cities into those where core-area decline takes place even though the metropolitan area is still growing, and those where core-area decline outpaces decline in the rest of the region. The former type, 'central area decline in a growth context', is typical of the stage of evolution of most British conurbations, and in such a context resources may be diverted from a prosperous periphery or a growing national economy to fund core-area policies. But some regions, either because of further population deconcentration (as has begun to happen in the USA and Japan) into smaller towns outside metropolitan areas, or because the regional location can no longer sustain a viable economic base (for instance Glasgow in the context of Strathclyde), are now losing population and economic activity. In these circumstances, particularly if the national economy is slow-growing or declining, it is difficult to pursue discriminatory policies in favour of the central core. In this respect, as core cities in Britain move into a period of further deconcentration with national economic decline, it is difficult to see how trends in spatial structures will favour central cities – unless energy cost conditions now move strongly against dispersed population structures.

The changes in the costs and flexibility of transport for households were also reflected in the movement of raw materials and goods at the intra-urban and inter-regional levels. Within the city, the development of effective trucking and motorway systems allowed firms to disperse outwards into the periphery. This fall in demand for centrality from the industrial sector was also facilitated by other changes in the characteristics of products and processes. There was a continued shift to the production of lighter products with a high value-to-weight ratio, products which were generally not based on local raw materials and which were often geared to final output rather than intermediate output sectors. At the same time, changing production techniques tended to favour flow production processes which required modern low-rise factories for effective production. This systematic locational shift to the periphery, where of course suitable sites and labour forces were available, is well-documented for the UK in various 'components-of-change' studies (Firn and Hughes, 1974; Malcolm, 1979). Of course, these studies also tend to suggest that differential birth and death rates of establishments are important, with inner areas having higher death rates and lower birth rates of manufacturing enterprises. Here again we run into a conundrum of causality. Given that de-industrialisation of the UK economy has occurred systematically throughout the post-war period (Cairncross, 1979) and that central cities have lost their locational advantage but contain most of the older plants, it could be argued that the observed patterns merely reflect the urban level impacts of de-industrialisation which is best explained in terms of macro-forces affecting competitiveness (and by the same token, some regions have de-industrialised more rapidly than others). This 'explanation' is probably the most important in quantitative terms.

Suburbanisation and the Effects of Policy

Whilst economic changes were stimulating decentralising tendencies the desirable degree of decentralisation may have been influenced not only by confidence and expectations but also, as was indicated earlier, as the result of deliberate policies. In the UK it may be dangerous to interpret suburbanisation as the result of a purely private-market process through which residential preferences were expressed. For instance overspill and 'new town' policies, and the housing policies of central and local governments, may have contributed both to decentralisation and residential differentiation. Rent-control policies systematically reduced the availability and quality of rental housing, much of which was concentrated in the inner core. Large-scale public sector house building programmes, which were chosen as the 'solution' to the post-war 'housing problem', pre-empted private developments on core-city land. Indeed some local authorities, such as Glasgow, adopted an ideological stance which precluded private development. In the United Kingdom, private housing is both an income-elastic good and an asset which generally appreciates more rapidly than the general price level. It is not surprising therefore that in an era of rising real incomes and rising inflation that there has been a progressive shift towards owner occupation in Britain. This shift has probably had a decentralising effect, not only because of public pre-emption of core-area land, but also because of developers' costs and attitudes and, of course, the apparent anti-inner-area bias of lending institutions (Maclennan and Jones, 1980). Thus suburbanisation has not only reflected growing real incomes and falling transport costs, facilitating an expression of suburban preference, but also mirrored policy measures and importantly, housing-market imperfections. Of course, these are only hypotheses – in the UK nobody has really researched why people leave cities and move into the periphery.

Urban and regional policies may also have influenced employment decentralisation. In the southern or previously prosperous conurbations national regional policy has had a negative direct effect on core areas of prosperous regions (contributing between five and ten per cent of job decline in London in the 1970s: see Stone, 1979) and inter-regional plant moves generally result in peripheral relocations. More importantly, it may also be argued that inner-area clearance programmes have removed, by compulsory purchase and demolition, large amounts of small, low-cost industrial spaces which nascent entrepreneurs used to develop and 'incubate' small firms which subsequently grew and renewed the economic base. Again, this thesis is only now being tested, for limited areas, in the UK. It has also been argued, and with some validity, that inner-area sites consisting of derelict land and buildings have site clearances and development costs far exceeding those in peripheral areas and that these costs constitute a disincentive to inner-area location (Harrison and Whitehead, 1978). This may well be the case, but if it is so, then doubts must be cast upon the efficacy of urban-land market policies. A major 'mystery' of the cities of central Scotland is why urban-land costs in core cities have appreciated more rapidly than for other areas, including oil development areas, at a period of industrial and population decline. Public sector landholding and land valuation policies may require scrutiny in this respect.

Perceptions of Problems

Despite these losses in core-area employment in manufacturing, unemployment levels in cities were not perceived to constitute a serious problem until the 1970s. Either the growth of core-area services, in both public and private sectors, or increased reverse commuting to peripheral jobs were sufficient to restrict the growth in unemployment rates and levels. The continued loss of international competitiveness throughout the 1970s and the skill requirements of growth service sectors, at the level of the urban economy as a whole, have resulted in income and unemployment problems, in particular for low-income and unskilled households. As mentioned above, the private-housing sector, and indeed the public-housing sector, 'sorts' households by income and socio-economic status into particular areas of neighbourhoods where the incidence of low incomes and unemployment tends to become geographically concentrated. That is to say, intra-urban unemployment and income differentials are more marked than inter-regional comparisons. Two points of importance arise here. First, for most households residence and workplace are not juxtaposed, and housing and labour markets may have a different spatial structure within the city. Thus policies to counteract the sources of poverty or unemployment are not necessarily coincident in space with policies to deal with the consequences of policy. Secondly, the existence of large-scale public housing in Britain complicates the relationship between poverty and residential location. In Glasgow, estates such as Priesthill and Garthamlock lie outside the inner area, but they have resident unemployment rates exceeding 20 per cent: in this respect it is misleading to emphasise the 'inner-city' problem.

Recently there have been attempts, on a localised basis, to assess whether or not there are 'area' factors which systematically reduce an individual's possibility of acquiring a job due to accessibility or stigmatisation factors. At present this 'area labour market stigmatisation' hypothesis has not been sustained in the UK (MacGregor, 1979; Cheshire, 1979). However, forced relocation within public housing has apparently increased job-quit rates and may have raised unemployment, increased transport costs, reduced overtime and decreased participation rates (Engleman, 1977). However, it would be reasonable to argue, at least for depressed-area conurbations, that regional demand deficiency is the principal cause of urban unemployment, although local structural and spatial mismatches may occur. There are few reasons to believe that the problem of urban unemployment, especially in the inner area, will be easily resolved. If the economy is genuinely moving into a 'post-industrial' phase with an emphasis on service development and export from developed economies, then the difficulties of unskilled workers will be exacerbated rather than diminished. Urban, and indeed regional, manufacturing incentives are probably too small to shift the national investment-demand function, and the role of incentives will merely be to shift employment – or unemployment – around the national and local economy.

Fiscal Aspects of Decentralisation

The decline in population and employment in core cities, particularly the inner areas, has had important fiscal repercussions. In the USA, Baumol has formally drawn attention to the macro-economics of unbalanced growth which stems from fiscal decentralisation (Baumol,

1967). The basic argument is as follows. Population decentralisation allows higher-income households to move outside the administrative or jurisdictional area of the core city. This migration is selective. When public services are provided on a basis other than user charging or benefit taxation then the commuters into the central city use and congest daytime facilities paid for by central residents. At the same time, selective migration leaves behind in the core groups who particularly 'merit' or need service provision – such as health, education, housing and welfare. Thus upper-income residents in the core bear high local taxes without receiving high benefits; in this way fiscal decentralisation may be exacerbated. Difficulties are then compounded by inflation and comparative wage-bargaining processes as local services tend to be labour-intensive and to have an inherently low productivity growth. Thus wage rises in the public service sector, if in line with productivity growth industries, generate relatively rising costs and local taxes.

When the British context is examined then it is clear that the major cities have fiscal difficulties. In Glasgow, for instance, the shift of the domestic and commercial property tax has increased rate burdens for local residents and commercial properties more rapidly than in the majority of attached peripheral authorities. In the UK, however, there are important reservations to the simple fiscal decentralisation hypothesis. First, the growth and scale of municipal expenditures in the UK have been quite marked, both in terms of geographical and historical comparisons, which would suggest that local fiscal distortions would be more important than in market- or charging-oriented provision systems (Maclennan, 1979). On the other hand, and this is a second important qualification, much of this local expansion has been based on general grants disbursed from central government tax revenues. This has been particularly true in the 1970s when the relatively income-inelastic property tax base could not generate increased revenues without revaluation, which was costly, or raising rate poundages, which influenced wage settlements and the acceptability of incomes policies. For instance, in Glasgow the share of central grants in local expenditure has risen from 36 per cent to 45 per cent since 1951. Furthermore, in selecting the tax base and assessing the 'needs' elements for the Rate Support Grant system, central government has the ability, subject to negotiation, to choose to favour certain types of areas. In the UK, local government reform may have helped to assuage fiscal difficulties of urban areas. Fiscal crisis is not, therefore, an inevitable feature of older, declining core cities. The extent to which difficulties arise and persist will depend on the extent to which public provision takes place, the definition of jurisdictional areas, the selection of the tax base, the system of charging and the extent and structuring of transfers from central to local governments. There is undoubtedly scope for improving the efficiency of urban-service financing and provision in the UK, but here again there is a major research lacuna which is only now being tackled.

This background of population loss, employment and local fiscal difficulty has characterised British cities throughout the 1960s and the 1970s. It is against these circumstances, and the previous policy commitment to dispersal, that recent policies for the inner area are analysed.

The Inner Areas Policy – A Brief Critique

At the same time as decentralisation processes were operating strongly, and policy was principally assisting this shift, there was, in the period 1968–76, the small beginnings of a counter policy. This was the Urban Programme. The programme was initiated as a political response to incipient problems of race and poverty in the southern conurbations. These issues were not viewed as problems created by broad socio-economic processes but were perceived as small, isolated poverty pockets. The programme, which was designed after the policy statement (Mackay and Cox, 1979), was largely seen as a minor tailoring or gap-filling exercise by major government departments to impart a specific urban bias to policy. Educational and community-development projects were the major items of expenditure in a total budget which annually ran around £10 million – about equivalent to expenditure on royal parks and palaces. In total, this small programme spent £55 million before being overtaken by the new inner-cities strategy in 1976. However, the urban impacts and inputs of central and local government policies far outweighed in resource terms any explicit, direct 'urban' policy. It is difficult to assess the urban impacts of existing public-expenditure programmes on core urban areas; such a breakdown is not commonly available in the UK. However, the West Central Scotland Planning Team undertook a special exercise to identify public expenditure in that region (see WCSPT Supplementary Reports) and they indicated that budgets for education, transport, social security, environment, housing and industrial development all had an important urban-level impact (we have argued earlier that industrial development, housing and transport expenditures probably stimulated decentralisation). However, unlike the US government, the UK government has not explicitly discussed, nor perhaps even analysed, the urban impact of public expenditures. These traditional functional/sectoral policies may still run counter to the explicit inner-area policies (Reiner, 1979).

One outcome of the 1968 urban programme was the 'rediscovery' of urban poverty and its spatial manifestation. This occurred via the Inner Area Studies, the West Central Scotland Plan, and DoE analysis of changes in census indicators for small areas for the period 1966–71. In turn, this research influenced the development and content of the Inner Areas Policy.

It may be best to start by suggesting what was correct with the new initiative.[9] First, it recognised that spatially-concentrated deprivation and poverty and the 'pervasive sense of decay and neglect' in the inner cities reflected, primarily, processes of urban economic decline. Secondly, it stressed the need for an area-based approach reflecting the belief that there were generic area effects operative. Thirdly, the complex nature of the problem was stressed and for the first time causes as well as symptoms were to be attacked. Fourthly, the system of organisational partnerships, and the more informal system already existing in Scotland, were to be developed to co-ordinate central and local and area-based and functional policy initiatives. Fifthly, a small programme of research and monitoring exercises was undertaken. Before turning to the inadequacies and non-feasible aspects of the programme it is worth recounting the rationale for the shift in the direction of policy. The relevant section in the White Paper suggests that 'The inner parts of our cities ought not to be left to decay' and the arguments to support this *diktat* were:

(1) The growth of a deprived and trapped population in the inner core would lead to 'mounting social bitterness' and 'increasing alienation'.
(2) The commercial hearts of cities, and indeed overall conurbation image and attractiveness, would be adversely affected by constructing rings of blight and deprivation.
(3) Physical and other social overhead capital in the core would be under-utilised and, at the same time, replicated on the periphery.

These justifications have, in effect, the status of hypotheses rather than empirical findings. It is clear that at this juncture government did not try to assess what spatial structure of British cities was appropriate or desirable and what adjustment costs were to be borne in the short term. Past policy, and apparently individual and firm locational preferences had favoured a decentralised structure (Vining, 1979). Why then should housing or industrial incentives be brought into play to reverse this pattern? The 'trapping' or 'alienation' problems could equally have been treated by a policy of planned decline and dispersal. Indeed, given the overall economic prospects, planned decline may have been a more appropriate strategy. But to make life tolerable, with decreasing employment opportunities, it would have required increasing public expenditure or transferring more resources from those in employment to those living in poverty and unemployment. This would have required an explicit, and heroic, distributional statement by government. And of course, with the recent change of government, such a strategy would be even less acceptable as it would have precluded tax reductions to stimulate effort and efficiency. Instead, redistributions towards the inner city were to be disguised. That is, in the present economic context in general, jobs for the inner cities (which does not of course mean jobs for residents in the inner areas) could only be acquired at the cost of job losses in other areas or cities. This latter objection also tends to restrict the importance of the 'growth restraining' effects of inner areas.

Further, the infrastructure argument is surely much too general and short-term in nature. Admittedly, failures to control suburban infrastructure could have resulted in inefficient infrastructure use. But are urban bygones never bygones? Are public developments never to be scrapped? The arguments of the White Paper are sufficiently flawed in this respect to merit more detailed economic attention. A more substantive argument for an inner-area policy would be that market imperfections, which affect area 'confidence' or expectation, result in unnecessary decentralisation of households or firms. For instance, we have already alluded to the existence of such area effects in relation to labour market 'area stigmatisation', the failure of the land market to adjust to clearance costs or the loss of individual or institutional confidence in the inner areas of the housing market. But these are, again, largely unresearched issues in the UK context.

Some more specific points on the details of the programme seem relevant. First, the selection of areas for action, within major cities, and the focus on 'inner areas' is only partially correct, in so far as urban poverty and deprivation are clearly shown to exist in peripheral estates of public housing within core cities (by indicator surveys or factorial ecology studies). There are good reasons to believe, at least in a Scottish context, that it is these areas which will constitute major housing and environmental problems in the 1980s. It seems that the policy solutions of the 1950s are now the pressing problems of the next decade. Secondly, the emphasis on re-industralising inner areas may be misplaced both on grounds of economic efficiency and inner-area environmental quality. The new government's proposals to stimulate small-scale industrial confidence in inner areas by suspending planning controls in 'free enterprise' zones tend to ignore or underestimate the costs of externalities. Unless the job-generating incubator hypothesis is correct for the UK then industrial decentralisation constitutes an efficient location pattern and it may be more appropriate to improve training and transport to raise the probabilities of inner residents finding peripheral jobs – always accepting that a labour-market displacement effect will occur. If the central problem of the city is general labour surplus or demand deficiency then it is not clear that siting jobs in inner areas will raise inner-resident employment prospects. Similar reservations must exist regarding training programmes. At the end of the day, the best hope for inner city residents will be a sustained rise in regional demand which policy may best effect at the regional level, but which may primarily stem from aspatial influences on economic growth such as better industrial relations, increased productivity, improved management, etc. Given this perspective then, at least in the regions benefitting from regional policies, appropriate planning can ensure that regional and urban employment policies are quite consistent. In this respect it is to be hoped that urban-level variations in industrial policies or subsidies – as occur as the result of the Tyne and Wear Act, or the Scottish Development Agency's operations in the East End of Glasgow – will not be allowed to proliferate, as a locational subsidy competition at the urban level may merely shift and not create new jobs.

Conclusion

The tone of this chapter has been generally gloomy and critical in respect of urban policy formulation. However, there are reasons to believe that housing and environmental policies can be successful in older-core housing areas. The continued decline of private renting in these areas is being matched by a transfer of properties into owner occupation and rehabilitation-oriented housing associations. In the

North American model of urban decline, older-core properties depreciate in value and are abandoned. But this does not appear to happen in British cities. Even with historically unhelpful attitudes on the part of financing institutions, property values in the inner city are rising rapidly and resident surveys indicate high levels of satisfaction with area attributes although they are dissatisfied with experienced levels of vandalism and crime, and the persistence of vacant sites and derelict buildings. Clearly more efficient policing and planning systems are required. Small- and large-scale environmental improvement schemes, either initiated by housing associations or by private owners, are now literally scrubbing away the drabness and apparent decay of the inner city. However, it is important to remember that the inner city is functionally related to its surrounding periphery, and there is some evidence to suggest that inner-area confidence and appreciation are growing at the cost of the abandonment of public housing in peripheral estates. The shifting spatial structure of problems in the city cannot be ignored.

There are other reasons to believe that the spatial structure of poverty and unemployment in the city may alter in the next decade. A continued rise in the real price of oil may well have quite marked effects on city structure, at least from a deductive viewpoint. It is difficult to be precise about these effects as they represent an interaction of little-known price and income elasticities. It could be predicted that higher-income households geared to 'cosmopolitan' rather than familial lifestyles may now choose to return to the urban core. If such 'gentrification' is widespread, then the welfare benefits to existing inner-area groups are not clear: they are likely to be displaced to less accessible locations in an era of rising movement costs, although they may be compensated by changing patterns of land values and house prices. The effect of rising oil prices on employment in the core cities is even less predictable. If inward moves to more accessible sites did occur, overall urban employment may fall if world trade or demand is reduced because of energy difficulties. On the other hand, as a producer and net exporter of oil the British government has some discretion. That is, it may choose to 'process' oil prior to export thereby increasing the British share of reduced world trade. This is all too speculative, but it does indicate that governments will have to assess the urban impacts of national policies and to monitor the changing structures of cities and their problems.

Fifteen years later Donald Robertson's call for a more informed and extensive economic input into town planning and urban development still rings true. To raise the probability of maintaining or increasing the quality of life in urban areas in the next decade, economists can make a limited contribution. First, the continued development of clear theoretical ideas is essential: an urban economics which can be related to policy still requires systematic development. Secondly, by using their critical and analytical skills economists can assist governments to assess the impacts and efficiency of existing urban-area and functional policies. Thirdly, in the next few years pragmatic as well as ideological reasons are likely to result in reduced public expenditures, and it is unlikely that a major commitment to urban programmes will be made. But urban-problem areas, if properly selected, can be favoured even within a shrinking public expenditure budget. Finally, and most important of all, a wider social obligation rests upon economists and academics, to press governments to understand the value of research, and significantly to advance our own science.

Acknowledgement

In preparing this chapter my views have been greatly influenced by my colleagues at the University of Glasgow. John Parr, Colin Jones, Bill Lever, Steve Bailey and Gordon Cameron have all been most helpful.

Notes

1. The concept of 'tolerable survival' is pursued elsewhere in this chapter. The remarks which follow are consistent with a wide set of conceptions of the term.

2. The welfare of individuals or communities within defined urban areas is the concern of this chapter. Recently it has become fashionable to call for 'the saving of cities' or the need for inner areas to 'survive and be revitalised'. Areas considered in isolation from populations are not however inherently interesting to the urban economist. However, it is recognised that an urban, spatial or area approach to problem identification may exclude disadvantaged rural or dispersed urban groups. For instance, in Strathclyde region a cross-check of functional as opposed to concentrated spatial measures of poverty and deprivation indicates that the latter may exclude more than 20 per cent of deprived households.

3. It is of course pertinent to note that in a growing economy some cities may decline and the populations of such cities will have their quality of life threatened. Population mobility or redistribution with growth can assuage such difficulties. However, even in an economy where all cities grow, within a city absolute or relative poverty is likely to be concentrated into particular locations. In high-income societies, even where the relatively poor enjoy high income levels, the distributional outcomes will still, probably, be reflected in area concentrations. Depending on the value judgements of society, this may or may not constitute 'tolerable survival'. In this chapter, in relation to the UK, we are discussing a

national economy with almost zero growth and with a large set of declining core cities.

4. As a minimum, expenditure on the Urban Programme and Inner Areas could be cited and this would constitute 0.005 per cent of GDP. On the other hand, the 'urban shore', based on population figures, of public expenditure could amount to some 40–50 per cent of GDP. Even this latter figure under-estimates the effects of urban policies if there are biases toward urban areas or if control policies, such as Industrial Development Certificates, Office Development Permits, Rent Controls or Planning Controls, had major urban impacts or if tax policy has an urban bias. The incidence of government expenditure and revenue schemes in the UK is not currently known.

5. A list of the areas causing most concern is presented in the Inner Areas White Paper (Cmnd. 6845). At the time of writing the policy commitment of the new Conservative Government to urban policy is somewhat unclear.

6. Here, 'core cities' relate to the administratively-defined large cities which formed the centre of British conurbations.

7. I hope that the many talented and hard-working civil servants, and indeed politicians, with responsibilities in this area, do not interpret this as personal criticism. It is, rather, a criticism of the system of policy planning within which individuals are forced to operate.

8. Of course spatial developments do not always fit into such easily-identified stages and changes may be continuous rather than discrete. Stages are adopted here for pedagogic simplicity.

9. Of course the Inner Areas Policy has a small budget of around £175 million, which would, for instance, constitute less than one per cent of local authority expenditure.

References

Alonso, W. (1964), *Location and Land Use* (Cambridge, Mass.: Harvard University Press)

Baumol, W. J. (1967), 'Macroeconomics of Unbalanced Growth: The Anatomy of Urban Crisis', *American Economic Review*, 57, 1

Berry, B. J. L. (1980), 'Inner City Futures, an American Dilemma Revisited', *Transactions of the British Institute of* Geographers, 5, 1

Cairncross, A. (1979), 'What is De-industrialisation?' in Blackaby, F. (ed.) *De-industrialisation* (London: Heinemann)

Cameron, G. C., Firn, J. R. and Maclennan, D. (1974), 'The Determinants of Urban Manufacturing Location', *London Papers in Regional Science*, 5

Cheshire, P. C. (1979), 'Inner Areas as Spatial Labour Markets', *Urban Studies* (February)

Clower, R. W. (1965), 'The Keynesian Counter-Revolution: A Theoretical Appraisal' in Hahn, F. and Brechling, F. P. R. (eds.), *The Theory of Interest Rates* (London: Macmillan)

Evans, A. W. (1973), *The Economics of Residential Location* (London: Macmillan)

Farmer, E. and Smith, R. (1975), 'Overspill Theory: A Metropolitan Case', *Urban Studies* (June)

Firn, J. R. and Hughes, J. T. (1974), 'Employment Growth and Decentralisation of Manufacturing' (Centre for Environmental Studies (CES), Urban Economics Conference Papers)

GEAR (1978), *Glasgow East Area Renewal Project Survey* (Scottish Development Agency, unpublished)
Hall, D. (1974), *Urban and Regional Planning* (Harmondsworth: Penguin)
Harrison, A. and Whitehead, C. M. (1978), 'Is There an 'Inner Cities' Problem?', *The Three Banks Review* (September)
Hirschorn, L. (1979), 'The Urban Crisis: A Post-Industrial Perspective', *Journal of Regional Science* (February)
Holmans, A. E. (1964), 'Restriction of Expansion in South East England: A Reappraisal', *Oxford Economic Papers* (July)
James, C. A. (ed.) (1979), *Urban Deprivation and the Inner City* (London: Croom Helm)
Leijonhufvud, A. (1968), *On Keynesian Economics and the Economics of Keynes* (Oxford and New York: Oxford University Press)
Lever, W. F. (1979), 'Employment Decentralisation in the Clydeside Conurbation' (mimeo)
MacGregor, A. (1979), 'Area Externalities and Urban Unemployment' in James
McKay, D. H. and Cox, A. W. (1979), *Politics and Urban Change* (London: Croom Helm)
Maclennan, D. (1978), 'The 1974 Rent Act: Some Short-Run Supply Effects', *Economic Journal* (June)
——— (1979), 'The Financing and Management of Urban Public Services' (Chicago: International Federation of Engineers)
Maclennan, D. and Jones, D. J. (1980), 'Institutional Influences on Housing Choices: Building Societies and Area Lending Patterns' (mimeo)
Maclennan, D. and Parr, J. B. (eds.) (1979), *Regional Policy: Past Experience and New Directions* (London: Martin Robertson)
Malcolm, J. P. (1979), 'Manufacturing and Service Industries' (Glasgow University Urban and Regional Discussion Papers, no. 30)
Norris, G. (1979), 'Defining Urban Deprivation' in James
Parr, J. B. (1979), 'Spatial Structure as a Factor in Economic Adjustment and Regional Policy' in Maclennan and Parr
Parr, J. B. and Denike, K. (1970), 'Theoretical Problems in Central Place Analysis', *Economic Geography* (October)
The President's National Urban Policy Report (1968) (Washington, D. C.: HUD)
Reiner, T. (1979), 'Towards a National Urban Policy: Introduction', *Journal of Regional Science* (February)
Richardson, H. W. (1973), *Regional Growth Theory* (London: Macmillan)
Robertson, D. J. (1964), 'The City' in Robertson, D. J. and Grieve, R. (eds.), *The City and The Region* (Edinburgh: Oliver and Boyd)
Segal, D. (ed.) (1979), *The Economics of Neighbourhood* (New York: Academic Press).
Stone, P. (1979), 'Changing Metropolitan Structures' in Maclennan and Parr
Vining, D. (1979), 'The President's National Urban Policy Report: Issued Skirted and Statistics Omitted', *Journal of Regional Science* (February)
Weintraub, E. R. (1979), *Microfoundations* (Cambridge: Cambridge University Press)
West Central Scotland Plan, Supplementary Report 5: Public Expenditure in the Region (1974) (West Central Scotland Team)

10 COMMUNITY DEVELOPMENT IN SCOTLAND: PROMISE AND PROBLEMS

Ian Carter

Community development is fashionable. The Hayekian political Right in Britain has never believed in centralised planning, but in recent years they have been joined by an increasing number of leftists who no longer accept the Old Left's vision of a centrally-planned future overseen by a benign state bureaucracy. The recognition that bureaucratic sclerosis may afflict large-scale public organisations as well as large-scale private organisations has driven many liberal and socialist professionals to seek more humane forms of organisation through which 'the people' can realise their own objectives: to seek 'the processes by which the efforts of the people themselves are united with those of governmental authorities to improve the economic, social and cultural conditions of communities, to integrate these communities into the life of the nation, and to enable them to contribute fully to national progress'.[1] Community development could ensure that 'the people' had a say in their own future, rather than being merely the objects of remote bureaucratic manipulation.

But community development can mean different things. It can mean working with the state, as in the United Nations definition quoted above. In Britain this conception gave birth to the Community Development Projects (CDPs), twelve action and research projects established in deprived sections of British towns and cities. Their purpose was to understand how to break the cycle of deprivation which allegedly bound inhabitants of these districts into their unhappy lot. In seeking this understanding the CDPs, while financed and controlled from the Home Office, were required to work closely with relevant local authorities (Anon, 1977; Littlejohn, 1976). But community development could also mean working against the state if the state was seen to be part of the problem rather than part of the solution: thus disaffected lawyers set up free legal advice services, disaffected planners tried to do advocacy planning, disaffected social workers organised tenants' associations, and disaffected teachers set up free schools.

In northern Scotland the idea of rural self-help through community development has been proposed as a radical alternative to centralised economic planning procedures which were seen either to do little to improve the lot of local 'communities' or to make that lot worse (Varwell, 1973; Carter, 1975). This attack has had some success: in goading the Highlands and Islands Development Board (HIDB) into establishing Hebridean community co-operatives, for example. But what many of these advocates of community development failed to notice was that their preferred solution to the problems of the area had been tried before. In this chapter we will do two things. First we will consider some aspects of the history of community development in Scotland. Then we will draw some conclusions about whether community development provides, by itself, a viable development strategy for rural Scotland.

Community Development in Rural Scotland

We saw earlier that community development can mean different things to different people. Thus a recent paper takes the HIDB to be a community development agency (Williams, 1979, p. 111) while some of the Board's many critics have attacked it precisely for not being such an agency (Varwell, 1973; Carter, 1974, 1975). On some definitions the Crofters' Commission would be taken to be doing community development. We will limit our attention, however, to the most clear-cut example of community development in rural Scotland: to the network of councils of social service (CsSS) funded by the Development Commission through the Scottish Council of Social Service (SCSS).

The idea of community development usually is taken to have its origin in British colonial practice: getting native peoples to do things for themselves (under the benevolent tutelage of British experts) was cheaper than doing it for them (Mayo, 1975). But similar policies were being applied at home, too. The Development Commission was established under the Development and Road Improvement Funds Act, 1909; its purpose 'to Promote the Economic Development of the United Kingdom and the Improvement of Roads therein'.[2] In its economic development work the Commission took a rigidly centralist and economistic line: refusing, for example, to fund more than one research station concerned with a particular branch of agricultural research and demanding that strict cost/benefit criteria should determine where its grants and loans were disbursed. But political pressure had also laid on the Commission the obligation of promoting agricultural co-operation, where centralist and economistic strategies were quite inappropriate. By the 1930s this cuckoo had turned a large part of the Development Commission's policy inside out: by 1935 the Commission was funding 20 Rural Community Councils (RCCs) in England and Wales.[3] These councils were based on county boundaries, and undertook a wide range of tasks from encouraging the construction of village halls to the administration of grants to rural craftsmen. With their emphasis on a highly diffuse conception of development and their establishment at the county level, the RCCs were community development agencies in all but name; that omission was rectified after 1945, when the Development Commission began to call the RCCs' work community development.

Scotland never had a county RCC within its borders. In 1943 the Development Commission began to fund the newly-founded SCSS's rural work – concerned mainly with the promotion of voluntary social work and with building village halls. In 1948 SCSS stimulated the establishment of the first rural community development agency in Scotland; Skye Council of Social Service. The Development Commission immediately funded the new council. No more Councils of Social Service were established until 1960, when Mull and Iona CSS and Shetland CSS were founded. The programme expanded after that date, so that by 1977 – when its Scottish functions were devolved – the Commission was supporting 20 local CsSS in rural Scotland. Fourteen of these 20 were in the seven crofting counties. Between 1948 and 1977 local councils received £662,510 (at 1977 values) in grants from the Development Commission. This money went to pay the salary of a quarter-time, half-time or full-time secretary for each council, to pay office expenses, and to pay travelling expenses. Local councils were expected to top up this grant from other sources: the Commission took this 'voluntary income' as a key indicator of the efficiency of a local council. Between 1948 and 1977 the Development Commission also granted £956,000 (at 1977 values) to SCSS for their rural work; after 1960 that work became almost exclusively concerned with promoting new CsSS.

Councils of Social Service in rural Scotland were modelled on English RCCs, acting as an umbrella for the multifarious voluntary bodies concerned – no matter in how tenuous a fashion – with social welfare in the locality. But there were important differences between Councils of Social Service and Rural Community Councils, differences which the Development Commission pressed intermittently – and unsuccessfully – to eradicate. The English councils' boundaries followed county boundaries while Scottish councils, and more particularly those in the Highlands, tended to cover a much smaller area in which people allegedly had a perception of interests held in common – what an SCSS officer was to call homogeneous communities, 'communities with close ties, family, economic and social similarities bound by the same constraints of terrain and transportation systems' (Howie, 1978, pp. 2, 3). More important than this, however, was the fact that the RCCs' involvement in economic work was limited to the administration of equipment grants to country craftsmen. In Scotland, and particularly in the Highlands, local councils took a much deeper interest in economic matters. The part-time secretary of Shetland CSS, for example, spent the rest of his time acting as the county council's development officer. And the pioneer council, Skye CSS, was formed after preliminary investigations had been made into economics, transport, agriculture, fishing, marketing, public health, local industries, forestry, tourism, and social and educational activities. Reading the minutes of Highland CsSS one finds – in their early days at least – a heavy emphasis on economic development. Agriculture, fishing, forestry, tourism, manufacturing industry, communications – often the ancient Highland sport of bashing MacBraynes – and rural electrification were discussed much more frequently than the social welfare matters, such as old people's welfare, that the Development Commission thought was their proper sphere of interest. It might appear that community development was providing a real alternative to centralised regional planning, a grass-roots alternative through which 'the people' pursued what they regarded as development in their own way. In the rest of this chapter I will argue that this view is too sanguine.

Contradictions of Community Development

In order to understand why community development in rural Scotland did not live up to the expectations that some had of it let us look at a brief case-study.

The first attempt to form Mull and Iona CSS came in 1955–6 (SCSS, 1956, p. 7). This attempt failed, partly because of the intransigent opposition of the local county councillor, an English landowner with a military background.[4] Four years later the Agriculture and Forestry Group of the Advisory Panel for the Highlands and Islands – a state body – contacted SCSS over the deplorable social and economic state of Mull (SCSS, 1959). SCSS despatched an officer to investigate matters, armed with two lists. One specified those people with whom he was to make contact, the other specified those people whom he should avoid at all costs. This officer, M. A. M. Dickie, produced a devastating report:

> The reason advanced for the collapse of the former Council was generally given as the action of the Secretary in cancelling, on short notice and without consultation with office-bearers, an important early meeting. An explanation, though not an excuse, given by some for his action was that he feared control was going into the hands of some of the newer English proprietors. The fear of such control in any future effort was widely expressed and indeed quite bitter criticism was made of some of the landlords who are said quite definitely not to want any development of the island, do not want the proposed car ferry service from Oban to Craignure, do not want caravans to come in, and, in some cases, actively discourage holiday-makers, climbers and hikers. Some are said also not to be working their estates productively, to be deliberately allowing land to go out of production and houses to go into disrepair; on one estate there were said to be twelve such houses. Certainly some areas of the island present a depressing and neglected look. The replacement of some of the small farm tenancies, in association with an extension of forestry activity, would provide a more virile population and strengthen the community in some of the more derelict outlying areas. (SCSS, 1960)

As the former Chief Lands Officer for the Department of Agriculture and Fisheries for Scotland Dickie knew scandalous misuse of land when he saw it. His report encouraged SCSS to promote the new Mull and Iona CSS in February 1961, under hand-picked leaders. The dominant figure was the Council's first chairman, Col. C. K. Finlay – sheep-farmer, children's books writer and enthusiast for repopulation through family farming. Under his leadership the CSS identified its major priorities: a new hospital for the island (with an airstrip close at hand for the evacuation of very serious cases to the mainland), the establishment of a local tourist organisation and, above all, a long-term development plan for the agricultural regeneration of Mull. Some of these aims were achieved. The new hospital at Salen was opened in 1964, the airstrip two years later. The CSS started a successful tourist organisation, based in Tobermory; this body was hived off from the

CSS in the mid-1960s under pressure from SCSS and promptly collapsed. There remained the highest priority, the development plan, into which the CSS put a great deal of effort. Together with a team of land-use planners they produced a report justifying the viability of land regeneration (Anon, 1965). In consequence the newly-founded HIDB was persuaded, rather reluctantly, to undertake a comprehensive land-use study of the island. It needed years of pressure from Mull and Iona CSS, together with pressure from other Highland CsSS and from SCSS, to get the HIDB to publish the report; but when it finally appeared in 1973 it justified all the complaints about the misuse of Mull's land. But it also noted wistfully that:

> Some estate owners drew attention to points concerning their own estates that were at variance with the report's general philosophy on optimising land productivity. It is clear that sport, and in particular deer-stalking, is regarded as being of considerably higher importance relative to agriculture and forestry than indicated in the report, and it has to be recognised that some estates will not be in favour of exploiting the indicated agricultural potential to the extent recommended. (HIDB, 1973, p. 137)

And there the HIDB report lies, a dead letter. The Board did, to its credit, try to buy a key estate on Mull to use as a test-bed for effective multiple land use, but they were outbid by a private buyer who continued the fine old tradition of evicting farming tenants – most of Mull is not covered by the crofting laws – in order to turn the estate over to sporting use.

Mull and Iona CSS has proved powerless to alter this unhappy picture. Indeed, like many other long-established Highland CsSS, it has withdrawn from the economic field. Its current activities appear almost indistinguishable from those of Mull Community Council, formed in the mid-1970s reorganisation of Scottish local government. There must be serious doubts about how long Mull and Iona CSS can, or ought to, survive.

What lessons can we draw from this history? A number, I think. One set concerns public representation. Compare a CSS with a district council or a county council. Local councillors are elected on a majority of votes cast and then (in theory, at least) represent the interests of their electorates in the council chamber. They are assisted by paid officials and have the right to raise a rate to finance their activities, as well as receiving funds from central government. A CSS also seeks to represent the interests of the inhabitants of its area, but representation is less direct. The delegates to the CSS from voluntary organisations in the district represent the interests of those organisations' members. In addition, successful CsSS have a system of district representation to avoid the taint of 'Portree-centredness' that, among other things, brought Skye CSS into crisis in the mid-1960s.

There seems no way to ensure that the social composition of a CSS matches that of the general population in the district, but the same is true of statutory local councils. But CsSS, unlike a statutory local authorities, have no power to raise money directly; they depend on grants from central government, disbursed through a Byzantinely-complex process, on grants from local authorities and on voluntary income – the profit from dances, for example. This, together with the need to liaise closely with government departments and local authorities on so many issues of interest to a CSS, means that a CSS has to maintain good relations with the local authority: unsympathetic local councillors or chief officers can make a CSS's task impossible. The problems of Skye CSS deepened when Iain Hilleary, its chairman (and dominant figure) for 25 years, lost his seat on Inverness County Council: 'he was', I was told in Skye, 'no longer "one of us" '. Kit Finlay realised that he had to get elected to Argyll County Council if the new Mull and Iona CSS was to have any chance of success. The problem with this close articulation between statutory and voluntary councils is that local authorities – and central government departments – hold an effective, if covert, veto over the CSS's activities: only those policies can be pursued that will not upset local and central authorities. This seems to be part of the explanation, along with the lack of money, why Highland CsSS generally have withdrawn from economic work to the 'safer' field of voluntary social welfare. Attempts to push conservative local authorities in new and radical directions doomed the 12 Home Office-sponsored CDPs (Anon, 1977; Butcher *et al.*, 1979). Scottish councils of social service should ponder the lessons of that sad history.

Thus we should not be surprised that Mull and Iona CSS failed in their attempt to regenerate Mull's agriculture. They were encouraged to make the attempt by officials in the Scottish Office who themselves were powerless to influence private-estate policies in Mull, but the position of sporting lairds on the island is so strong that local agitation alone – even if supported by a number of damning unofficial and official land-use surveys – never could shift them. The relentless advance of bracken on Mull marks the steady degradation of what is, by Highland standards, very good agricultural land; but sacred property rights are preserved. Mull's story echoes evidence from other parts of the world suggesting that when social and economic opportunities are grotesquely maldistributed then real community development is no more than a pious hope (Huizer, 1971). It can work, as in the dramatic transformation of the Chinese countryside after 1947, but only when structured social and economic inequalities are levelled first (Aziz, 1978).

That is not to say that rural community development in Scotland has been worthless. All 20 districts with CsSS are better off with their councils than they would have been without them, which is not a claim that one can make for all organisations. Some CsSS, like North and West Sutherland and Harris, have plugged away in extraordinarily difficult districts, trying to support what economic activity and social life could be sustained. The councils in the Long Island (Lewis and Harris) generated some sense that things could be different, and better, in the face of rather scandalous neglect from county councils based far away in Inverness and Dingwall: it is not too fanciful to suggest that recent successes by the Western Isles Island Council in promoting community activities stem, in part at least, from previous work by the Hebridean CsSS.

But we need to remember that even in 1977 Scotland held only 20 rural councils of social service. Vast areas of the country – the north-east and the south-west, for example – were barely touched by the movement. If CsSS did have any significant effect on the problems of their own districts then, it might be argued, part of their success was bought at the expense of other districts which lacked articulate populist leadership. We see the effect of such leadership in the chairman's report given by Iain Hilleary, a well-connected businessman and landowner, to the 1953 AGM of Skye CSS:

> He would, he said, like particularly to draw attention to the recognition being given to the Council and its work outside the Island, as has been shown by the contacts sought with it by highly-placed bodies. In the past year or so the Council had been given the opportunity of discussions with the Secretary of State (for Scotland), the Minister of State, the Royal Commission on Scottish Affairs and the Committee of Enquiry into Crofting Conditions. In this way Skye had had an extra opportunity of 'putting its case' on matters of far reaching importance in the life of Skye; he himself had gained the very firm impression that the existence of the

> Council as a medium through which contact can be made informally with the people of Skye has been welcome in high places. The setting up of a body such as the Council by the people of Skye is, he said, taken as an indication of initiative in seeking solutions to their problems. It would, he felt, favourably influence the decisions taken at high levels on matters affecting the Island's welfare. (Skye CSS, 1953)

And what, one wonders, would happen to areas which lacked someone with Hilleary's contacts with people in high places? If we are serious about trying to improve the social condition of the Scottish countryside through grass-roots development strategies then we must move away from the clientalistic approach exemplified by Iain Hilleary's speech, an approach that benefits one district at the expense of others and hence inhibits the development of common solutions to common problems. We must take a much more fundamental, more political, approach and tackle the structured inequalities that, for example, prevented Mull and Iona CSS doing anything about the real problems of Mull – the English military sporting lairds. Such an approach would mean dumping the nebulous populism that characterises so much community-development rhetoric. No longer would we be able to talk about the interests of 'the people': we would have to examine the real interests of different social groups and decide which groups' interests we wished to support. That done, we would have to organise in support of those interests. Local authorities and central government would be unlikely to give us grants to pursue these objectives. A crumb of comfort is that, given the trend of Sir Keith Joseph's thoughts on the problems of bits of Britain outside the golden south-east of England, that is not likely to be much of a loss.

Notes

1. The original source of this statement, quoted in Dickie (1968), is *Principles of Community Development – Social Progress Through Local Action* (United Nations Economic and Social Council, New York, 1955).
2. See 9 Edw. 7 c. 47, Preamble.
3. See 28th Report, Development Commissioners, *Parliamentary Papers*, 1937–8 (176) x, pp. 29–31.
4. SCSS *Rural Community Development Committee Minutes* (1 February, 1959). Also, an interview with Col. C. K. Finlay, 1979.

References

Anon. (1965), *Mull 1965* (Edinburgh: School of Town and Country Planning)
——— (1977), *Gilding the Ghetto: the State and the Poverty Experiments* (London: Community Development Project)
Aziz, S. (1978), *Rural Development: Learning from China* (London: Macmillan)
Broady, M. (ed.) (1973), *Marginal Regions: Essays in Social Planning* (London: Bedford Square Press)
Butcher, H., Pearce, J., Cole, I. and Glen, A. (1979), *Community Participation and Poverty: the Final Report of Cumbria Community Development Project* (University of York Papers in Community Studies, no. 22)
Carter, I. (1974), 'The Highlands of Scotland as an Underdeveloped Region' in de Kadt, E. and Williams, G. (eds.), *Sociology and Development* (London: Tavistock)
——— (1975), 'A Socialist Strategy for the Highlands' in Brown, G. (ed.), *The Red Paper on Scotland* (Edinburgh: Edinburgh University Students' Publications Board)
Dickie, M. A. M. (1968), 'Community Development in Scotland', *Community Development Journal*, III
Highlands and Islands Development Board (1973), *Island of Mull: Survey and Proposals for Development* (Inverness: HIDB)
Howie, A. S. (1978), *Historical Background to the Regional Projects* (Edinburgh: Scottish Council of Social Service, mimeo, 18 December)
Huizer, G. (1971), 'Community Development, Land Reform and Political Participation' in Shanin, T. (ed.), *Peasants and Peasant Societies* (Harmondsworth: Penguin)
Littlejohn, G. (1976), 'The CDPs', *Community Care* (19 May)
Mayo, M. (1975), 'Community Development: A Radical Alternative?' in Bailey, R. and Brake, M. (eds.), *Radical Social Work* (London: Arnold)
SCSS (Scottish Council of Social Service) (1956), *13th Annual Report* (Edinburgh: SCSS)
——— (1959), *Rural Community Development Committee (RCDC) Minutes* (1 February)
——— (1960), *Rural Community Development Committee (RCDC) Minutes* (4 May)
Skye, CSS (1953), *Minutes* (2 December)
Varwell, A. (1973), 'Highland and Island Communities' in Broady, M. (ed.), *Marginal Regions: Essays in Social Planning* (London: Bedford Square Press)
Williams, G. (1979), 'Community Development in Rural Britain: The Organisation of Social Initiative', *Community Development Journal*, XIV

11 OCCUPATIONAL CHANGE AND SOCIAL MOBILITY IN SCOTLAND SINCE THE FIRST WORLD WAR

Geoff Payne, Graeme Ford and Marion Ulas

Although some sociologists are interested in occupations and work *per se*, most British sociologists regard jobs only as a useful indicator of something else, namely social class. The basic facts of inequality in the distribution of resources, how social arrangements bring this about, and how these social arrangements themselves evolve, these questions have been predominant in sociology since its earliest days. It is these concerns which have prompted interest in occupations, and led to considerable debate about the theoretical issues involved in treating social class as occupation. Social stratification can be based on levels of education; or income and wealth; or any one, or combination, of power, status, life style or race. But at the end of the day most sociological analyses resort to men's jobs as the best single measure by which to identify social groups that differ from one another. In this respect, sociologists are unlike economists, who are more often directly interested in employment and income, as Coleman and Rainwater (1979, p. 5) have recently emphasised.

This has certainly been the case in the field of social mobility, that is, the study of movements from one social identity or status, to another. Typically, sociologists have looked at the movement of individuals from sharing the social (class) identity of the families in which they were reared, to taking on adult identities of their own. The first identity is usually defined by the father's occupation when the individual was 14 years old, and the second identity by the individual's occupation as an adult, or on entering work, etc. The *underlying question* is one of social class: to what extent do we have a rigid, closed society in which privilege, wealth, the best jobs are the inherited right of one class to the exclusion of all others; or do we have a fluid, open, 'democratic' society in which there is equality of opportunity for all?[1] The *mechanics of operationalising* this question tie us into jobs and the labour market.

For some time, writers on social mobility did not recognise how dependent on the occupational sphere they were. Only in the last few years have they realised that social mobility depends on how people come to get jobs – and lose them; on how many jobs of particular kinds are available – and where; and on how historical changes in the distribution of occupations constrain patterns of mobility.[2] It has for some time been a commonplace that non-manual occupations have been expanding rapidly since the nineteenth century, and that this expansion is part and parcel of industrial society. It has only recently been realised how fully this expansion has created openings for people to work in middle class jobs, thus fuelling the process of social mobility.

The relationship between occupational change and mobility is illustrated in Figures 11.1 and 11.2, the data being drawn in both cases from a sample survey of nearly 5,000 male Scots in the 1975 Scottish Mobility Study. Figure 11.1 shows the position in relation to the first full-time jobs of the sample subjects, the upper graph showing the proportion of the total entering non-manual jobs, and the lower graph the proportion of the men who were 'upwardly mobile', that is moved into non-manual occupations from manual family origins, at that stage in their careers. It should be noted that the percentages graphed by both lines have been calculated as five-year moving averages based on year of birth.

Figure 11.2 then shows the state of play ten years after starting work, the upper line again tracing the overall percentages of non-manual job-holders at that stage, and the lower line showing the proportion at each birth date who during the first ten years of working life had moved from manual into non-manual jobs – i.e. been upwardly mobile. Again, the percentages have been calculated as five-year moving averages.

The central sections of each of the figures show a congruence between the availability of non-manual jobs and the proportion of upward mobility. When the non-manual (upper) line goes up, so too does the mobility as evidenced in the lower line; and when it falls, so too does mobility. At the beginning of the period, for men born before and during the First World War, and at the end of the period, for men born during the Second World War, the fit between the lines is less good.[3] It seems reasonable to conclude that a major part of mobility rates can be explained by the changes in occupational distribution, although other, if sometimes less important, factors (such as educational reform or the dislocation of wars and post-war reconstruction) are also involved and presumably are more important at the beginning and end of the period in question.

While an analysis based on two categories, manual and non-manual, is useful because of its simplicity, it disguises the variety of changes

Figure 11.1: Occupation at First Job: Opportunity and Mobility

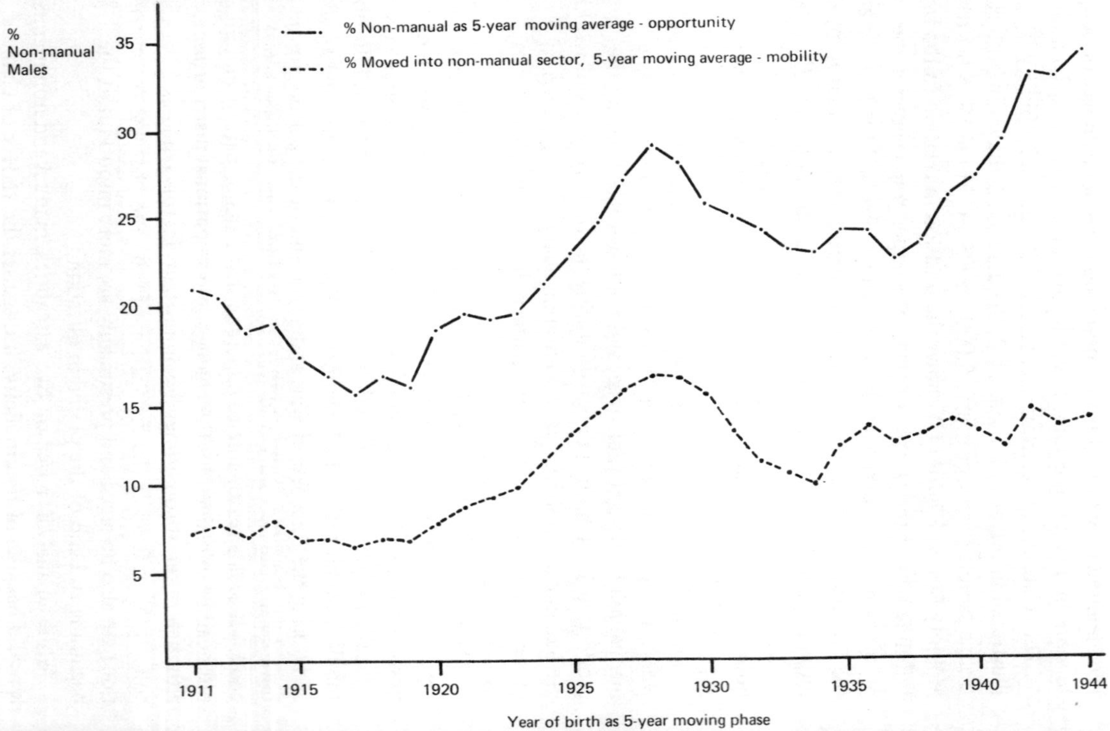

Figure 11.2: Occupation Ten Years After Starting Work

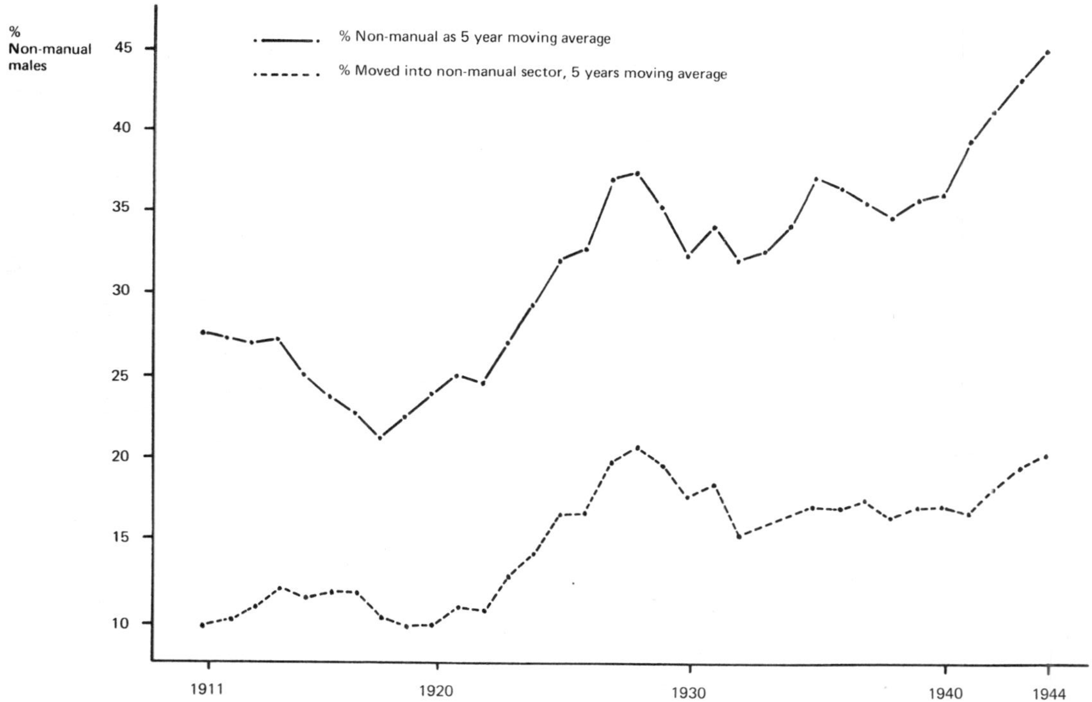

that have been taking place in the occupational structure this century. Recently there have been several attempts to examine occupational change using more detailed breakdowns based on Census data.[4] While there are considerable technical problems with this approach, it has thrown up some interesting features which had been relatively neglected to date. For example the growth of the various components of the non-manual sector has not been uniform. Since the First World War, the number of men employed in routine white collar work in Scotland has increased by around 16,000: an increase in the share of the male labour force of about one per cent. But semi-professionals have increased by 57,000, from one per cent to five per cent of the labour force.[5]

Nor has this expansion been at a consistent rate over this fifty-year period. In the better-paid components of the non-manual sector (that is, the professional and managerial elements), there was an actual decline in number between 1921 and 1931, whereas the more routine components increased, even if at a slower rate than at other times. Similarly, the period from 1961 to 1971 showed a slowing of the expansion in non-manual work for male workers, certainly as compared with the previous decade. Obviously, attempting to relate these kinds of complex change to changes in mobility is a very difficult exercise, and one that we do not intend to develop further here. However, it is clear that if the manual/non-manual dichotomy can be deceptive in looking at occupational structures, we must also look at mobility in more detail. We can, of course, measure mobility as movements between smaller categories than manual and non-manual work. An increase in the number of categories increases the mobility score, but makes it much harder to demonstrate graphically that there is a relationship between mobility and occupational distribution.

Conventionally a seven-category schema is used, and mobility is taken at the present job, rather than the first.[6] On this basis, 42.3 per cent of the SMS sample were upwardly mobile, by at least one category, 27.4 per cent remained in the same category, and 30.2 per cent were downwardly mobile. In other words, about three in every four experienced some kind of disjunction between their family background and their own occupational identity (forgetting for the moment any additional respondents whose earlier career took them away from their origins before they returned to the same category at the time of interview). This we regard as a relatively fluid condition.

Of course, had we used a smaller number of categories, such as retaining 'manual' and 'non-manual', the appearance of the results would be different. In that case, 23 per cent of the sample were upwardly mobile, 65.7 per cent were immobile and 11.3 per cent were downwardly mobile. We might hesitate to call this 'fluid', but to treat the class structure as a dichotomy would be to miss a great deal of variation.

So, having decided upon a seven-fold model, the picture which results is then one of social fluidity – although that is not to say Scotland is an open or egalitarian society. What it does show is that direct inheritance of occupation is relatively rare, even at this level of general categories. Exceptions do occur: for example, farming and small businesses are heavily recruited from among the ranks of farmers and 'small businessmen'. The reasons are self-evident. But the general rule is to the contrary; it has become 'normal' *not* to follow in one's father's footsteps. If we consider the upper middle class of professionals, senior administrators and managers of large establishments, three out of every four of its members have come from other origins, one in three from manual backgrounds, and each of the manual categories contributes about 10 per cent or more. It is true that the professional managerial class's largest source of recruitment is from itself, followed by the adjacent class of semi-professionals and managers of small establishments. But this is a totally different picture from that given by earlier studies in the 1940s. There one finds that apparently only one in ten of the upper middle class have manual working class origins, and half are self-recruited (Glass, 1954, p. 183). It should be stressed, however, that whatever may be happening to the great mass of society, the social characteristics of the men at the very top – company directors, cabinet ministers, newspaper owners, senior civil servants etc – are quite different (see Stanworth and Giddens, 1974; Abrams, 1978). There public school and Oxbridge, and recruitment from their own ranks, is the rule. Social mobility reaches up just so far, but not quite far enough to engulf the true centres of power in Britain.

As we saw in Figure 11.2, mobility has tended to increase since the First World War, but the tail end of the line shows a marked deviation: the youngest men in these data have been less successful in crossing the manual/non-manual line. On this other measure, using seven categories, the same is true: there is less mobility in more recent years. Table 11.1 shows four birth cohorts by way of illustration: in this case we are talking about mobility to present job, which means that the younger men are less far advanced in their careers, although we are still dealing with men in their thirties.

Upward mobility increases until the last cohort – 35 per cent, 42

Table 11.1: Occupational Mobility in Scotland, 1975, for Four Cohorts, Measured as Gross Mobility over Seven Social Classes

	Year of birth			
	1909–18	1919–28	1929–38	1939–43
Upwardly mobile	35.6	42.3	49.0	44.8
Immobile	26.5	29.4	25.0	30.8
Downwardly mobile	37.9	28.3	26.0	24.4

per cent, 49 per cent and 45 per cent. This last cohort have careers concentrated in the 1961–71 decade when the census data show that the expansion of non-manual jobs began to slow. Nevertheless, downward mobility has continued to decline. This represents a somewhat inconclusive picture of the more recent events, but there is such a marked difference in the last cohort that it prompts speculation about even more recent changes since 1971. Is there a general slowing down in the creation of new middle class job opportunities which is based in some feature of the British economy, or do we see here some much more fundamental historical evolution of an industrial society into a new stage (à la Colin Clarke or Rostow)?

And what will be the effects of current Conservative cuts in public expenditure following several lean years under the last Labour government? Without the cancelled 1976 census it is not possible to extend the analysis using the same categories, but it does not seem unreasonable to anticipate that cutbacks on teacher training, in the NHS, in social services, in the civil service, in local government administration must all weigh most heavily on the white-collar sector. There may be fewer good jobs to go round. If this proves to be the case we may look back on the present period as one which marked a closing off of mobility opportunities and a hardening of class boundaries. A zero-growth economy in the sense of zero-growth in middle class jobs presents us with completely new rules for the mobility game. Few evolutionary theories of society allow for regression. We await the 1981 census with interest.

However, we have not fully specified even the basic rules of the mobility game because we have been exploring changes in the occupations and consequent social mobility of *men* only. Nothing of what we have said has taken account of females, and once again, this is typical of previous work in this field. Although there was good reason for concentrating on male workers in the Scottish Mobility Study,[7] we were able to collect some information about wives' careers, and it seems sensible to extend the earlier arguments to married women in order to gain a fuller picture of what is happening in Scottish society.

Again, it has become a commonplace that women have increasingly entered the labour market. Between 1921 and 1971, the number of economically-active women in Scotland rose by about 233,000 to 870,000, an increase of over one-third.[8] This growth was concentrated in the non-manual sector, apart from some increase in unskilled work – socio-economic group (SEG) 11 – with some elements such as skilled manual work declining sharply. This means that the basic patterns of employment have changed extensively, particularly in non-manual employment. At the end of the First World War men held 64 per cent of all non-manual jobs: by the 1970s this was down to 54 per cent. During the same period, men working in non-manual jobs went from 28 per cent of all male occupations to 39 per cent while non-manual women went from 38 per cent to 57 per cent. In other words, women are making in-roads into non-manual jobs to the extent that over half of the female labour force is non-manual, and the expansion of that sector is greater for women than for men.

However, these broad changes contain considerable variation. As Table 11.2 shows, by far the biggest non-manual increases were in two areas: routine white-collar work (from 138,000 to 311,000) and semi-professional work (from 43,364 to 105,640). As these are the two SECs with the greatest total growth, this lends support to the idea that women have been most able to compete in parts of the labour market where expansion has taken place, and less able in parts such as skilled manual labour where the contraction has taken place.[9] But commentators such as Scharf (1977) and Garnsley (1978) have noted that women are generally concentrated in particular segments of employment and that powerful social mechanisms operate to maintain this. In few areas do they compete directly with men for the same jobs. Certain jobs are women's work, and others are men's, and this applies over broad types of occupations, like management, or skilled manual work, not just for specific tasks like midwife or stevedore. Figure 11.3 is an illustration of this, taken from the 1971 census.

By 1971, women had successfully penetrated the lesser professions like teacher, nurse, social worker and librarian; they had dominated routine white collar work in shops and offices; and their less fortunate sisters were prominent in service work like catering, and well-represented in other of the less skilled manual occupations. But they had made little impact in management and the more established

Table 11.2: 'Economically-active' Scottish Women: Based on Census Data 1921–71

SEG* + % Total	1921	1931	1951	1961	1971
1 – 4	18,572 2.9	20,137 3.1	25,461 3.7	30,660 4.2	41,520 5.0
5 + 8	44,806 7.1	41,178 6.3	63,182 9.3	80,570 11.0	111,090 13.3
6	137,581 21.7	159,156 24.3	228,403 33.6	281,740 38.5	311,140 37.3
7	131,581 20.8	150,409 22.9	100,083 14.7	86,700 11.8	108,420 13.0
9	115,736 18.3	99,535 15.2	83,503 12.3	69,780 9.5	51,480 6.2
10	109,722 17.3	98,007 14.9	92,901 13.6	109,850 15.0	113,260 13.6
11 + 15	38,429 6.1	56,132 8.6	72,374 10.6	60,200 8.2	83,550 10.0
12	32,518 5.1	23,711 3.6	12,027 1.8	8,670 1.2	9,060 1.1
13 + 14	5,013 0.8	4,023 0.6	2,770 0.4	3,510 0.5	3,700 0.4
Totals (ex. 16 + 17)	634,016 100	655,990 100	680,659 100	731,680 100	833,480 100

*The SEG's contain the following approximate groupings:

SEGs 1 – 4: Professionals, managers, employers
5 + 8: Semi-professionals and supervisors
6 : Junior white collar
7 : Service workers
9 : Skilled manual workers
10 : Semi-skilled manual workers
11 + 15: Unskilled and agricultural workers
12 : Own account workers
13 + 14: Farmers

professions; were under-represented in the small business world; and heavily outnumbered among skilled manual workers. Compared with men, their patterns of work are quite different. We must therefore expect that their patterns of mobility will be different too.

If we turn to the Scottish Mobility Study sample of married women, we find that this is true:[10] 35.1 per cent of women are upwardly mobile (comparing their fathers' occupations when the women were 14 years old with the women's present or last occupations) whereas 42.3 per cent of men were upwardly mobile; 18.7 per cent of women stayed in the

Figure 11.3: Male and Female Occupations: 1971 Census Scotland

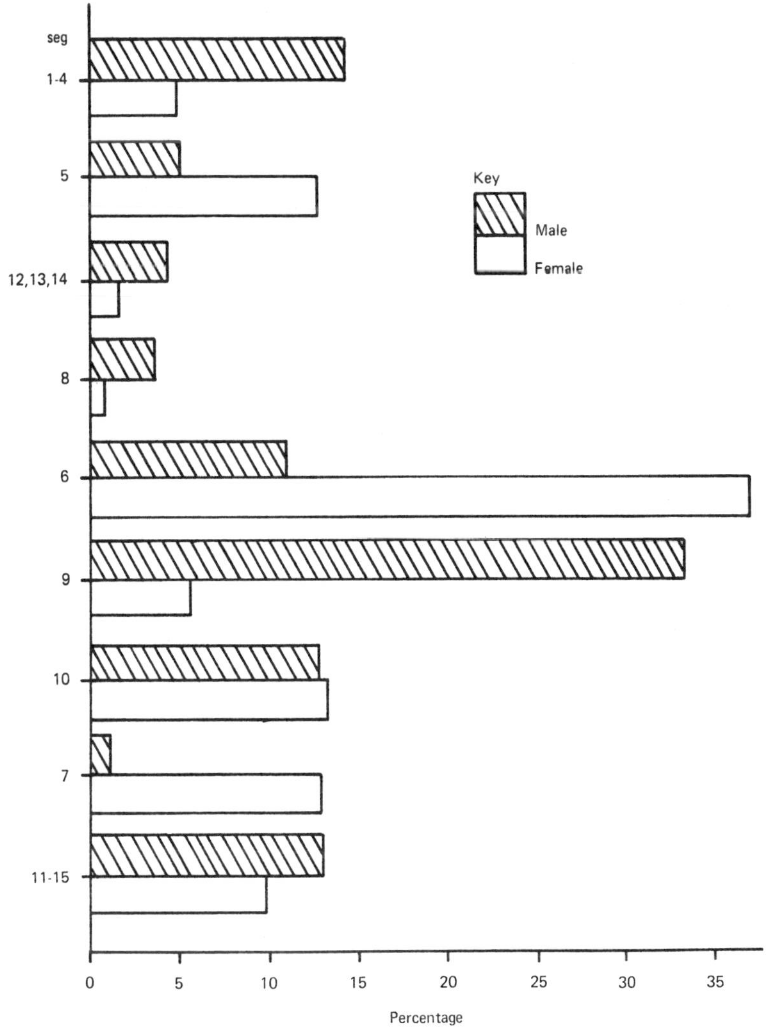

same occupational class, compared with 27.4 per cent of men; and 46.2 per cent were downwardly mobile, compared with 30.2 per cent for men. The distributions of the men's family backgrounds are very similar indeed to those of the women: it is their own occupations which differ, and therefore create the disparity of mobility rates.

Table 11.3: Occupational Distributions for Men, Wives and Fathers*

	Occupational class**						
	1	2	3	4	5	6	7
Man's father when man was 14	6.2	12.2	12.8	3.3	28.7	19.9	16.9
Wife's father when she was 14	5.4	11.3	12.3	4.7	28.3	20.1	18.0
Man's present or last job	11.9	14.7	14.3	5.9	20.6	19.2	13.5
Wife's present or last job	1.5	13.9	1.8	21.7	10.6	26.1	24.6

*The sample sizes were 4648, 3693, 3998 and 3998 respectively.
**The seven classes used here are basically:

1. Professionals and senior managers
2. Semi professionals and managers of small organisations
3. Supervisors and self-employed artisans
4. Routine clerical workers
5. Skilled manual workers
6. Semi-skilled manual workers
7. Unskilled manual workers

These are derived from the Hope-Goldthorpe scale, but different from the seven categories used by the Nuffield College study of England and Wales (see Hope and Goldthorpe, 1974).

Although the two sexes start from similar backgrounds, as we can see by comparing the first two rows, the men go on to more non-manual opportunities – the first four columns total 46.7 per cent for men as compared to 38.7 per cent for women. And even here there is a difference, with men far-outnumbering women in classes 1 and 3, and also in the more skilled part of manual work (column 5).

As a result, classes 1 and 3 contribute 44 per cent of all male upward mobility, and class 5 adds a further 18 per cent. For women, the figures are 6 per cent and 14 per cent. Classes 2 and 4 contribute only 29 per cent of male mobility but 67 per cent of female mobility. The availability of jobs channels people's lives through different avenues.

This means that brothers and sisters with the same family

background are likely to achieve different social identities in their adult lives, a kind of growing apart from each other – and of course their parents. The mean occupational class score for fathers is 4.7; the sons' is 4.2; the daughters' is 5.0. These apparently small numerical net differences represent considerable gross movements and consequently social differences. Sons tend to move up, daughters to move down.

A further result of these occupational distributions is that women, on average, marry upward socially. There just are too few men of their own station in life to allow for equal pairing, or choice of mates with lower social standing. The pairings are shown in Table 11.4. In the lower left hand sector of the table, we have women who married men from higher social classes: in excess of half the sample. A further one-fifth lie on the main diagonal from top left to bottom right; they have married men in the same class as themselves. The remaining one-quarter in the top right hand sector of the table have married down by at least one class. Only about one in eight had married down by more than one class.

Table 11.4: Marriage by Social Class*

Wife's occupation	Husband's occupation 1	2	3	4	5	6	7	T	
1	20	17	5	3	5	2	5	57	1.4
2	134	163	67	35	57	65	35	556	13.9
3	11	9	12	2	14	13	9	70	1.8
4	136	153	128	85	162	111	89	866	21.7
5	25	47	58	16	98	101	79	424	10.6
6	106	141	157	59	241	208	130	1042	26.1
7	44	56	145	32	247	266	193	983	24.6
T	476	586	572	234	824	766	540	3998	
	11.9	14.7	14.3	5.9	20.6	19.2	13.5		

*The seven classes are as defined in note **, Table 11.3.

Again, those occupational categories in which males predominate – columns 1, 3 and 5 – each contribute heavily to this marrying-up effect, to the extent of almost two-thirds of the 'hypergamy', to use the technical term in Lowie's sense (1948, p. 272).

This finding of predominant hypergamy comes as no surprise, once one has grasped the point of how the labour market provides people with an occupational or social class identity. However, it is a finding which can only add fuel to a long-running – one might say smouldering – debate about how people choose marriage partners. Worsley *et al.* (1977) claim that whatever the state of the law or popular beliefs about love and individual choices,

> we know that in actual practice homogamy – the tendency of like to marry like – is as much part of our actual marriage patterns as formal freedom of choice. Marital partners tend to come from the same area, to be of the same social class . . . (p. 195)

and Anderson writes that

> a mass of studies established that mate selection was most likely to occur homogamously (like married like) with respect to individual background variables like . . . parental social class (1971, p. 165)

In contrast, Rosser and Harris draw an 'obvious conclusion' from their study of the Swansea Area

> that there are a very large number of homes in Swansea in which the husbands and wives come from different social backgrounds as a result of 'mixed marriages' – from the viewpoint of occupational class (1965, p. 99)

A fourth and widely-acknowledged view is given by another local study, of Aberdeen in the 1950s, where almost exactly half of the sample of the women married *downward* in class terms (Oldman and Illsley, 1966, p. 58). However in this last study, the combination of local conditions in the Aberdeen labour market, and two different systems of occupational classification, meant that women outnumbered men in the non-manual categories – the reverse of what is presently the case. So inevitably, as we now see, women appeared to marry down, because of the disparate occupational structures.[11]

Clearly, these differing positions depend rather heavily on what we mean by saying 'the same class' or in other words, on the system of occupational categorisation. A second area of confusion lies in which occupational status is chosen: the individual's – or his/her father's. We know that the women, as compared with their fathers, had previously tended to sink down the occupational scale. Marriage can be seen as a mechanism by which they could recover their former positions, that is, provided we regard the woman's occupational status as merely that of her husband. This is something which the present authors do not accept.

However, one cannot lightly shrug off the question of what is a woman's occupational and class position. It can be taken as given by her father's occupation, by her own occupation, or by her husband's. This is not merely an abstract academic point. In the first place, it matters passionately to many working women who object strongly to being a mere occupational outgrowth of their marital partners. Secondly, it makes a big difference to how basic analysis of official statistics is carried out, and at least, in part, such analyses contribute to policy formulation.[12]

And thirdly, of course, as sociologists, what else would one expect but an interest in social class, given the traditions of our discipline?

Although these issues are relevant for our discussion, consideration of them lies outside of the scope of this chapter.[13] What has been attempted here is a simple exploration of occupational structures and social mobility. We have used sample and census data on Scotland – not always the most easily available sources – to show a variety of changes in the occupational structure. The central theme has been that these changing opportunities have shaped each new generation's life chances afresh, in such a way that over the last fifty years, sons and daughters have increasingly grown away from their original families by virtue of their occupational careers. In particular we have shown that a 'traditional' pattern – wherein the older generation and the married couple are all members of the same occupational class – is an unusual phenomenon in modern society, given present rates of mobility. What is more, partners come to marriage with very different work and class experiences behind them.

This is important if we are to understand the ways in which traditions, attitudes and beliefs are transmitted from person to person within the family. In the 'traditional' pattern, shared occupational levels mean a sharing of experience which forms the basis for a close-knit family unit. It also means that successive generations grow up in the same class environment, learning and accepting a class identity, acquiring sentiments which are the basis of class solidarity and cohesion. In contrast, the 'modern' pattern of occupational non-inheritance removes occupational level as a source of shared experience. Instead, different attitudes and beliefs arising from work experience are imported into family life, making a cohesive social life more difficult. And the traditions of one social class become replaced by the competing traditions of several classes. As an earlier study of car-workers concluded,

> it is precisely such changes in the occupational structure, rather than affluence itself, that must be regarded as possibly the most influential factor in encouraging the spread of middle class values and life style among the working class. (Goldthorpe *et al.*, 1968, p. 81)

As values change, so too will manifestations of class identity change, such as trade union membership, political views, and voting behaviour. Changes in occupational structures are helping to breakdown the separate worlds of the social classes, and this applies to all classes: we are not just witnessing the decline of the working classes in isolation from the middle classes. The standards of tolerable survival for a previous generation of one class will not be the same for their children, because the fundamental basis of social class processes are undergoing radical change as a result of the changing occupational structure.

Acknowledgement

This chapter is based on work initially carried out in the Department of Sociology, University of Aberdeen (financed by an SSRC Grant to Professor Robert Moore) and continued in the School of Behavioural and Social Science, Plymouth Polytechnic. The authors are grateful to Dr Pat Martin, Visiting Fellow from the University of Florida, for her stimulation to examine the data on female mobility, and to Nick Wiseman, Economics Teaching Group, Plymouth Polytechnic, for statistical advice.

Notes

1. Of course, the question is not usually posed as two such contrasting alternatives, although British sociology has tended to concentrate on class inequalities, while American sociologists, particularly in the 1950s and 1960s tended to emphasise the openness of American society.

2. See Hauser *et al.* (1975); Payne, Ford and Robertson (1975, 1976); Goldthorpe and Llewellyn (1977).

3. It will be recognised that this is something of an over-simplification. The manual/non-manual categorisation is a crude one; the moving averages smooth out considerable year to year variation; the 'test' of visual inspection is a weak one, quite apart from the fact that this ignores other factors which might equally well 'explain' both variables. However, the values of r^2 for both jobs are in excess of 0.9. Alternatively, a more sophisticated analysis using Goodman's log-linear modelling of contingency tables method is to be found in Goldthorpe *et al.*

(1979): their conclusions about England and Wales are essentially the same as in this simple illustration and matches a comparable unpublished analysis of our own. Similar results using that method were reported for several countries, one exception being Erikson (1977) for Sweden, at the 1977 ISA conference in Dublin.

4. See, for instance Bain *et al.* (1972); Goldthorpe and Llewellyn (1977); Brown (1978), and particularly a lively exchange between Jones (1977) and Payne (1977a, b). The census time series data discussed in this chapter follow the conventions outlined in the latter, which also present arguments for and against using the censuses in this fashion. The reader should not confuse the census data with the SMS sample data, as the definitions used are not the same.

5. 'Routine white collar' is the Registrar General's socio-economic group 6, and 'semi-professionals' is the Registrar General's SEG 5. SEGs 16 and 17 have been excluded from the calculation of the percentages.

6. The SMS classes are based on rankings of occupations as in the Hope-Goldthorpe scale (1974). The cut-off points between the categories are somewhat different from those later used by Goldthorpe as a 'collapsed scale' and resemble the style of the Registrar General's categories more closely.

7. Neither the Scottish Study, nor that of England and Wales included females in their samples. In discussions in 1975, Goldthorpe explained the latter's decision in terms of the dominance of males as bread winners for most of this century. He has subsequently (1977) stressed financial limitations on sample size, the rationale advanced by the Scottish team (with a sample only half the size) from the outset. The wives of a random sample of men are not a random sample of women: they differ from a sample of women by excluding single, widowed, divorced or separated women. Strictly speaking, the wives are not an independent sample, because their selection is dependent on the selection of their partners.

8. These figures are based on census data, as above. They refer to all women not just those married. They are bedevilled by the fact that women 'out of work' seem less likely to classify themselves as belonging to an occupation or seeking work: for example they do not register themselves as unemployed as efficiently as do men. The more women who participate in some way in the labour market, the more likely this is to be a problem. Again, there is a problem in deciding between full-time and part-time work, and part-time work is a female phenomenon. As we shall see below, deciding what is a woman's occupation – and thereby her class position – poses an awkward sociological question.

9. The reasons for women's occupational achievement – or rather lack of it – have been cogently argued by feminist writers in recent years, and we do not wish to repeat them here. A good discussion of the main themes, with a wider theoretical and historical perspective, is to be found in Chapter 10 of Clegg and Dunkerley (1980).

10. The mobility data are based on seven 'classes' drawn from the Hope-Goldthorpe scale, not the Registrar General's SEGs. The H–G scale was not set up to produce a ranking of 'women's jobs' or of 'women in jobs': most of its specimen titles are male or neutral, and its authors were concerned to prepare a research instrument to analyse male mobility. We are therefore 'stretching' the instrument in applying it to women.

In all previous reports, we regarded one set of routine clerical jobs ('2304' in the H-G scale) as belonging to class 6 by virtue of its ranking score. This affected less than 0.5 per cent of the male sample. But many more women fall into category 2304 (7 per cent) and therefore to avoid any complaint that we have artificially depressed the female mobility score, we have reallocated 2304 to class 4 in this chapter. In fact, it makes a difference of only one or two percentage points to the mobility rates reported. 'Present job' does not distinguish between full- and part-time work: there is virtually no difference overall in mobility between full-time work immediately before marriage, and 'present job'.

11. Further discussion can be found in Winch (1971, pp. 280–1), Blau and Duncan (1967, pp. 337–54), Winch and Goodman (1968), and a table without comment in Garnsley (1978, p. 228). The reader should be cautious about the claims for homogamy: Winch for example inflates 37 per cent strict homogamy into 71 per cent by including one category on either side of each class. This combines, for example, 'professional and managerial' with all other 'white collar' and 'upper manual' as a single unit in which homogamy can take place. Again, the American studies have often employed 'socio-económic status', which, being something more than occupation, points the way to an homogamous effect on non-occupational grounds such as levels of education.

12. In a recent paper, Kingsley and McEwan (1978) have shown how medical statistics can be distorted in this way. The contrary view can be found in Thompson (1978), which argues for simplicity.

13. For a good discussion of this, see Garnsley (1978).

References

Abrams, P. (ed.) (1978), *Work, Urbanism and Inequality – UK Society Today* (London: Weidenfeld and Nicolson)

Anderson, M. (ed.) (1971), *Sociology of the Family* (Harmondsworth: Penguin)

Bain, G. *et al.* (1972), 'The Labour Force', in Halsey, A. H. (ed.), *Trends in British Society since 1900* (London: Macmillan)

Blau, P. and Duncan, O. D. (1967), *The American Occupational Structure* (New York: Wiley)

Brown, R. (1978), 'Work', in Abrams

Clegg, S. and Dunkerley, D. (1980), *Organisation, Class and Control* (London: Routledge & Kegan Paul)

Coleman, R. P. and Rainwater, L. (1979), *Social Standing in America* (London: Routledge & Kegan Paul)

Erikson, R. (1977), 'Trends in Social Mobility in Sweden', ISA Stratification and Mobility conference, Dublin (April: mimeo)

Garnsley, E. (1978), 'Women's Work and Theories of Class Stratification', *Sociology* (May)

Glass, D. (1954), *Social Mobility in Britain* (London: Routledge & Kegan Paul)

Goldthorpe, J. *et al.* (1968), *The Affluent Worker: Political Attitudes and Behaviour* (Cambridge: Cambridge University Press)

Goldthorpe, J. and Llewellyn, C. (1977), 'Class Mobility in Modern Britain', *Sociology* (May)

Goldthorpe, J., Llewellyn, C. and Payne, C. (1978), 'Trends in Class Mobility', *Sociology* (September)

Hauser, R. *et al.* (1975), 'Temporal Change in Occupational Mobility', *ASR* (October)

Hope, K. and Goldthorpe, J. (1974), *The Social Grading of Occupations* (Oxford: Oxford University Press)

Jones, T. (1977), 'Occupational Transition in Advanced Industrial Societies – A Reply', *Sociological Review* (May)

Kingsley, S. and McEwan, K. (1978), 'Social Classes for Women of Marital Status', *Journal of Bio-Social Science* (October)

Lowie, R. (1948), *Social Organization* (New York: Holt, Rinehart & Winston)

Oldman, D. and Illsley, R. (1966), 'Measuring the Status of Occupations', *Sociological Review* (March)
Payne, G. (1977a), 'Occupational Transition in Advanced Industrial Societies', *Sociological Review* (February)
——— (1977b), 'Understanding Occupational Transition', *Sociological Review* (May)
Payne, G., Ford, G. and Robertson, C. (1975), 'Occupational Mobility in a Scottish Context', SSRC International Seminar on Occupational Mobility, Aberdeen (September)
——— (1976), 'Changes in Occupational Mobility in Scotland', *Scottish Journal of Sociology* (November)
Rosser, C. and Harris, C. (1965), *The Family and Social Change* (London: Routledge & Kegan Paul)
Scharf, B. (1977), 'Sexual Stratification and Social Stratification', *British Journal of Sociology* (December)
Stanworth, P. and Giddens, A. (1974), *Elites and Power in British Society* (Cambridge: Cambridge University Press)
Thomson, E. J. (1978), Letter in *New Society* (29 June)
Winch, R. F. (1971), *The Modern Family*, 3rd edn (New York: Holt, Rinehart & Winston)
Winch, R. F. and Goodman, L. W. (1968), *Selected Studies in Marriage and the Family* (New York: Holt, Rinehart & Winston)
Worsley, P. *et al.* (1977), *Introducing Sociology*, 2nd edn (Harmondsworth: Penguin)

NOTES ON CONTRIBUTORS

Maxwell Gaskin has been Professor and Head of the Department of Political Economy at the University of Aberdeen since 1965, and was President of Section F (Economics) of the British Association in 1978–9. His main research interests are in regional economics, the regional and market aspects of energy development and financial institutions. He is the author of books, reports and articles on Scottish banking, regional development and the regional impacts of North Sea oil.

David Marquand has been Professor of Contemporary History and Politics at Salford University since 1978. He had previously been a Lecturer in Politics at the University of Sussex, Labour Member of Parliament for Ashfield, and Chief Adviser to the Secretariat-General of the European Commission. He is the author of numerous books and articles on political and social issues.

David Reisman is a Lecturer in the Department of Economics, University of Surrey. He is the author of *Adam Smith's Sociological Economics* (1976), *Richard Titmuss: Welfare and Society* (1977), *Galbraith and Market Capitalism* (1980) and of a number of papers on political economy. He is Recorder, Section F, British Association for the Advancement of Science.

Colin Crouch is Senior Lecturer in Sociology at the London School of Economics and Political Science. He is the author of *The Student Revolt* (1970), *Class Conflict and the Industrial Relations Crisis* (1977) and *The Politics of Industrial Relations* (1979); and editor (with L. Lindberg and others) of *Stress and Contradiction in Modern Capitalism* (1975), *British Political Sociology Yearbook*, Volume 3: *Participation in Politics* (1977), (with A. Pizzorno) *The Resurgence of Class Conflict in Western Europe since 1968* (1978), and *State and Economy in Contemporary Capitalism* (1979). He is currently engaged on research into relations between trade unions and the state in Western Europe.

Colin Robinson has been Professor of Economics at the University of Surrey since 1968. His main research interests are the economics of energy market and forecasting. He has written numerous articles and books on these subjects (including *North Sea Oil in the Future*,

Macmillan, 1978) and has built up a substantial research programme in energy economics at the University. Professor Robinson spent eleven years as a business economist, at one time heading the Economics Division in Esso Petroleum before becoming Economic Adviser to Esso Europe in the first North Sea Natural Gas negotiations. He is a member of the Electricity Supply Research Council, of the Editorial Boards of *Applied Economics* and *Energy Policy*, joint Editor of *Energy Economics* and a director of Staniland Hall Associates Limited.

Patrick Minford has been Professor of Applied Economics at Liverpool University since 1976. He is the author of articles on monetary and macro- economics, and of *Substitution Effects Speculation and Exchange Rate Stability* (North Holland, 1978).

Tom Stonier holds the Founding Chair in Science and Society at the University of Bradford, and previously held posts in the USA at Brookhaven National Laboratory, Rockefeller University and Manhattan College. He is Chairman of the education consultancy firm, Global Education Systems, and has been a consultant to various governmental, educational and business organisations.

Edward Cunningham is Director of Planning and Projects of the Scottish Development Agency which he joined soon after its establishment. Previously he was in the World Bank for a number of years and he also worked in industry and the Civil Service. He is a graduate of Cambridge and the Harvard Business School.

Duncan Maclennan is Lecturer in Applied Economics in the Department of Social and Economic Research, University of Glasgow. He was Lecturer in Political Economy in the University of Aberdeen between 1976 and 1978. He has published extensively in the fields of urban and regional economics and in the economics of housing and is Co-editor of a recent volume on regional policy.

Ian Carter is Senior Lecturer in Sociology at Aberdeen University. He is the author of *Farm Life in Northeast Scotland, 1840–1914* as well as many chapters and articles about the social history and rural sociology of northern Scotland.

Geoff Payne was formerly Director of the Scottish Mobility Study at Aberdeen University and is now Dean of Social Science at Plymouth

Polytechnic. Of his co-authors, Marion Ulas is Research Assistant in the same department and Graeme Ford is Research Sociologist in the MRC Medical Sociology Unit, University of Aberdeen.